Fairy Tale Films

Visions of Ambiguity

Fairy Tale Films

Visions of Ambiguity

Pauline Greenhill and Sidney Eve Matrix
Editors

UTAH STATE UNIVERSITY PRESS
LOGAN, UTAH
2010

Cover photo adapted from *The Juniper Tree,* courtesy of the Wisconsin Center for Film and Theater Research, Nietzchka Keene papers, 1979-2003, M2005-051. Courtesy of Patrick Moyroud and Versatile Media.

ISBN: 978-0-87421-781-0 (paper)
ISBN: 978-0-87421-782-7 (e-book)

Manufactured in the United States of America
Printed on acid-free, recycled paper

Library of Congress Cataloging-in-Publication Data

Fairy tale films : visions of ambiguity / Pauline Greenhill and Sidney Eve Matrix, editors.
    p. cm.
Includes bibliographical references and index.
ISBN 978-0-87421-781-0 (pbk. : alk. paper) -- ISBN 978-0-87421-782-7 (e-book)
1. Fairy tales in motion pictures. 2. Fairy tales--Film adaptations. I. Greenhill, Pauline. II. Matrix, Sidney Eve.
PN1995.9.F34F35 2010
791.43'6559--dc22
                    2010021567

Contents

Acknowledgments

Pᴀᴜʟɪɴᴇ ᴀɴᴅ Sɪᴅɴᴇʏ Eᴠᴇ ᴛʜᴀɴᴋ ᴛʜᴇ ᴄᴏɴᴛʀɪʙᴜᴛᴏʀs for their patience with the process of revision and rewriting. We thank John Alley for being a persistent, but warmly appreciative, editor. We thank Jack Zipes and an anonymous reviewer for their helpful comments and suggestions that greatly improved this book. We thank John Dobson for his attentive indexing. We thank Barbara M. Bannon for her careful and insightful copy-editing. We thank Dorinda Hartmann of the Wisconsin Center for Film and Theater Research for archival assistance. We thank Patrick Moyroud for giving us permission to use the cover image. And we thank Emilie Anderson-Grégoire and Kendra Magnusson for their invaluable research assistance at various stages of the work.

Pauline thanks Sidney Eve for getting her interested in fairy tale film in the first place, for having the idea that we should do this book together, for assigning her Nietzchka Keene's *The Juniper Tree* to write about, and for being an excellent friend and colleague. She thanks her wonderful colleagues in women's and gender studies at the University of Winnipeg—Roewan Crowe, Angela Failler, and Fiona Green—for their unwavering support and fabulous company. She also thanks the Social Sciences and Humanities Research Council of Canada for its ongoing support of her research and its invaluable and tireless nurturing of Canadian scholars in the human sciences.

Sidney Eve thanks Pauline for her generous and critically astute role in shaping this project. She has learned a great deal from Pauline about folklore and fairy tales, and she is deeply grateful for Pauline's unwavering enthusiasm and tireless efforts in preparing this text. Sidney Eve's inspiration for editing this text came from the students she worked with in a course called FILM436—Fairy Tale Film—at Queen's University. The unexpected connections, sharp and fresh insights, and sense of delight and wonder in fairy tales that emerged through many hours of seminar discussions were enlightening and energizing. Most of all she wishes to acknowledge her parents, Penny and Mike Reynolds, for the countless hours they spent reading fairy tales and children's stories to an inquisitive girl who developed an insatiable appetite for books and a lifelong love of learning. Thank you.

Foreword

Grounding the Spell
The Fairy Tale Film and Transformation

Jack Zipes

In *The Oxford History of World Cinema* (1996), edited by Geoffrey Nowell-Smith and advertised as "the definitive history of cinema worldwide," there is not one word about fairy tale films. Even in the chapter on animation, the term "fairy tale" does not appear. All this is very strange, if not bizarre, given the fact that two fairy tale films—*Snow White and the Seven Dwarfs* (1937) and *The Wizard of Oz* (1939)—are among the most popular films in the world and have had a significant impact on cinema up through the present. The exclusion of fairy tale film as a category from *The Oxford History of World Cinema* is even stranger when one considers that the godfather and pioneer of film narrative, Georges Méliès, produced close to thirty films that were superb *féeries* and numerous directors in Europe and America created well over forty silent fairy tale films at the beginning of the twentieth century. Moreover, Walt Disney and Lotte Reiniger began their great cinematic careers in the 1920s by adapting fairy tales, and nothing much has been made of their great debt to folklore and the fairy tale genre. Indeed, aside from a number of essays and a couple of books that touch on the subject, film critics, folklorists, and literary historians in America and Europe have not realized how much films owe to folklore and the fairy tale. It is for this reason, I believe, that the publication of Pauline Greenhill and Sidney Eve Matrix's *Fairy Tale Films* is path breaking and will fill a gap in both film studies and folklore.

Not only do the essays in Greenhill and Matrix's critical study fill a need, but they are also original in their concept, insightful, and based on thorough research. To be sure, they cannot cover all the fairy tale lacunae in film studies; they cannot magically discuss every aspect of the fairy tale film. The focus of the book is mainly on North American, Mexican, and British films produced in the past forty years. And not all the films covered in the book, such as the adaptations of the Harry Potter novels and the fantasy films of Tim Burton and Stanley Kubrick, are, strictly speaking, fairy tale films. However, the motifs, characters, and plots of these films have clearly been borrowed from fairy tales, and they exemplify how complicated the definition of a literary or film genre can be.

If we begin with a valid thesis that there is no such thing as a pure genre, but there are distinctive characteristics and plots that alert us to regularities in similar works of art, we can trace a marvelous evolution of the oral wonder tale in the western world and see how it contributed to the formation of the literary fairy tale as a genre in the sixteenth and seventeenth centuries and how the oral and literary traditions conspired or colluded to reach out to other forms of art to propagate their wonder and fairy tales. We can also easily recognize how the wonder tale and fairy tale were adapted and transformed over five centuries through solo storytelling, gala performances, opera, the ballet, the salon, theater, opera buffo, the magic lantern, vaudeville, extravaganzas, shows at fairs, painting, book illustrations, and card and video games. By the time Méliès arrived on the scene in Paris with magic and vaudeville shows in the 1890s, the fairy tale was begging or perhaps even demanding to be made into a film. In short, all the conditions for adapting fairy tales for film had been satisfied.

Méliès's experiments with the fairy tale are good examples of the way he expanded the definition of the genre and demonstrated the way that film could enrich it. Not only did he re-create three literary fairy tales written by Charles Perrault and show a flair for comic invention, but he also freely adapted *The Arabian Nights* and *The Adventures of Baron Munchausen* and used montage, stop-action, dissolves, folklore, and dream to create his own stories. He borrowed and played with motifs and characters from diverse fairy tales, reversing expectations and creating extravagant spectacles. He invented his own fairy tale skits, developed surreal images as backdrops, and created all sorts of weird monsters, ghosts, ogres, witches, wizards, bizarre animals, whales, gnomes, and fairies. In short, Méliès designed fairy tale films to comment on fairy tales, and in every film he made, he emphasized miraculous transformation. Everything that we may today call fantastic or fantasy was already present in the films of Méliès, and his creative laissez-faire attitude toward genre broke conventions and enriched them at the same time.

While Méliès relied heavily on the theater and made almost all of his films in his indoor studios, other producers and filmmakers began shooting outside, making longer films, and modernizing the plots of classical fairy tales such as "Cinderella," "Snow White," and "Little Red Riding Hood." Many of the silent films of the 1920s are set in contemporary America or Europe and change classical fairy tales in diverse ways. The fairy tale cartoons that began with Walt Disney, Lotte Reiniger, Paul Terry, and the Fleischer brothers in the 1920s and early 1930s paved the way for great experimentation that turned traditional fairy tale plots on their heads and exposed the ridiculous aspects of romantic love, fixed gender roles, the greatness of royalty, and so on.

At the same time, however, Disney began changing his original, more provocative approach and gradually became more conventional in adapting the classical fairy tales of the Brothers Grimm and Perrault and adhering closer to the traditional plots and patriarchal ideology of nineteenth-century folk and fairy tales. Not only did Disney "straitjacket" his earlier wild experimentation with fairy tales in his production of *Snow White and the Seven Dwarfs* by following the conventional plots of American sentimental musicals, sweetening the characters as stereotypes, developing more realistic human figures, and adding cute comical animals to liven the plots, but he continued that practice until his death and established a model of conformity that hundreds of other filmmakers have followed up until today: 1) girl falls in love with young man, often a prince, or wants to pursue her dreams; 2) wicked witch, stepmother, or a force of evil wants to demean or kill girl; 3) persecuted girl is abducted or knocked out of commission; 4) persecuted girl is rescued miraculously either by a prince or masculine helpers; 5) happy ending in the form of wedding, wealth, and rise in social status or reaffirmation of royalty. In many ways, Disney's predictable fairy tale film schemata became classical in the same way that the Grimms' stories served as the model for most early collections of fairy tales in the nineteenth century.

This is not to say that all fairy tale films in the twentieth and twenty-first centuries were obliged to acknowledge Disney, whether they were animated or live action. But they certainly paid lip service of some kind since it has been virtually impossible for any filmmaker born after 1945 not to have seen or been exposed to a Disney fairy tale film as a result of the powerful marketing and distribution of all products by the Disney Corporation.

While the Disney Corporation created the model for what audiences should expect from a fairy tale film and has duplicated this model since then, even with its recent feature, *The Princess and the Frog* (2009), it has also set the standards of defining the fairy tale film against which serious and gifted filmmakers have reacted.

In every genre and cultural field, there are forces that collide and joust to attain dominance. By 1959—with the production of *Sleeping Beauty*—the Disney Studios became the dominant creator of fairy tale films and remains so today, although there have been clear signs since the 1980s that the Disney Corporation may be toppled from the throne. The number of remarkable animated and live-action films in America and Europe during the past twenty years has grown, and these films demand that we regard both fairy tales and fairy tale films no longer with the rosy-colored lens of the Disney Corporation and mass media but with open (ended) eyes.

The essays in *Fairy Tale Films* seek to keep our eyes open and sharpen our perspective. Folk and fairy tales pervade our lives constantly through television soap operas and commercials, in comic books and cartoons, in school plays and storytelling performances, in our superstitions and prayers for miracles, and in our dreams and daydreams. The artistic re-creations of fairy tale plots and characters in film—the parodies, the aesthetic experimentation, and the mixing of genres to engender new insights into art and life—are significant because they mirror possibilities of estranging ourselves from designated roles and the conventional patterns of the classical tales. As Greenhill and Matrix stress in their introduction, "the mirror of fairy tale film reflects not so much what its audience members actually are but how they see themselves and their potential to develop (or, likewise, to regress)."

Of course, as I have tried to show, most standard fairy tale films, such as those produced by the Disney Corporation, Shelley Duvall's *Faerie Tale Theatre,* or the Cannon Group's five fairy tale films, essentially provide hackneyed renditions of fairy tales for commercial profit. They appeal to our craving for regularity and security in our lives. The cutting edge of the criticism in *Fairy Tale Films* reveals differences between films that want to titillate and guarantee happiness and those that want to compel us to engage with open eyes all those haunting dilemmas that cause existential and social problems. Fairy tale films such as Guillermo del Toro's *Pan's Labyrinth,* Nietzchka Keene's *The Juniper Tree,* and Neil Jordan and Angela Carter's *The Company of Wolves* unnerve us because they destabilize our notion of the happy-ended and predictable fairy tale and deal with issues such as fascism, rape, and infanticide. Optimistic fairy tale films such as *Ever After* and Disney's *Enchanted* demand that we critically reflect about false and artificial gender definitions and the backlash against feminism. The four *Shrek* films challenge the Disney Corporation and other filmmakers to rethink their fairy tale politics and audiences to reformulate their notions of beauty and what a fairy tale film is supposed to look like and mean. Now, in *Fairy Tale Films*, a book of thoughtful and enlightening essays, we are challenged to reflect about the ways fairy tale films in tantalizingly diverse forms continue to cast their spell on us and ask us to consider possibilities for change, for if the fairy tale film as a genre can produce radical transformation, why can't we?

Introduction

Envisioning Ambiguity
Fairy Tale Films

Pauline Greenhill and Sidney Eve Matrix

> *Who owns fairy tales? To be blunt: I do. And you do. We can each claim fairy tales for*
> *ourselves. Not as members of a national or ethnic folk group—as French, German, or*
> *American. Not as nameless faces in a sea of humanity. And not in the Disney model as*
> *legal copyright owners. We claim fairy tales in every individual act of telling and reading.*
>
> Donald Haase, 1993a (71–72)

Fairy tales are fictional narratives that combine human and non-human protagonists with elements of wonder and the supernatural. They come in traditional (usually collected from oral tellers) or literary (formally composed and written) forms. Each traditional fairy tale telling forms a copy for which there is no original. Every version offers a snapshot—a view of that story in time and space that refers to its sources and predecessors—but fidelity to an original is profoundly beside the point. Though readers, hearers, viewers, and tellers may perceive the first version they encounter as the genuine, authentic text, as Donald Haase argues, the single-authored, written version cannot be assumed as the model for understanding fairy tales.[1] With their own specific meanings and uses, fairy tales speak with as well as about their tellers, audiences, contexts of performance, and sociocultural backgrounds. They thus offer different visions.

---

1   Indeed, literary texts do not constrain filmmakers like Walt Disney. The Disney version of Hans Christian Andersen's "The Little Mermaid," for example, closes with a happily-ever-after that is entirely absent from the original tragedy (see Bendix 1993). More consideration of Disney's cultural politics of tradition can be found in Bell, Haas, and Sells (1995).

Fairy tales provide intertexts par excellence. Though the term *intertex-tuality* has a disputed history, following Julia Kristeva, we understand it as the quality of the fairy tale to be a structure that "does not simply *exist* but is generated in relation to *another* structure . . . an *intersection of textual surfaces* rather than a *point* (a fixed meaning) . . . a dialogue among . . . the writer, the addressee (or the character), and the contemporary or earlier cultural con-text" (emphases in original, 1980, 64–65). Jack Zipes alludes to this generic quality of fairy tales when he argues that "we know, almost intuitively, that a particular narrative is a fairy tale" (1996, 1). A genre comprises a series of narrative conventions, including characterization, plot, and style, common to each iteration of a story. But traditional genres go further: their patterns fall into recognizable and specific forms. Thus, beginning in the early-twen-tieth century, folktales were classified into types. With the move from text to context and performance in 1970s folkloristics (see Ben-Amos 1971), the tale-type index (now in its third revision; Uther 2004) fell into some disrepute. Yet the authors' references in this book to tale types, or "ATU" numbers,[2] are not anachronistic. Instead, they draw readers' attention to the specifics of fairy tale intertextuality—that each story is international as well as local, and that the commonalities among texts extend into different modes of representation, including film.

But traditional fairy tales are not the only forms of the genre with a distinct intertextuality. Indeed, even literary fairy tales arguably differ from other forms of fiction. Linda Dégh puts it this way:

> We cannot speak of authenticity in our [Euro North American] sense before the 1940s. The general public did not distinguish between oral narrator and tale writer and regarded published stories as common property free for anyone to change. Scholarly recording of oral tales from the folk, at the same time, meant notation of a skeleton content of stories judged to be genuine. Style editing along the lines of exist-ing models then embellished the tales to reflect more the style of the

---

2   The ATU numbering system refers to Hans-Jörg Uther's (2004) revision of the Antti Aarne and Stith Thompson work (1961), which classified folktales into types based upon plot and sequence of *motifs* (recurrent patterns or ideas found in traditional culture). The original was criticized, among many other reasons, because it "(1) overlooks gender identity in its labeling of motifs, thus lumping male and female actions or characters under the same, male-identified, heading or (2) disregards female activity or (3) focuses on male activity at the cost of female" (Lundell 1986, 150). We use it to alert our readers to the multiple and international qualities of traditional folktales and give them a source for further exploration of individual tale types.

collector than that of the raconteur. Texts the scholars regarded as folk-alien, inauthentic, corrupt, or retold from a book were omitted. Small wonder that most published collections reflect the wishful thinking of folklorists, not the real folk repertoire: an oral tradition of miscellaneous provenience. . . . The "genuine" tale is the one told and listened to irrespective of its literary antecedents. (1991, 70–72)

As Dégh's comments suggest, the fairy tale genre has long been a shape shifter and medium breaker—generically ambiguous. Even when its oral forms were fixed in print—and often expurgated or moralized over—by collectors of traditional culture—most notoriously the Grimm brothers—that process failed to limit the texts to a single form. The Grimms (and others) edited successive versions for publication, changing them to fit their notions of appropriateness.[3]

Indeed, the movement of traditional fairy tales to cinematic form may have enabled their commodification in capitalist socioeconomic structures, but filmed fairy tales are as much the genuine article as their telling in a bedtime story or an anthology. Thus, the present work approaches fairy tale film not as a break with tradition but a continuation of it. Our question is not how successfully a film translates the tale into a new medium but, instead, what new and old meanings and uses the filmed version brings to audiences and sociocultural contexts.[4] The authors, then, address the specific shapes of fairy tale films as a subgenre of fairy tales—as experiments, departures, and innovations in genre and intertext.

Why can the fairy tale seemingly weather vast historical and geographical changes? Kay Stone discusses the "deliberately enigmatic quality of wonder tales" and notes that "the mysterious nature of this genre endures, even after long years of attention by a host of writers offering their own particular interpretations" (2004, 113). Lutz Röhrich contends that they are "essential and substantial stories which offer paradigmatic examples of conflicts in decisive life situations" (1986, 1). The fairy tale film may comprise a newer subgenre, but it, too, manages to address a huge range of audiences. Most of the films discussed in this book are intended for adult audiences, though

---

3   Though this aspect of the Grimms' versions has long been well known among folklorists, the brothers' methods were more widely exposed in Ellis (1983); for a somewhat-more-measured reading of the Grimms' redactions, see Alderson (1993). As Donald Ward correctly comments, "Ellis criticizes the Grimms for not adhering to the rigorous demands of scholarship that in that day did not exist" (1991, 96).

4   Of course, as Dudley Andrew (1984) argues, questions of fidelity are profoundly epiphenomenal, even in literary adaptations.

some can be considered family fare, aimed as much at the parents who are taking their children to the movies as at the kids themselves. All undoubtedly implicate adult lives and relationships.

Folklorist Bengt Holbek catalogued some particular qualities of fairy tales, as a genre of traditional narratives, which—not at all coincidentally—show their connection with film versions. First, fairy tales are told by "skilled specialists" (1998, 405), not by everyday tellers, a characteristic that underlines the place of fairy tale film, also a subgenre requiring skill and specialization, as a recognizable fairy tale variation. Second, they are texts appreciated primarily by "the lower . . . strata of traditional communities," not by "the higher strata [who] . . . usually regard them with condescension or even contempt" (Ibid.). Fairy tale film, too, with a few exceptions, is associated with contemporary popular culture, rather than with elite art. Third, fairy tales "are told by and for adults. Children may listen . . . but they are not the primary audience" (Ibid). The versions we address in this collection definitely fall into this category, though some of the films may be literally inaccessible to anyone younger than a teenager.[5] Fourth, "male and female repertoires differ" (Ibid.). Holbek suggests that men "prefer masculine fairytales, whereas women's repertoires are more evenly distributed" (Ibid., 406; he distinguishes female and male tales on the basis of the primary protagonist). Though male film auteurs overwhelmingly outnumber females, we argue that women directors' versions of fairy tales—sometimes actively feminist readings (like Nietzchka Keene's of *The Juniper Tree* (1990), discussed by Pauline Greenhill and Anne Brydon)—make gendered statements that qualitatively differ from those of men. Fifth, fairy tales are viewed as fictional, and storytellers and audiences "identify themselves with the heroes or heroines of the tales" (Ibid.). In sum "fairytales [provide] a means of collective daydreaming" (Ibid.).

Holbek, along with structuralist Vladimir Propp (1968), saw the tales he considered as explorations of family relationships. Similarly Alessandro Falassi examined the Tuscan *veglia*, "the main occasion for meeting and the place of social reality" (1980, 3), an informal gathering of family and

---

5   In the United States, *Pan's Labyrinth* (directed by Guillermo del Toro, 2006) received an R rating (anyone under seventeen must be accompanied by a parent or guardian); *Eyes Wide Shut* (directed by Stanley Kubrick, 1999) only narrowly missed receiving an NC-17 rating (no one under seventeen permitted); *Edward Scissorhands* (directed by Tim Burton, 1990) was rated PG-13 (some material may be inappropriate for children under thirteen); even *Enchanted* (directed by Kevin Lima, 2007) was rated PG (some material may not be suitable for children) (see *Film Ratings*).

friends, usually in wintertime, involving many folklore genres. He argues that storytelling is "the first genre of folklore performed at the *veglia*" (Ibid., 30) and that it is aimed at an intergenerational audience, but it crucially involves the family, even to the extent of "family above society" (Ibid., 250). He believes that "the most frequently found narratives concern family values and the formation of families" (Ibid.). Perhaps this focus is part of what drew the most famous fairy tale interpreter, Walt Disney, to the form.

Fairy Tale Film Beginnings and the Disney Paratext

In her keynote address to the British Film Institute's seminar, Marina Warner traces a history of fantasy cinema beginning with Georges Méliès and his numerous fairy tale films (including a *Bluebeard* [ATU 312], three versions of *Cinderella [Cendrillon]* [ATU 510/510A], and a *Little Red Riding Hood* [ATU 333]). At the very birth of modern filmmaking, she indicates, the magic of wonder tales and folklore were key inspirations. So, too, was the artwork from the golden age of children's book illustration in the late-nineteenth century by Kay Nielsen, Arthur Rackham, Edmund Dulac, Walter Crane, and Aubrey Beardsley.[6] What made this narrative and graphic imagery so intriguing for filmmakers like Méliès was the artists' ability to tell the tale through a "multicolored skein of images with which to think about the real, both reiterating and shaping the real in restructured narratives, reassembled images" (Warner 1994, 17). It is likely that this emphasis—privileging visual form over narrative—inspired Jack Zipes's comment that filmmakers working at the fin de siècle were little interested in the richness of the folktales they adapted for the screen; instead, they were focused on driving innovation in cinematography. "Fairy tales were incidental to their work," he suggests; the real thrill for artists like Méliès came in "resolving [the] technical and aesthetic problems" in crafting his animated and live-action films (1997, 2). Walt Disney and his animator colleague Ub Iwerks differed little from Méliès in this respect.

Zipes describes Disney's rather haphazard approach to narrativizing folktales for the silver screen, beginning with the 1920s cartoons (including renditions of *Puss in Boots* [ATU 545B], *Little Red Riding Hood,* and *Cinderella),* and continuing through his Hollywood animations.

---

6   Arguably, more-recent illustrators like Maurice Sendak also contribute to current film readings of fairy tales (see Segal and Sendak 1973).

Unconcerned with fidelity to the source text—from his first feature-length animated films, *Snow White and the Seven Dwarfs* (directed by David Hand) in 1937 and *Pinocchio* (directed by Hamilton Luske and Ben Sharpsteen) in 1940—Disney "bowdlerized and sanitized" the work of collectors/anthologists of traditional tales like Charles Perrault in France and the Grimm brothers in Germany, as well as the literary fairy tales of Carlo Collodi and others, to achieve his goal to create visually spectacular cinema that reinforced and reflected patriarchal, capitalist American family values (1994, 141).[7]

The subject of narrative accuracy and the rocky relationship between fairy tale films and the oral and literary traditions that preceded them raises issues about translating folk narratives across distinctive popular mediums for different audiences. Of course, fairy tales were not always for children. In fact, educators, parents, and clergy were wary when nineteenth-century publishers attempted to popularize the transcribed (and often bawdy and rough-hewn) tales in Europe and North America as family fare. Zipes comments, "At first, fairy tales were regarded as dangerous because they lacked Christian teaching and their symbols were polymorphously meaningful and stimulating. But by the end of the nineteenth century, fairy tale writers had learned to rationalize their tales and to incorporate Christian and patriarchal messages into the narratives to satisfy middle-class and aristocratic adults" (1997, 4–5).

It was perhaps the Grimm brothers, more than any other collectors, who did the most to sanitize the folktale for the nursery. But though the Grimms edited out the nasty bits of sex, they sometimes added or expanded the violence: from cannibalism to pedophilia, from matricide to graphic torture, and beyond. Walt Disney picked up the censor's scissors where the Grimms left off, further whitewashing the folk and fairy tales that he used as a textual scaffold on which to erect his cartoons. In this cleansed canon of Disney's folkloric animations, Zipes observes a deep conservatism that commodifies the fairy tale while promoting apathy and an apolitical acceptance of the status quo (1997, 6). Disney's perspective might not be so important, except that Zipes correctly observes that the company's version has become the referent for most well-known fairy tales in the Euro-North American popular imagination.

---

7   A detailed international history of fairy tale film can be found in Zipes (2010).

In fact, the fairy tale as interpreted by Disney has so saturated mainstream Euro-North American culture and gained such legitimacy through market dominance and repetition that his versions of *Peter Pan, Pinocchio,* "Cinderella," "Snow White" (ATU 709), and other tales have become the modern source text with which any newer adaptations must engage (as Christy Williams argues in this volume). Thus, Zipes concludes that Disney has cast a spell over the fairy tale genre—both literary and cinematic—displacing the classic literary and traditional versions. That enchantment is dangerous, he warns, because the deeply conservative ideology of Disney productions—meant to "amuse and pacify the rebellious instincts" of audiences—puts spectators into a deep sleep of political apathy and acceptance of the status quo (1994, 140).

One film theorist has argued that "suspension of motility on the part of the spectator allows for a partial identification of the film process with the dream, countered by the greater elaboration of the film system and by the fact that the image perceived as real constitutes a concrete perceptual content in the cinema (the images and sounds of the film itself)" (Rose 1988, 144). Others concur. Many fairy tales also have a dreamlike quality, as Holbek characterizes them. But at times that dream is a nightmare. For example, Zipes sees "Hansel and Gretel" (ATU 327A) as a tale that rationalizes parental abandonment and abuse of children and exemplifies the patriarchal rule of the father as well as the "male Christian God" (1997, 47). For Zipes, though, the tale also echoes social reality, especially since "many women died in childbirth in the eighteenth and nineteenth centuries, [and] numerous men, left with motherless children, remarried and brought stepmothers into their own homes" (Ibid., 49). Since social expectations governed priority of food to men and children in times of scarcity, it is easy to understand why a woman might want to turn out members of the family who were not her own offspring. Rather than a functional reassurance that the child and family would survive, tales like "Hansel and Gretel" could be baldly stating the worst imaginable circumstances. Thus, as with films of fantastic voyages, fairy tale films about monstrous dreams can be based in reality.

Nevertheless, the present collection proceeds from the awareness that there remain exceptions to the dystopic vision of the fairy tale film that Zipes describes. Innovative films—often made for television, including Jim Henson's *The Muppet Show* (directed by Peter Harris and Philip Casson, 1976–81) and *The Storyteller* (directed by Steve Barron and Jim Henson,

1988), and Shelley Duvall's *Faerie Tale Theatre* episodes (directors including Roger Vadim, Nicholas Meyer, Tim Burton, and Francis Ford Coppola, 1982–87)—succeed in "breaking the Disney spell," according to Zipes.[8] But the authors in this collection have found other examples of animated and live-action cinema—for children and adults alike—that displace or disregard the Disney paratext. While some of the films considered in the following chapters are entertaining and escapist, others are deeply political. Opening up the focus from fairy tale films proper—those that employ the structure of a recognized fairy tale—to cinematic folklore more generally—which draws upon folkloric motifs commonly found in traditional culture—invites speculation on the many Hollywood, international, and independent productions that incorporate these motifs and narratives across a variety of genres and to varying degrees (see the essays by Cristina Bacchilega and John Rieder, Tracie Lukasiewicz, Sidney Eve Matrix, Brian Ray, and Naarah Sawers).

In their analyses of a wide range of films, the authors in this anthology largely concur with Marina Warner's observation that this popular medium can reflect and reify the status quo. Yet alternately conservative ("safe, compliant with prevailing convention") and controversial ("resistant, Utopian") fairy tale films can provide audiences with innovative, imaginative, and even magical ways of dealing with the crises of everyday life (1993, 34–35). However, we doubt that these examples are sufficient to address Zipes's concerns that fairy tales—though immensely popular—discourage social transformation, and therefore their popularity is fundamentally conservative. Nevertheless, there is no question that the cinema analyzed in this collection effectively demonstrates a widening of fairy tale film, extending far beyond Disney's—and Zipes's—visions and versions.

Fairy Tale Films for Adults

Fairy tale films and cinematic folklore for adolescents and adults, usually live-action productions—sometimes incorporating significant visual effects—span across the genres from horror to erotic thriller, romantic comedy to

---

8   Often less heavily capitalized, and overall less expensive, television allows experimentation in style, format, and content that doesn't exist in Hollywood. Increasingly, however, the success of independent cinema is changing the rules and opening up the previously tightly controlled circuits of production and distribution within the mainstream film industry.

psychological melodrama, fantasy to science fiction. These fairy tale readings manifest the resurrection of the sexual, violent, and supernatural elements of folktale that existed in oral tradition but were censored for children's literature. In this sense, contemporary, sometimes radical, and innovative filmmakers such as Guillermo del Toro (see Lukasiewicz), Steven Spielberg (see Sawers), Nietzchka Keene (see Greenhill and Brydon), Neil Jordan (see Kim Snowden), and Tim Burton (see Ray) appear to have returned to the roots of folklore's darker elements. As Maria Tatar notes, for anyone familiar with the Disney paratext, the experience of reading the German (or French) versions on which it draws can be eye opening due to the mutilation, murder, incest, terrible punishments, cruelties, and other atrocities commonplace in most tales (1987).

Similarly, in *Off With Their Heads! Fairy Tales and the Culture of Childhood*, Tatar argues that most classic children's literature aims for progressive socialization, enforcing conformity through violent coercion and a pedagogy of fear (1992). Such cautionary tales follow audiences from childhood to adulthood, as is immediately evident by the works of cinematic folklore analyzed in this collection. Many are dark. Some incorporate evil magic, supernatural elements, and haunting special effects that mesmerize and enchant audiences (think of *Pan's Labyrinth,* discussed by Lukasiewicz and by Bacchilega and Rieder, or *AI: Artificial Intelligence,* directed by Steven Spielberg [2001] and examined by Sawers, for example). They can even inspire moral panic. Consider the reception of the Harry Potter series (discussed by Ming-Hsun Lin) or *The Golden Compass* (directed by Chris Weitz, 2007, analyzed by Bacchilega and Rieder), or other films alleged to promote Satanism, for example (see Overstreet 2007).

Apart from computerized special effects, however, sexual and moral ambiguity remains a standard feature of fairy tale films for adults, accounting for the narrative tension and suspense that keep audiences attentive. Whereas Disney characters represent either pure innocence (such as orphans) or unadulterated evil (often stepmothers), cinematic folklore intended for mature audiences deals in shades of grey. Ultimately characters' motivations are largely unknown in films such as *The Juniper Tree* (see Greenhill and Brydon), *The Company of Wolves* (directed by Neil Jordan, 1984; discussed by Snowden), *Enchanted* (see Linda Pershing and Lisa Gablehouse), *Eyes Wide Shut* (considered by Matrix), and *MirrorMask* (directed by Dave McKean, 2005; discussed in Bacchilega and Rieder). In each example, male and female characters struggle with eternal questions about identity, power, love, lust, and belonging—the human condition.

Live-Action and Animation in Fairy Tale Films

In the winter of 2007, Disney unveiled *Enchanted*, a hybrid film that mixes animated sequences with live-action footage. A modern princess tale (though the main female character is not literally royal), this romantic comedy follows the protagonist's enchanted journey through time and space to land in the alien world of Manhattan. Not surprisingly, the only way to break the spell cast upon her by a jealous evil crone is with love's first kiss. Billed as a fairy tale film for adults, *Enchanted* rewarded delighted audiences with its many tongue-in-cheek references to earlier Disney classic fairy tale films. This explicit self-referentiality evidences the fact that most mature theatergoers have grown up on Disney animations and are thus well schooled in the significance of talking animal helpmates, gags and slapstick comic relief, musical interludes, double entendres, the romantic, heterosexual, happily-ever-after guarantee, and other Disney conventions.

It should come as no surprise, then, that Steven Spielberg's *AI: Artificial Intelligence* can explicitly (and more-or-less faithfully) incorporate significant portions of Carlo Collodi's *Pinocchio* narrative and still not be universally or instantly recognized as a fairy tale film (see Sawers). Disney's animators have stamped a cartoon vision of the boy puppet on the popular imagination in indelible ink. Theoretically speaking, moving from animation to live action is already a step outside the Disney paratextual boundary, yet the majority of the essays in this volume address primarily live-action cinematic folklore.

Even if they cannot be properly classified as animations, the special effects and computer graphic imagery (CGI) that are largely responsible for the magic of a Harry Potter film (see Lin; or other magical voyage films from *The Chronicles of Narnia: The Lion, the Witch, and the Wardrobe* and *Prince Caspian* [directed by Andrew Adamson, 2005, 2008] to *The Lord of the Rings* series [directed by Peter Jackson, 2001–3] or *Star Wars* [directed by George Lucas, 1977]) clearly continue in the tradition of the early animation and puppet films of Méliès and his contemporaries.[9] Digital special effects (DFX) have become standard fare for blockbuster movies, which means that

---

9   In fact, in his work on digital cinematography, Lev Manovich argues that—due to
     the proliferation of special effects in Hollywood blockbusters—mainstream live-action
     cinema can no longer be distinguished from animation (1999).

the fantastic and grotesque creatures, supernatural trickery, other-worldly terrains, and inhuman acts capable through CGI are no longer confined to science fiction and fantasy films.[10] When the wonder tale comes to life on the silver screen, DFX animation artists are largely responsible for the enchantment of spectators—though the Hollywood celebrities who appear in fairy tale films may take issue with that statement!

Genre Migrations and Folklore Mutations in Fairy Tale Films

Setting special-effects animation aside for the moment, many examples of cinematic folklore in live-action cinema are classified as melodramas, thrillers, and horror films. In some cases, the films share or echo the title of a folktale or tale character, such as *La Belle et la bête* (*Beauty and the Beast;* directed by Jean Cocteau, 1946), *The Juniper Tree, Bluebeard* (directed by Edward Dmytryk and Luciano Sacripanti, 1972), *The Gingerdead Man* (directed by Charles Band, 2005), *Snow White: A Tale of Terror* (directed by Michael Cohn, 1997), *Hansel & Gretel* (directed by Gary Tunnicliffe, 2002), *Baba Yaga* (directed by Corrado Farina, 1973), *964 Pinocchio* (directed by Shozin Fukui, 1991), *Kvitebjørn Kong Valemon* (*The Polar Bear King;* directed by Ola Solum, 1991), *The Red Shoes* (directed by Michael Powell, 1948), *Peau d'âne* (*Donkeyskin;* directed by Jacques Demy, 1970), *Snow White: The Fairest of Them All* (directed by Caroline Thompson, 2001), or *Sydney White* (working title *Sydney White and the Seven Dorks*, directed by Joe Nussbaum, 2007). In other cases, some familiarity with the source is needed to identify the film as a fairy tale adaptation, as in *Secret Beyond the Door* (directed by Fritz Lang, 1948) or *The Stepford Wives* (directed by Bryan Forbes, 1975)—both "Bluebeard" tale types—or *The Thief of Bagdad* (directed by Raoul Walsh, 1924)—from the *Arabian Nights* tales.

The task of spotting cinematic folklore embedded in films that give no overt clues to their roots and intertextuality involves a subtle impression of déjà vu as part of its spectatorial pleasure. That uncanny sense of familiarity—of a submerged story haunting the narrative on-screen—requires some detective work by the film critic. A search of the literature in film and folklore-friendly fields reveals some creative interpretations of films such as *The Texas Chain Saw Massacre* (directed by Tobe Hooper, 1974), *The*

---

10   Blackford (2007) discusses links between science fiction and fairy tale film.

Piano (directed by Jane Campion, 1993), and *Notorious* (directed by Alfred Hitchcock, 1946) as "Bluebeard" tale types; *Dirty Dancing* (directed by Emile Ardolino, 1987) as "The Ugly Ducking"; *Pretty Woman* (directed by Garry Marshall, 1990) and *Maid in Manhattan* (directed by Wayne Wang, 2002) as versions of "Cinderella"; *Splash* (directed by Ron Howard, 1984) as "The Little Mermaid"; and *Hable con ella (Talk to Her;* directed by Pedro Almodóvar, 2002) as a modern interpretation of "Sleeping Beauty" (ATU 410). In this volume, essays on what at first appear unlikely candidates for cinematic folklore include Stanley Kubrick's erotic thriller *Eyes Wide Shut* as a version of "The Twelve Dancing Princesses" (ATU 306); Chris Wedge and Carlos Saldanha's animated wonder *Robots* (2005) as an updated *Pinocchio;* and Tim Burton's *Corpse Bride* (2005) and *Edward Scissorhands* as animated and live-action retellings of the legend of "Venus and the Ring" and the "Beauty and the Beast" folktale (ATU 425C), respectively.

To make the case that some of these films, especially those with adult themes, are fairy tales in disguise requires some familiarity with folklore tale types and motifs and comfort with the notion that "no fairy tale text is sacred," as Maria Tatar has observed (1992, 229). Indeed, in her investigation into contemporary migrations and metamorphoses of fairy tales in film and television, Marina Warner, tongue in cheek, accused critics of seeing "Bluebeards" and "Cinderellas" "here there and everywhere" (1993, 27)! Yet as already mentioned, fidelity to the source is not the only measure of the value of a fairy tale film adaptation or remake, nor is it the best one.[11] *Adaptation,* understood as "repetition without replication," may involve a degree of faithful homage in its alteration or translation of the text, but fidelity may just as easily reside in critique as it does in imitative tribute (Hutcheon 2006, 7).

With each reinterpretation, incorporation, or transposition of these familiar stories, tellers create new tales to serve contemporary needs. The process of revisiting classic tales renders them defamiliarized or strange, thus opening up the possibility of a shift in perspective that encourages the audience to reflect anew on these stories that have ossified as part of the bedrock of cultural narratives (Tatar 1992). Many modern fairy tale films and examples of cinematic folklore are best understood as transfigurations or transmutations of folktales since they incorporate varieties of

---

11   For an overview of debates in fidelity criticism, see Welsh and Lev (2007); and Sanders (2006).

transtextuality—embedded interlinked texts—theorized by Gérard Genette (1997). Once the focus of the fairy tale film expands beyond the classic Disney animations, it becomes immediately apparent that there are numerous examples of the kind of resolutely unfaithful cinematic folklore adaptations that Robert Stam would describe as "less a resuscitation of an originary word than a turn in an ongoing [intertextual] dialogical process" through which the filmmaker engages with the source (2004, 25). As Stam argues, the range of cinematic adaptations extends far beyond homage or critique to include filmic rewritings, resuscitations, resignifications, and even cannibalizations of literary or oral texts. These processes reflect various intentions on the part of the filmmaker, ranging from changing to correcting, echoing, or experimenting with the original story (Ibid.).

Postmodern Adaptations

From thinking about the range of adaptive approaches in cinematic folklore, it is a short leap to considering the postmodern elements in many fairy tale films. In *Postmodern Fairytales: Gender and Narrative Strategies*, Cristina Bacchilega notes how frequently the narratives and motifs associated with *Snow White and the Seven Dwarfs, Cinderella,* and other Disney classics are deconstructed and recombined in popular culture. Their storylines, props, and characters are so thoroughly engrained in the imagination that audiences instantly recognize elements of them in the artwork and advertisements of commercial culture, not to mention jokes, songs, and cartoons. These fragments act as "bait," Bacchilega argues, to catch the viewers' or hearers' attention, drawing them in through nostalgic childhood memories (1997, 2). The postmodern approach to fairy tales is perhaps best illustrated by *Shrek* (directed by Andrew Adamson and Vicky Jenson, 2001), *Shrek 2* (directed by Andrew Adamson, Kelly Asbury, and Conrad Vernon, 2004), and *Shrek the Third* (directed by Chris Miller and Raman Hui, 2007). Originally based on William Steig's literary fairy tale, this trilogy is an animated "Beauty and the Beast" tale type that shamelessly inverts the classic story line.

Thus, the beautiful princess metamorphoses into a monster, rather than being the agent of disenchantment who returns her beastly bridegroom to human form, as is the case in most versions. Moreover, the *Shrek* films present a folkloric montage of characters and motifs from well-known tales, nursery rhymes, and legends, including "Puss in Boots,"

"The Gingerbread Man/Runaway Pancake" (ATU 2025), "Robin Hood," "The Three Little Pigs" (ATU 124), "Little Red Riding Hood," *Peter Pan,* "Snow White," and a miscellaneous cast of fairies, witches, dragons, dwarfs, and enchanted animals. The result is a multilayered literary and oral fairy tale remix, wherein the conventional and innovative merge and blend. The spectator's pleasure results from predicting the familiar plot twists and turns and being pleasantly surprised to be both correct and incorrect. This postmodern retelling of the value-added "Beauty and the Beast" is, as Bacchilega observes of other tales, a composition of multiple possible stories—authorized and unauthorized, at times parodic, and overall transformational vis-à-vis the source texts (1997, 23). Similar postmodern productions that are explicitly self-referential include the made-for-TV films *The 10th Kingdom* (directed by David Carson and Herbert Wise, 2000) and *Into the Woods* (directed by James Lapine, 1991). Both, like *Shrek,* sample and remix many fairy tale stories, themes, and motifs into a new adventure that delivers a kick of déjà vu to spectators, as did *The Princess Bride* (directed by Rob Reiner, 1987). These cinematic montages reveal a postmodern doubling as they unsecure the narrative integrity of the classic tales while remaining faithful to the overarching generic conventions, albeit modernized in some cases.[12]

Other postmodern remixings and transmutations of folkloric elements are considerably more subtle than the *Shrek* comedies. Filmmakers may insert sampled references or fragmentary narrative parallels that engage yet disrupt the earlier text. Innovative use of folktale figures and tropes is evident in *Lady in the Water* (directed by M. Night Shyamalan, 2006), a postmodern engagement with Hans Christian Andersen's "The Little Mermaid" that amplifies the ancient supernatural power of the sea nymph so she is no longer a tragic romantic figure but, instead, humankind's savior. Similarly *Star Wars* incorporates many recognizable elements of L. Frank Baum's *The Wizard of Oz* into a very different kind of adventure narrative about an extraordinary extraterrestrial journey and the ultimate battle between good and evil.

To extend this consideration of postmodern fairy tales, Maria Nikolajeva (1998, 2003) observes that one recurrent feature of these stories is the presence of *heterotopias*—otherworldly realms, where reality appears topsy-turvy

---

12   For more on fairy tales and postmodern doubling, see Bacchilega (1997), who argues that, according to this textual approach, the tales can resist and reify conventional discourses of sex, gender, race, and power.

and terrible, fabulous, supernatural events and beings question all that is commonsensical and familiar. They are often shot as surrealist dream sequences—as in *The Company of Wolves* (a version of "Little Red Riding Hood") or *The Matrix* (directed by Andy Wachowski and Larry Wachowski, 1999) and *Vanilla Sky* (directed by Cameron Crowe, 2001), which both combine elements of Lewis Carroll's *Alice's Adventures in Wonderland* with "Sleeping Beauty." They may also incorporate elements of grotesquerie and the carnivalesque—such as in the shocking "flesh fair" scene in *AI: Artificial Intelligence.* Heterotopical elements in postmodern fairy tale films unsettle the conventions of the genre to the extent that these films may be better understood as what Lutz Röhrich (1991) sees as antifolkloric texts.

Fairy Tales and Genre

Although the happy ending remains a crucial convention of most fairy tales, in the antifolktale there may be only an unsettling sense of closure, perhaps better understood as a narrative resolution, according to Röhrich. In this way, among others, modern cinematic folklore corresponds to, and departs from, generic conventions of the fairy tale. Genre classifications serve a purpose insofar as they shape audience expectations and offer a kind of narrative scaffolding for theatergoers. Genre distinctions provide spectators with a discursive framework and analytic vocabulary, tools with which to evaluate and enjoy the work. Audio and visual cues are encoded in genre films, and spectators anticipate sequences—in the soundtrack, editing, and camerawork, for example.[13] In the case of fairy tale films, stock characters and familiar plotlines form the basic generic imperatives with which filmmakers grapple. Those working with fairy tales are surely aware of the need to strike a balance between the pleasure of the familiar and the excitement of the unexpected when incorporating stylistic conventions of the genre.

Genre filmmakers know that their work will be received and evaluated in the light of generic predecessors. The Disney paratext provides the most obvious measuring stick for any fairy tale film. As the essays in this volume attest, however, the concept of genre is likely more constricting than constructive when studying even a small selection of fairy tale films that are otherwise classified as romantic comedy, erotic thriller, animated family film,

---

13   For more on film classifications see Berry (1999).

melodrama, and horror film—to name only a few of the different kinds of cinema included in this collection.

How then do audiences, critics, and analysts read fairy tale film as a sub-genre of fairy tales in general? Some readers argue that the texts can be readily decoded. But we concur with Donald Haase that "fairy tales consist of chaotic symbolic codes that have become highly ambiguous and invite quite diverse responses; and . . . these responses will reflect a recipient's experience, perspective, or predisposition" (1993b, 235). Indeed, Haase feels that "irresponsible readings may ensue, but they nonetheless reflect the actual conditions of most fairy tale reception" (Ibid., 238–39). Perhaps he would find some filmed fairy tales "irresponsible readings," particularly when they ignore historical context or favor a univocal or stereotypical view. But what seems most noteworthy to scholars of fairy tale film is the relative freedom of auteurs to riff almost end-lessly on the same tales. A brief look at our filmography shows considerable historical and geographic range, and yet the tale types and literary sources in these versions are relatively few. We might go so far as to argue that, statistically, a familiar tale like "Cinderella" stands a much greater chance of being retold for the nth time than a less-well-known example like "The Twelve Dancing Princesses" or even the alleged great classic "The Juniper Tree" (ATU 720).

Also highly noteworthy is the lack of women directors in this genre, even though many argue that fairy tales are quintessentially women's texts. This deficiency may be more indicative of the glass ceiling in the film indus-try, not only in Hollywood but worldwide, which denies women access to what is arguably the most central position in filmmaking. The exceptional writer/director Nietzchka Keene's *The Juniper Tree* was independent and low budget—and sadly, her death in 2004 to pancreatic cancer marks an end to her contributions (Memorial Resolution 2005). Even when taking writ-ers into account, the picture improves only slightly (and probably becomes worse proportionally since most films credit only one director and may have two or more writers). Too often, also, the credited writer is the author or collector of the source, rather than the cinematic creator.

Christian Metz argues that "film is like the mirror. But it differs from the primordial mirror in one essential point: although, as in the latter, every-thing may come to be projected, there is one thing and one thing only that is never reflected in it: the spectator's own body. In a certain emplacement, the mirror suddenly becomes clear glass" (2004, 822). Metz speaks of mir-rors since a fundamental premise, not only of film scholarship but of film-making itself, is that viewers should be able to identify with the characters at some level. The notion of identification is central to Bacchilega's use of the same simile to describe the fairy tale genre:

> Like a magic mirror, the fairy tale reflects and conforms to the way things "truly" are, the way our lives are "truly" lived. As with all mirrors, though, refraction and the shaping presence of a frame mediate the fairy tale's reflection. As it images our potential for trans-formation, the fairy tale refracts what we wish or fear to become. Human—and thus changeable—ideas, desires, and practices frame the tale's images. Further, if we see more of the mirror rather than its images, questions rather than answers emerge. Who is holding the mirror and whose desires does it represent and contain? . . . This mirroring . . . is no value-free or essential distillation of human des-tiny, but a "special effect" of ideological expectations and unspoken norms. (1997, 28–29)

Thus, the mirror of fairy tale film reflects not so much what its audi-ence members actually are but how they see themselves and their potential to develop (or, likewise, to regress). The fairy tale film's frame—not only the physical limits of what it actually shows but also its containment in time and space—allows an often-succinct and telling expression. Its metaphorical flexibility means that viewers can potentially return at different times and receive different, sometimes even contradictory, impressions of the film's meanings and intentions. Nevertheless, we suggest that within the genre of fairy tale film—apart from Disney—experiments, departures, and innova-tions predominate.

Experiments, Departures, and Innovations

Sometimes what a particular reader sees as a fairy tale film involves exten-sive reading in. Some may argue, for example, that Matrix's discussions of fairy tale references in *Eyes Wide Shut* or Sawers's analysis in *AI: Artificial Intelligence* stretch the notion of fairy tale film nearly beyond recognition. Often these references are located in a single image—although the resulting consideration of fairy tale connections can greatly enhance both the fairy tale and the film as intertext. For example, *Hard Candy* (directed by David Slade, 2005) alludes to "Little Red Riding Hood" primarily through the image of the girl's red hoodie (see Bacchilega and Rieder; see also Greenhill and Kohm 2009). However, the reference not only deepens the film's meaning as a narrative about revenge against Internet stalkers and pedophiles but directly relates it to a series of other films that share that reference.[14]

Similar links can illuminate the specifics of fairy tales—for example, the idea that they maintain their own geography. Activist folklorist Vivian Labrie charts a construction in some traditional fairy tales where a helper—a stock figure in the genre who assists the hero with her/his tasks—structurally positioned between a powerful figure and an incumbent, aids the latter when they form an alliance. The young protagonist of the fairy tale moves through a specific physical space, locating a particular road, crossing "troubled waters," and climbing stairs to confirm identity and find success (1997, 152). Labrie notes that this structure exists not only in the tale generically designated "The Magic Flight" (ATU 313) but also in two American films of the late 1980s, where young neophytes contrive to make it in the capitalistic corporate world—*Working Girl* (directed by Mike Nichols, 1988) and *The Secret of My Succe$s* (directed by Herbert Ross, 1987)—as well as in a French show-business film, *Trois places pour le 26* (directed by Jacques Demy, 1988) (Labrie 1997).[15]

---

14   "Little Red Riding Hood" pedophile films include not only *Hard Candy*, *Freeway* (directed by Matthew Bright, 1996) and *The Woodsman* (directed by Nicole Kassell, 2004) but arguably also *Little Red Riding Hood* (directed by David Kaplan, 1997). Linking these works also allows consideration of the "Little Red Riding Hood" narrative's influence on contemporary Euro-North American understanding of criminality in other films about pedophilia (see Greenhill and Kohm 2009).

15   Labrie designates the hero(ine)—the main protagonist who seeks a better job, adventure, and/or marriage—"Person one"; the gatekeeper—the daughter, secretary, or wife—"Person two"; and the patriarch—the king or boss—"Person three." She notes both the exploitative sexual relationship between Person two and Person three (for example, the boss in *The Secret of My Succe$s* has apparently married for money) and the incestuous and/or undisciplined relationship between Person one and Person two (for example, in the same film, ambitious protagonist Brantley Foster [Michael J. Fox] has a sexual, and later a professional, relationship with his aunt, who is also his boss's wife).

Labrie's analysis explains the way those who are positioned relatively low in a hierarchy can attempt to use sexual relationships to advance their positions. She points out that such relationships are structurally violent because they predispose the authority figure to exploit the subordinate. But she also shows that these connections are problematic because they fail to change the patriarchal institutional dynamic, thus perpetuating the monstrous nightmare. However, Labrie also argues that Person two, in the role of gatekeeper, opens possibilities to change an exploitative situation:

> The knowledge associated with a Person two position is at least as strategic as it is stressful; she speaks both the inside and the outside languages and, although uncomfortable, her borderline situation gives her the possibility of translation

Other voyages detailed in this book are partly geographical, but they are also cerebral and sometimes even spiritual. At times, though, the journey simply returns to the location where it began. Thus, Bacchilega and Rieder's contribution presumes fairy tale hybridity, but rather than expecting that quality to be invariably subversive, they emphasize its contradictions and clashes. Thus, *MirrorMask*, *Spirited Away* (directed by Hayao Miyazaki, 2001), and *The Golden Compass* may be genre bending, but they also tend to be gender normative. Similarly Pershing and Gablehouse look at the recent Disney offering, *Enchanted*, which transports characters from an animated to a live-action world. But it also takes its audience on a journey that reveals a need literally to enchant everyday life. The film proposes that its Disneyfied fairy tale romance is viable in the real world as long as the girl finds the right divorce lawyer/prince.

The journey to otherworldliness is more difficult to render in live-action fairy tale films. However, a distinctive aesthetic is evident in *The Juniper Tree*, filmed in Iceland by an American feminist director who sought realism even in her representation of the magical but also specified a melancholic historicized chronotope. Greenhill and Brydon's analysis of this film describes—not surprisingly, given its auteur—its reading of the world as complex and nuanced, rather than a reproduction of conventional notions of gender often understood in fairy tales and their films.

Lukasiewicz, considering *Pan's Labyrinth*, looks at the interaction between nonfictional and fairy tale expectations in what she calls *neomagical realism*. Its fantasy world impinges on reality exclusively through one character. In the concluding resolution, no one within the filmic diegesis but Ofelia sees the gigantic faun who gives her the final, most crucial task. Whichever vision the audience takes as real—Ofelia's or everyone else's—it is clear that both the real and the fairy tale world incorporate monstrous creatures and monstrous acts. Sawers, using both *AI: Artificial Intelligence*

---

in either direction. As an intermediary between the makers of rules and their subjects, Person two retains the real balance of power—when she becomes aware of it—and thus, in life as well as in art, she can become a major agent of social change—once she decides to make use of her position. (1997, 163)

This means that when Person one proceeds to the position of boss or king, thanks to the critical help of Person two, he or she has the choice of changing the relationships with others around them from exploitative to cooperative because of Person two's lesson on the importance of alternative values—a wonderful vision indeed. In her own social activism, Labrie uses folktale analyses in action research to work with marginalized people, such as those receiving public assistance, to help them see through and understand their positions and the ways they may positively influence them.

and *Robots* as her touchstones, considers capitalism's alliance with techno-science to profit from people's desire for the perfect child: the commodifica-tion of the child/body under contemporary capitalism. The films appear to offer happy endings, but read through a critical materialistic lens, their dénouements become more threatening.

Ray discusses the oeuvre of Tim Burton, specifically the folkloric ele-ments in *Sleepy Hollow* (1999), *Corpse Bride*, and *Edward Scissorhands*. In Burton's work, he argues, the dreamlike images both overshadow and embody the stories' identities and realities. Matrix considers the motifs and narrative structure from "The Twelve Dancing Princesses" in Kubrick's *Eyes Wide Shut* to explore issues of sexuality and power in cinematic folklore. Again in this film, the potential happily-ever-after is very much dependent upon the spectator's position. Marriage is thoroughly deconstructed, and the perspectives of husband and wife seem irreconcilable.

Feminist views on fairy tales have long been incorporated into the scholarship on the genre. As detailed by Haase (2004a), from its very incep-tion (arguably with Alison Lurie's "Fairy Tale Liberation" in 1970), femi-nist fairy tale scholarship has refused the easy association of the compli-ant, mainstream, Disneyfied view of the genre to a simple reproduction of patriarchal stereotypes about women.[16] Feminist readers of fairy tales have consistently understood the ambivalent and multivalent positions on gender that traditional tales offer (e.g., Bottigheimer 1986 and 1987). Far from simply depicting the way women are oppressed by unrealistic expec-tations of beauty and youth, fairy tales can offer multiple perspectives on the positions of women and men in current times (e.g., Preston 2004) and the multitude of locations where they have historically been found (e.g., Bottigheimer 2004).

Not coincidentally some feminist film theorists have sought uncon-ventional gender messages in what initially appear to be very conventional films. Most notably Carol Clover's work on "slasher films" suggests that their focus on what she calls the "final girl"—the androgynous, resourceful, gender-ambiguously named character who becomes the triumphant survi-vor—requires its teenaged male audience to identify themselves across sex,

16   Though arguably even the Disney Corporation is capable of producing potentially
      revolutionary visions of gender and race relationships (Barr 2000). And some feminist
      criticism denies any possibility that fairy tales can have liberating readings (e.g.,
      Lieberman 1972).

sexuality, and gender boundaries.[17] Clover does not see the final girl as a simple protofeminist development of a bold heroine (instead of a bold hero) but instead shows the way she reverses the conventional investigatory and voyeuristic gaze (usually a male gaze on a female object) (1992). Similarly complex readings deepen the works included in the book.

Snowden looks at *The Company of Wolves* and Angela Carter's wolf stories, exploring feminist pedagogy to work with these texts. She considers the process whereby students—many initially blinded by the Disney paratext—may come to understand both fairy tales and feminism in more complex ways as a result of considering radical revisions of both generic and ideological narratives. Christy Williams reads the presumption that *Ever After* (directed by Andy Tennant, 1998) is a feminist version of "Cinderella" critically. She suggests that simply reversing patriarchal binaries—making the primary female character strong, confident, politically astute, and forceful, instead of weak, doubting, naïve, and self-effacing—is insufficient to create an image of a postpatriarchal world. However, she also affirms that the text allows the audience to imagine an alternative ending. Finally, in another reversal of expectations, Ming-Hsun Lin approaches the understanding of *Harry Potter* films unconventionally, arguing that Harry takes the position of the conventional heroine, a kind of male Cinderella. Though the film versions offer a much more muted view of the books' gender-bending propensities, they nevertheless bring a feminist perspective to the screen.

Talewards

This collection of essays by no means covers the range of the genre of the fairy tale film because it is heavily skewed toward Euro-North American productions in English. Even within that cultural subcategory, this study addresses feature-length films much more than short works, and live action much more than animation. Though this perspective is in large part a result of the interests of the writers, it also lends some coherence to the work. Many of the best-known tales and films—not always linked together—in Euro-North American culture are represented in this book. We leave it to those who follow to extend their reach beyond these limitations.

---

17 Fairy tale storytellers and audiences, similarly, may be unconstrained in their identification with main characters by their sex or even their species (Greenhill 2008).

As scholars and teachers of fairy tales, film, and folklore, we have witnessed firsthand the delight and dismay that students experience when decoding, dissecting, and discussing these stories. From the beloved Disney favorites revisited through the rosy lens of childhood nostalgia, to the deep investment and near-fanatical attention to detail that fans of the epic chronicles of J. R. R. Tolkien, J. K. Rowling, or C. S. Lewis bring to the classroom—the academic study of fairy tale film is a high-stakes endeavor! Add to this mix a measure of cynicism that other students (and even faculty colleagues) may feel (initially at least) when approaching a cinematic genre that seems, at best, to be diversionary kid stuff or, at worst, utterly facile, predictable, disposable low-culture trash.

Inevitably, however, once the sceptical soul steps one, then two, feet in the direction of appreciating the richness, diversity, and complexity of fairy tale films, a powerful seduction takes effect. Fairy tale films and cinematic folklore are endlessly intriguing, with something for everyone in their visions of ambiguity: a little blood and guts, some mystery and whodunit, hair-raising adventure, saccharine romance, suspense, epic battles, unlikely heroism, magic and fantasy, dazzling special effects, a bit of the weepies, fetching costumes, timeless stories, tragedy, terrible truisms, and still more. As the late psychoanalyst and fairy tale theorist Marie-Louise von Franz reported, "Fairy tales represent something very much removed from human consciousness. I once heard [Carl] Jung say that if one interprets a fairy tale thoroughly, one must take at least a week's holiday afterward, because it is so difficult" (2002, 11). So wickedly, pleasurably, exhaustingly, and rewardingly so. Enjoy!

1

Mixing It Up
*Generic Complexity and Gender Ideology in Early Twenty-first Century
Fairy Tale Films*

Cristina Bacchilega and John Rieder

WHILE FOLKLORISTS OFTEN DEFINE THE FAIRY TALE or tale of magic as a
narrative where the supernatural is never questioned—thus requiring the
audience's absolute suspension of disbelief—recent fairy tale films seem to
thrive precisely on raising questions about the realism, if not the reality, of
fairy tales and their heroines. For instance, in the popular 1998 film *Ever
After* (directed by Andy Tennant), the heroine's self-proclaimed great-great-
granddaughter states, "While Cinderella and her prince did live happily ever
after, the point, gentlemen, is that she lived." Bringing closure to the tale she
has just told the two men identified as the Brothers Grimm, she reinforces
this assertion by producing material evidence: not only a Leonardo portrait
that is possibly of her Cinderella ancestor but another precious heirloom:
the heroine's ornate and "real" glass shoe.

Charles Perrault's glass slippers lose their magic in that scene, but their
material presence on screen adds to the realism that has inflected the noble-
woman's telling of "Cinderella" not as a fairy tale but as family history, or, at
the very least, legend. This Cinderella is a larger-than-life figure—not simply
an ideal beauty but an active, educated, willful, *and* flawed woman—with
whom the teller proudly associates herself, and one whom, presumably, girls
at the end of the twentieth century will not dismiss as an outdated fantasy.

To reach adolescents, its target audience, this PG-13 film had to be
"realistic," which meant not only using live action but also presenting more
rounded characters than Disney's and not relying on the supernatural to
produce the heroine's success. Rather, the film ascribed some degree of

historical plausibility or legendary dimension to the Cinderella story by grounding its credibility in family history and its cultural significance in humanistic progress. Cathy Lynn Preston persuasively develops such a reading of *Ever After*. Placing her discussion in the broader popular-culture context of contemporary fairy tale jokes, TV shows, and folk criticism, she describes *Ever After* as an "American popular culture production of the Cinderella tale that cleverly blurs the boundaries between folktale and legend in an attempt to retrieve the romantic possibilities of 'true love' for the generation currently raised in the aftermath/afterglow of second-wave feminism and post-Marxist critique" (2004, 200). More specifically Preston suggests that the film's combination of "the shift in genre from fairy tale to legend" with "a shift in gender patterns" is a response to "the last thirty years of feminist critique of gender construction in respect to key Western European popularized versions of the fairy tale (in particular those of Perrault, the Brothers Grimm, and Disney)" (Ibid., 203).[1]

A lot has changed, we agree, in the production and reception of fairy tales in popular culture since the early 1970s, when North American feminists argued vehemently in the public sphere about the genre's role in shaping gender-specific attitudes about self, romance, marriage, family, and social power. Fairy tale studies has emerged as a field where sociohistorical-analysis challenges romanticized views of the genre. The electronic accessibility of a wide range of fairy tales (such as on D. L. Ashliman's *Folklinks: Folk and Fairy Tale sites* and Heidi Anne Heiner's SurLaLune fairytales. com) has expanded the popular canon far beyond the Perrault-Grimms-Disney triad. World-renowned writers such as Margaret Atwood, A. S. Byatt, Angela Carter, Robert Coover, and Salman Rushdie—recently christened "the Angela Carter generation" by Stephen Benson—have engaged the genre "intimately and variously," producing "what might be called the contemporaneity of the fairy tale" (Benson 2008, 2). Simultaneously a more critical awareness of the fairy tale has taken hold in popular consciousness. In twenty-first-century North America, the authority of the genre and its gender representations has become more multivocal, as Preston reminds

---

1   Christy Williams explores *Ever After* in this volume. Two other essays discuss the economy of genres in *Ever After* and raise questions of cultural value. John Stephens and Robyn McCallum (2002) focus on the hybridization of fairy tale and utopia in the film; their argument pits postmodern ideology and poetics against a feminist humanism, reinforcing a polarity that does not necessarily characterize fairy tale intertextuality today. Elisabeth Rose Gruner (2003) analyzes the way the dynamics of history and fairy tale in the film deauthorize a male-dominated tradition.

us: "For many people the accumulated web of feminist critique (created through academic discourse, folk performance, and popular media) . . . function[s] as an emergent and authoritative—though fragmented and still under negotiation—multi-vocality that cumulatively is competitive with the surface monovocality" of the canonized older fairy tale tradition (2004, 199). Contemporary fairy tales, in both mainstream and eccentric texts, play out a multiplicity of "position takings" (Bourdieu 1985) that do not polarize ideological differences as they did during the 1970s but, rather, produce complex alignments and alliances.

To extend this point—as Cristina Bacchilega has already proposed—it may be helpful to think of the fairy tale genre today as a web whose hypertextual links do not refer back to one authority or central tradition. This early-twenty-first-century "fairy tale web" has woven into it—inside and outside of the academy—multiple, competing historical traditions and performances of the genre as well as varied contemporary revisions in multiple media (see Bacchilega 2008, 193–96).[2] And contributing to this proliferation of the contemporary fairy tale is its hypercommodification in popular film and the marketplace, including clothing, toys, video games, and more—a diversification that also has implications for the way folklorists and/or cultural critics read popular culture's employment of the fairy tale as an "already multilayered polyphony" (Makinen 2008, 151).

In approaching this new or transformed pervasiveness of fairy tale magic in American media today, Jeana Jorgensen builds on Linda Dégh's analysis of fairy tales in advertising (1994) and Preston's observation that "in postmodernity the stuff of fairy tales exists as fragments" acquired through a number of possible forms of cultural production (2004, 210) to tackle a crucial question: how to deal with films and other popular culture texts that "make money on fairy tales while critiquing them" (Jorgensen 2007, 219) and engage the fairy tale but "cannot be reduced to individual fairy tale plots" (Ibid., 218). "These fragments," Jorgensen declares, "whether fairy tale motifs, characters, or plots, are the building blocks of new media texts, inspired by fairy tales but not quite fairy tales themselves." She calls them "fairy tale pastiches . . . to privilege their 'schizophrenic instrumentalization

---

2   Donald Haase's "Hypertextual Gutenberg" (2006) pioneered the discussion of hypertextuality in fairy tale studies in ways that connect technological innovations with the dynamics of authority. Both Haase and Preston employ the metaphor of the web, and Bacchilega's conceptualization of the contemporary "fairy tale web" draws on their insights.

of fairy tale matter'" (Ibid.).[3] Indeed, for every fairy tale movie that recycles a recognizable tale or tale type ("Cinderella," ATU 510 to folklorists, in *Ever After*, ATU 709 in *Snow White: A Tale of Terror* [directed by Michael Cohn, 1997]), there are other films that—regardless of their classification as comedy, drama, or fantasy—incorporate fairy tale elements drawn from a range of canonical images and themes, such as the young girl's red hoodie reminding viewers of "Little Red Riding Hood" (ATU 333) in *Hard Candy* (directed by David Slade, 2005), the magic slipper and happy ending in *Sex and the City* (directed by Michael Patrick King, 2008), or the animal helpers in the various *Harry Potter* movies (directed by Chris Columbus, 2001, 2002; Alfonso Cuarón, 2004; Mike Newell, 2005; David Yates, 2007, 2009)[4] and *The Golden Compass* (directed by Chris Weitz, 2007). Like Jorgensen, we are interested in this fragmentation of individual tales in relation to social power dynamics, but the emphasis in this essay is less on mixed tale types than the strategy and effects of blending fairy tale elements with other narrative genres.

In this chapter we reflect on some recent, popular, big-budget films that feature fairy tale elements as a major part of their appeal but do not rely on a single fairy tale plot. Recognizing both the fragmentation of the fairy tale—visible in the current configuration of the fairy tale web—and the central role that not just individual tales but some notion of the generic fairy tale continues to play in the encoding and decoding of popular culture, this essay focuses on these films' incorporation and integration of fairy tale elements with other narrative strands—that is, on the films' generic complexity or hybridization.

We do not mean to contrast the generic hybridity of these films with some "pure" version of the fairy tale. All literary or cinematic fairy tales— and indeed almost all narratives longer than a headline or a joke—use more than one genre. At the center of our analysis are relationships of tension or harmony—the clashing or blending of different genres in a text. In classic films, the fairy tale blends into and integrates itself with other film genres. In *Snow White and the Seven Dwarfs* (directed by David Hand, 1937), the fairy tale and the musical are not in tension but, rather, flow naturally and

---

3   Whether the term *fairy tale pastiche* stays in the critical vocabulary of fairy tale and folklore studies or not, Jorgensen's essay opens up new possibilities for discussing the dynamics of social power within these popular culture texts, their relationship to literary and oral tales, and the uses that we as scholars make of our disciplinary authority.

4   See Ming-Hsun Lin's essay in this collection discussing the *Harry Potter* films.

harmoniously into one another; their shared distance from realism seems complementary. In *The Wizard of Oz* (directed by Victor Fleming, 1939), the transitions between the realistic Kansas sections of the film and the magic world of Oz are carefully mediated in a way that allows everything in the fantasy section to be explained in realistic terms (that is, as Dorothy's feverish dream).

Some recent films, though, make a point of pushing the hybridity or generic complexity of their narratives into the foreground. Disney's *Enchanted* (directed by Kevin Lima, 2007)[5] creates a passage between a fairy tale world and a realistic one and exploits the two worlds' differences to comic effect as a kind of metacommentary on the suppression of realism in earlier Disney productions of fairy tale films. Other films, like Jim Henson Productions' *MirrorMask* (directed by Dave McKean, 2005) or Studio Ghibli's *Spirited Away* (directed by Hayao Miyazaki, 2001), seek a more homogeneous combination of what remains a strikingly noticeable and eclectic mix of generic strategies or traditions.

What concerns us is the social significance of the generic hybridity in a range of films, including *Enchanted, MirrorMask, Spirited Away,* DreamWorks's *Shrek* trilogy (directed by Andrew Adamson and Vicky Jenson, 2001; Andrew Adamson, Kelly Asbury, and Conrad Vernon, 2004; Chris Miller and Raman Hui, 2007), and Guillermo del Toro's *Pan's Labyrinth* (2006),[6] and, especially, the meaning of this approach as an intervention in the contestation or reproduction of gender ideology. If—in John Frow's words—"Texts—even the simplest and most formulaic—do not 'belong' to genres but are, rather, uses of them . . . [so that] they refer not to 'a' genre but to a field or economy of genres, and their complexity derives from the complexity of that relation" (2005, 2), how and why has the place of the fairy tale changed in the field of genres? What do those changes have to do with the genre's long and vexed connection to gender ideology?[7] To understand the relationship of the economy of genres to the ideologies of gender, what other fields and economies need to be considered? And because these different types of genre bending affect the reproduction of gender norms

5   Linda Pershing and Lisa Gablehouse critique *Enchanted* in this volume.

6   Tracie D. Lukasiewicz also analyzes *Pan's Labyrinth* in this collection.

7   In this anthology, essays by Kim Snowden, Christy Williams, and Ming-Hsun Lin in
     particular explore issues of gender.

and attitudes, what positions are the films staking out within the culture and the industry of entertainment?

Parody and Romance in *Enchanted* and *Shrek*

One of the most prominent types of genre mixing in recent fairy tale films is the parodic practice of undercutting fairy tale conventions by contrasting them humorously with realistic ones. The Disney Corporation's *Enchanted* begins with a scene that evokes the "my prince will come" expectations of Disney's *Snow White and the Seven Dwarfs* and *Sleeping Beauty* (directed by Clyde Geronimi, 1959), but then the fairy tale princess, Giselle (Amy Adams), finds herself unexpectedly exiled from the two-dimensional animated world and forced to survive as an exaggeratedly naïve woman in the unfriendly confusion of New York City. The relationship between the cartoon Disney fantasy and the realistic New York setting is apparently one of stark oppositions—pastels decorating the heroine's idyllic relationship with nature and the fulfillment of romance in one space and genre versus grays cementing regular New Yorkers' routine dealings with vermin, dirt, and work in the other. As each of the fairy tale characters emerges into New York from the enchanted world of Andalasia, his or her arrival occasions a traumatic experience. The city takes the place of the unfamiliar forest where classic fairy tale heroines and heroes used to be tested, but at first what is tried is not the characters' mettle so much as their sense of genre. Giselle mistakes a thief for a helper, her prince (James Marsden) mistakes public-utility workers for peasants, and both show an alarming propensity to launch into song during the middle of a conversation. The climax of this incongruity comes in Giselle's musical housecleaning number in New York, a grotesque parody of the similar song in *Snow White* that has already been more subtly parodied in the film's cartoon section.

Underlying this clash of genres, however, is an economy that reunites them. *Enchanted's* parodic strategy eventually yields to a return to Disney's familiar fairy tale expectations, even though Giselle changes from a Sleeping Beauty/Snow White innocent persecuted heroine to the rescuer of her "true love" in a "dragon-slaying" scene at the top of the Empire State Building. This mélange of Disney's *Sleeping Beauty*, *King Kong* (directed by Merian C. Cooper and Ernest B. Schoedsack, 1933), and *Shrek* hinges on a role reversal that is hardly transformative. That the dragon is female recalls the lady dragon in *Shrek,* and in a way minimizes the irrationality of the kidnapping of Robert (Patrick Dempsey), Giselle's New York love interest. That the monstrous dragon is only the final metamorphosis of the monstrously powerful, older, female Narissa (Susan Sarandon), the queen who does not want to relinquish her power to her son, Prince Edward, prompts us to ask who or what is a King Kong threat nowadays. Finally, although Giselle risks her life to save Robert, it's the sidekick chipmunk, Pip, who saves the day in the climax of the film's rehabilitation of city vermin as animal helpers.

So we can't even say that Giselle performs the heroic rescue expected of the Prince Charming stereotype. She is charming, and that's it. In this and all too many other ways, *Enchanted* merely pays lip service to feminism.[8] While becoming more three dimensional and making choices for herself, Giselle continues to be a cheerful and fashionable housecleaning helpmate, whose actions never question the institution of marriage. The film parodies Disney's earlier representations of Snow White and Sleeping Beauty—the princesses who sing but have nothing to say, who engage in cheerful housework and exhibit fashions on hourglass figures, who know their prince will come—but it ultimately seeks only to bring new glamour and power to the Disneyfied fairy tale princess image and her romantic plot.

Furthermore, the film's congruity with the Disneyfication of the fairy tale harnesses its gender ideology to the marketplace. *Enchanted* blatantly advertises Disney's "princess" franchise, a multi-billion-dollar business that sells toys, DVDs, dolls, and clothes for girls and women. In the transporting song-and-dance scene in Central Park, the commodification of the fairy tale as an escapist or compensatory fiction is naturalized or, more precisely, spectacularized. Early in the film, New Yorkers scoff at the "ever ever after," but in this scene, they (as representatives of *Enchanted*'s mainstream Euro-North American audiences) love pretending they are in its make-believe world, whether this means dressing up for an exclusive and expensive costume ball, dressing up and paying for a fairy tale wedding, or flocking to a children's performance of "Rapunzel" (ATU 310), featuring a young girl with fake long tresses spilling out of a miniature tower in the park—another teaser for an upcoming Disney computer-animated production.

It is no wonder that Giselle's song and charm seduce the New York lawyer who is her skeptical prince figure as well as *all* the park-goers. The ball, the wedding, and the other make-believe scenarios naturalize the appeal

---

8   Pauline Greenhill and Anne Brydon, Sidney Eve Matrix, Linda Pershing and Lisa Gablehouse, Kim Snowden, and Christy Williams discuss feminism and feminist perspectives on fairy tale film in this volume.

of fantasy and display the power of magic for sale in the contemporary world. There is no parody here but a *Fantasia*-like (directed by James Algar, Samuel Armstrong. Ford Beebe, Norman Ferguson, Jim Handley, T. Hee, Wilfred Jackson, Hamilton Luske, Bill Roberts, Paul Satterfield, and Ben Sharpsteen, 1940) spectacle of commercialized dreams for which girls and women dress up. The film's insistent clash of worlds and genres merely consolidates a normative project that exploitatively sells a watered-down representation of feminism to the same ends as Preston sees in *Ever After*: to "retrieve the romantic possibilities of 'true love' for the generation currently raised in the aftermath/afterglow of second-wave feminism and post-Marxist critique" (2004, 200).

DreamWorks produced *Shrek* and its sequels starting in 2001 in an effort to contest Disney's corporate monopoly (Zipes 2006a, 211). This struggle for power among producers of today's fairy tale films is actually dramatized as a *mise-en-abîme* from the competitor's perspective in one of *Shrek*'s early scenes, when we see unruly fairy tale or fantasy characters like Pinocchio, the ogre, the damsel in distress, and the talking donkey fighting to free themselves from the normalizing and self-aggrandizing project of one ruler's fantasy. And the commercial success of the *Shrek* films has indeed challenged Disney enough for it to produce *Enchanted* to regain its shaken monopoly on the cinematic fairy tale. But the parodic strategies that Disney and DreamWorks employ in comically mixing genre conventions, then utilizing them to bolster a specific social use of the fairy tale as genre, are not that different.

Like *Enchanted*, the *Shrek* films start by comically disrupting what is commonly understood as a classic—meaning clichéd, rather than traditional, in folklore terms—fairy tale frame. Each of the first three *Shrek* films begins with the same stereotypical scenario as its pretext and framing device: the rescue of the maiden in the tower, or the damsel-in-distress motif that a romanticized and Disneyfied image of the fairy tale has canonized. But in each film, the rescue explodes into parody. In the opening of the first film, the prince's rescue of the maiden, and the "true love" kiss that follows—presented in a beautifully illustrated children's book that someone is reading out loud—is interrupted by the reader's expression of disbelief, which sets the tone for the film's retelling. The ogre Shrek is then revealed as the reader. He tears the pages out—and since he is in the outhouse, we are left to imagine the rest.

In the second film, when we are presented with the same storybook scenario, the happy ending is no longer there: Prince Charming arrives too late, finds a transvestite wolf in the princess's place, and realizes that Princess Fiona does prefer Shrek to him. In the third film, the prince's rescue is revealed as a cheap fiction, a role that he plays on a tacky dinner-theater stage for a living. And yet, although the narcissism of the Disney-like prince is emphasized in all three films, the inadequacy of the rescue as a resolution or happy ending does not result in demythologizing a romanticized image of fairy tales because the *Shrek* trilogy goes on to celebrate Shrek and Fiona's nevertheless "magical" romance. In short, while the parodied rescue scenes draw on a satirical demystification of fairy tale formulas and motifs already active in popular culture, the effect is merely humorous and transient because the alliance of fairy tale and romance still ends up shaping the stories' closure and emotional power. *Enchanted* seems to have learned from the *Shrek* films this dualistic strategy of initially parodying the idealization of romance in earlier fairy tale films only to conclude by celebrating the same set of conventions. The presence of the strategy in both franchises testifies to the impact of the feminist critique on the reception of fairy tale film, on the one hand, and to the underlying strength of the gender ideology that feminists have sought to contest, on the other.

Another thread of the contemporary fairy tale web that the *Shrek* films reweave is the skepticism that has prompted many a feminist fairy tale joke. Consider this incident in *Shrek the Third*. The princesses—all the usual suspects: Snow White, Rapunzel, Cinderella, and Sleeping Beauty—together with the queen save the day for the whole kingdom. They do so by showing their fighting skills and, in the case of the queen, by turning a certain thickheadedness (she has willfully forgotten that her king was once a frog!) into a strength when she bashes down the wall of the dungeon imprisoning them with a blow of her head. It is hard to say whether this caricature of feminist militancy is laughing at, or with, women who stand up against gender oppression. But perhaps at least some of the *Shrek* films' greater commercial success may result from their raising such a question—something that *Enchanted* never attempts.[9]

This pattern of parodying, then celebrating, enchantment in these films may finally be less about the fairy tale than the ideological power and

9   *Shrek* grossed $120,000,000 during its first weekend in 2001. *Enchanted* grossed approximately the same in four months.

contradictions in romance. Each of these films exposes the tension between fantasy and realism in the conventions of popular, formulaic romance, which combines strongly repetitive plots, a highly predictable set of complications, and a nearly obligatory happy ending with a demand for full-bodied characters—or at least engaging and convincing ones. The parodies of fairy tale conventions in these films echo this contradiction between the demands of plot and characterization. In fact, the films' jokes distance the main characters from their fairy tale prototypes for their viewers in a way that resembles what Sigmund Freud calls the "bribe" that the joke teller offers the listener to allow utterance of hostile or obscene material (1960, 100). The parodies express a disavowal of belief in fairy tale fantasies that opens up the space for rehearsing those same fantasies; since the films have declared that they and their audiences do not take them seriously, they and their audiences can go ahead and repeat them. Thus, this parodic strategy may owe the success evident in its repetition to the way it conspiratorially establishes the tellers' and the listeners' agreement to indulge in the guilty pleasures of unreconstructed romantic fantasy.

Genres and Worlds in *Pan's Labyrinth*

To say that generic strategies involve an economy of genres means, first, that generic choices have values attached to them, and, second, that making those choices involves taking a position on other choices and values. For John Frow, the consequences of generic choice are related to one's sense of reality: "genres create effects of reality and truth which are central to the different ways the world is understood. . . . The semiotic frames within which genres are embedded implicate and specify layered ontological domains—implicate realities which genres form as a pre-given reference" (2005, 19). Frow playfully lists a few of our "generically projected worlds," including the tabloid-press world, the world of the picaresque novel, the world of the Petrarchan sonnet, the world of the curse, the world of the television sitcom, "and so on, as many worlds as there are genres" (Ibid., 86–87).

Like Frow, Mark Bould connects genre choice to world construction when he argues that the critical potential of fantasy lies in its clarifying the inevitability and inescapability of such constructions in contrast to the invisibility that cloaks the generic strategies that maintain our everyday sense of reality: "what sets fantasy apart from much mimetic art is a frankly self-referential consciousness . . . of the impossibility of 'real life'"

(2002, 83). Angela Carter wrote that the fairy tale "positively parades its lack of verisimilitude" (1990, xi). But through the institutionalization of the fairy tale as children's literature, the critical potential Bould attributes to this parading of artifice has been, for the most part, carefully subordinated to didacticism. The fairy tale has to teach its child reader a lesson about the real adult world, and our enjoyment of the pleasures of fairy tale imagination has to be justified by its ultimate performance of duty. Because of that history, the relationship between a fairy tale world and a realist one always has something to do with relationships between children and adults.

The choice to contrast fairy tale and realist elements in telling a story or making a film, then, necessarily involves taking a position about make believe versus reality in relation to pleasure versus duty and childhood versus maturity. In *Enchanted,* these oppositions collapse into the all-encompassing embrace of consumer capitalism, and the adults are finally infantilized by their embrace of the happily-ever-after romance fantasy. Although the *Shrek* films successfully take arms against the Disney Corporation's dominance of the fairy tale film, they certainly do not equally contest the dominance of conventional romantic fantasy or didactic rhetoric. In both *Shrek* and *Enchanted,* the deliberate parodic contrast between fairy tale convention and realist representation is not sustained because the values attached to the films—the generic worlds that are called upon—are not really at odds with one another. The gestures of rebellion against patriarchal convention are only pretexts setting up its eventual triumphant celebration.

At the other end of the spectrum from these films in the way it constructs and sustains a contrast between fairy tale and realist worlds is Guillermo del Toro's R-rated *Pan's Labyrinth.* No recent film raises the stakes in the generic economy of the fairy tale higher. Its double plot sets the fairy tale narrative of the voice-over frame story and the young protagonist, Ofelia (Ivana Baquero), against the historical account in 1944 Spain that is the world shared by all the adult characters in the film. Both worlds are dangerous and brutal: one is not a fantasy escape from the harsh realities of the other. During the climactic confrontation in the depths of the labyrinth between Ofelia and her monstrous stepfather, the fascist Captain Vidal (Sergi López), the fact that he cannot see the magical faun (Doug Jones) to whom Ofelia is speaking never receives the straightforward explanation the viewer expects: that Vidal sees what is really there, and Ofelia is only imagining her fairy tale. Instead, the scene dramatizes the abyss that separates the two narrative worlds—their mutual incomprehensibility.[10]

Nonetheless, the worlds act upon one another. While Vidal's bullet kills Ofelia in the historical world, in the fairy tale world, it completes her choice to save her newborn brother—rather than sacrifice him, as the faun commanded her—that earns her return to her real, royal home. Thus, Ofelia's fairy tale world is not insulated from the adults' reality but remains an alternative to it. And Ofelia's belief in the magical world is surely no more delusional than Vidal's faith in his own favorite story, the saga of the honorable death of a soldier passed down to him by his father, which he pathetically expects the community he has tortured and terrorized to pass on to his son. Stories in this film have profound effects and tie together generations, but no hierarchy of genres sorts out the choices they contain.

Pan's Labyrinth features two strong female protagonists—Ofelia and Mercedes (Maribel Verdú), Vidal's head servant and secret supporter of the anti-Fascist rebels—but its debt to feminism has less to do with the critique of gender ideology than with that critique's acknowledgment of the fairy tale's power. Del Toro does not strip the fairy tale of its didacticism. Ofelia's story certainly has an ethical point, articulated by the faun when he praises her for her decision to disobey his command to sacrifice her brother. Rather, Del Toro separates the fairy tale's moral imperative from the condescension that so often attends the encryption of adult rules in fairy tale situations. The fears and anxieties so strongly depicted in a film like *The Wizard of Oz* are no longer insulated, not so much from the children who view it— remember how notoriously frightening that film has been to many a young child—as from the adults invited to pass off the Wicked Witch of the West (Margaret Hamilton) as mere make believe. *Pan's Labyrinth* allows no subordination and separation of its sometimes-nightmarish fairy tale from the nightmare of history.

Del Toro's achievement bears comparison to Angela Carter's treatment of fairy tale conventions and traditions in *The Bloody Chamber*, but these artists are tellingly different from one another. Instead of the rapprochement between fairy tale and gothic that Carter achieves through eroticism, Del Toro uses the techniques of cinematic horror, a genre he has praised in interviews as a form of "naïve surrealism" that confronts commercial culture's

---

10   The analyses of Jennifer Orme (2008) and Jack Zipes (2008) have been helpful to us in working out this reading of *Pan's Labyrinth*.

pathological denial of darkness and death (*Pan's Labyrinth* Official Podcast). By calling horror cinema's surrealism naïve, Del Toro does not mean that it is for children but that, unlike the surrealist movement of the early twentieth century, it does not separate itself from popular culture through the ironic distance of an elite or avant-garde attitude. He claims that his predilection for depicting monsters participates in "no postmodern irony whatsoever." The strategy of merging fairy tale and horror, and then making them the emotional and thematic partners of historical realism, insists upon the intellectual seriousness of these forms of popular culture that have been trivialized in the past.

Here a second comparison to Carter suggests itself. While her prodigious erudition allowed her to retell well-known fairy tales by drawing on their less-well-known folkloric genealogies, Del Toro constructs a synthesis of cinematic and pictorial traditions, alluding with equal virtuosity to Arthur Rackham and Francisco Goya (see DVD director's commentary). For both Carter and Del Toro, the point is that these allusions not only place their work in relationship with the traditions they invoke but also reposition the genres they work with. The power of Carter's and del Toro's work can be measured by the way each of them actively challenges and changes the value of the fairy tale within the contemporary economy of genres.

Fairy Tale Genealogies and Coming of Age in *MirrorMask* and *Spirited Away*

What, then, about those who choose to tell a cinematic fairy tale neither in the adult fairy tale mode of Del Toro, nor in the self-parodying fashion of *Enchanted* or the *Shrek* films, but in a manner aimed at teens and children that maintains conventional boundaries between the worlds of magic and reality?[11] The stresses and opportunities that contemporary intertextuality offers turn out to be just as decisive.

Jim Henson Productions' *MirrorMask*, directed by Dave McKean and written by Neil Gaiman, met with mixed critical reception for what appears to be its excessive faith in a formulaic and schematic understanding of the fairy tale. The most common complaint about the film was that its cinematic achievement—impressive though it was—still was not enough to sustain the viewer's interest in its weak plot and thin characterizations. "The

---

11   Both *MirrorMask* and *Spirited Away* are rated PG.

movie is a triumph of visual invention," wrote Roger Ebert, "but it gets mired in its artistry and finally becomes just a whole lot of great stuff to look at while the plot puts the heroine through a few basic moves over and over again" (2005).

The plot certainly follows a predictable set of conventions. A child protagonist (female in this case), faced with real-world problems she does not know how to deal with, enters a magic world where she meets a different set of challenges—a quest involving various magical tasks. When Helena (Stephanie Leonidas) completes the quest and reenters the real world, the audience understands that the magical experience has equipped her to work through the original problems, or at least discover the personal resources necessary to deal with them—in short to take a crucial step toward growing up and becoming an adult. In *MirrorMask,* the realistic development and rounding of characters in the initial situation is simply abandoned in favor of their visually stunning re-presentation in the fantastic world, where they appear as distorted doubles of their real selves, a doubling accentuated by an overriding moral dualism splitting them into good and evil halves.

The charge that fairy tale formula undermines the film's imaginative energy may, however, be countered by calling attention to its generic eclecticism. The fascinating dream world takes its striking stylistic vigor from the protagonist's drawings, which clearly provide the basis for much of its imagery and represent a psychological process of displaced autobiographical representation parallel to the story. (Gaiman's graphic novel version of *MirrorMask* is narrated entirely in the first person and through the protagonist's drawings.) The title of the film, which names the object of the protagonist's quest in the dream world, also refers to the complex function of the drawings. Acting both as reflecting surfaces and expressive windows between her inner and outer worlds, they both convey and hide the artist's feelings. They also dramatize her confusion about her proper role in her family and the way to deal with her developing sexuality. The drawings, in short, explore how what she sees in the mirror matches up with the masks she puts on.

The self-reflexive relationship of the drawings to the story-within-the-story parallels the self-conscious handling of text and interpretation within the dream. Books are not read but turn into magic vehicles when properly cajoled. The relationship between the dreamer's identity crisis and her family romance is not only elaborated in the elevated and polarized roles played by her mother as Queen of Light and Queen of Shadows (Gina McKee), her father as Prime Minister (Rob Brydon), and herself as Good Princess and Bad Princess but also through the film's playful allusions, not to the Oedipus myth but to its riddle. The main joke is that Helena counters the sphinx's well-known challenge by changing it into a neck riddle: one that usually functions in traditional tales, as it does in *MirrorMask*, to save the riddler's life but to which only one person—the riddler—can know the answer (Abrahams 1980, 8–9). It is not man who goes on four legs in the morning, two legs in the afternoon, and three legs at night, she declares, but rather the circus dog, which she saw running about normally in the morning, performing on two legs in the afternoon, and, for unknown reasons, limping on three in the evening.

Perhaps this substitution of an entirely personal solution for the Oedipal riddle's universal referent (with interpretations that can be sexualized or not) deflates generic expectation the same way that the insistence in *Ever After* about the historical reality of Cinderella does. The dreamer and the viewer know that the fairy tale sequence is not about good and bad queens and princesses but a particular talented teenage girl and her sick mother. The point, however, is not the framing realism of the narrative but its willing suspension in the center. The clever and funny way Helena befuddles the sphinx is also a joke about the dream—a dig at its adolescent self-involvement and a whimsical admission of how worn are the conventions that nonetheless get donned as provisional masks in the artist's private theater. The play with riddling reminds us, first, that formulas handicap those who put too much dull-witted faith in them—like *MirrorMask*'s comical sphinx but also like the New York girlfriend (Idina Menzel) in *Enchanted*, who decides true happiness lies in actually becoming the cartoon partner of her prince in Andalasia. Second, however, such play suggests that—like the library-books-cum-flying-carpets—these formulas can be transformed into serviceable vehicles for those who know how to tease them into life. The fun in this film depends as much on the allusions as the surprises, and no more heavily on the protagonist's uniqueness and depth than her typicality.

The status of types versus individuals is crucial to *MirrorMask*'s gender ideology and economy of values. Despite playing with the roles of princess and queen, *MirrorMask* enjoins its audience to make use of this typology, rather than consume or be consumed by it. Set to the tune of Burt Bacharach's "Close to You," the stylized dance scene, where clockwork dolls transform Helena into a fairy tale princess, is presented as dystopic in the film and the book—where the magic of dressing up is exposed visually as restrictive mask and aurally as hypnotic placebo: "I watched them as they took me, and they made me beautiful. It was like I was another girl, and I watched her clothes, her hair, her lips, as the dolls made her perfect. She was me, and yet she wasn't me at all. She wasn't angry. She didn't feel anything at all. . . . They had made me into the thing the Dark Queen wanted me to be—perfectly passive and, looking back on it, perfectly pathetic" (Gaiman 2005, n.p.). Helena never fully embraces the princess avatar—the ideal (obedient and controllable) child and the ideal (beautiful and controllable) woman—or the fetishistic costume that comes with it. And as soon as she can, Helena runs away from the enchanted palace.

The film thus distances itself quite unequivocally from the romance fantasy and attendant gender ideology of *Enchanted* and *Shrek*: its coming of age plot resolves in a back-to-work ending, rather than using happily-ever-after conventions. Tellingly, Helena's romantic interest is inspired by a helper and a trickster—a juggler, rather than a prince. Such plot and thematic decisions are also generic choices that position the film within a significantly different construction of the fairy tale's genealogy. In contrast to the way *Shrek* and *Enchanted* allude almost exclusively to the corpus of Hollywood fairy tale film, *MirrorMask* invokes a folklore tradition where stories solve the problems of a day, rather than plotting an ideal life. Helena performs the role of the smart and witty, if not wise, girl featured in folktales such as "The Clever Farmgirl" (ATU 875) and "Rescue by the Sister" (ATU 311). These girls make use of everyday experience or practical knowledge to answer riddles and pass tests posed by powerful men. And whether they marry or not, that is not the goal of their adventures (see Greenhill 2008).

It is to this idea of the fairy tale as a genre absorbed in "pleasure in the fantastic" and "curiosity about the real" (Warner 1994, xx) that Hayao Miyazaki's *Spirited Away* also connects. Like *MirrorMask*, this fairy tale film presents a girl's coming-of-age story that does not culminate in a wedding or have happily-ever-after closure. But in this case, Japanese *anime* (film) plays a role in generic expectations. The *shōjo*—literally "little female," functioning as "a shorthand for a certain kind of liminal identity between child and adult"—is pervasive in both *manga* (comics) and anime (Napier 2005, 148); and perhaps in reaction to American comic books and animated films, happy endings are not required in manga/anime (Kelts 2006, 34, 114).

Spirited Away shares with *MirrorMask* that typical fantasy structure whereby a girl's dreamlike or magic quest is framed by a realistic problem-posing plot. But successfully completing the quest hardly fixes everything:

the worlds to which Helena and Chihiro return remain problem filled. Ten-year-old Chihiro goes from being an unpromising heroine to an "intrepid" one (Zipes 2006a, 211), a shōjo upon whose courage—but also discipline and integrity—the rescue of others—the dragon Haku, the XL baby Bôh, and her parents—depends. Like the children in "Hansel and Gretel" (ATU 327A), Chihiro must contend with greed and the danger of being cannibal-ized, but as critics have noted, the fairy tale elements in *Spirited Away* are commenting specifically on Japanese twenty-first-century reality and cul-ture (Kelts 2006).

And yet to read *Spirited Away* as "an explicit critique of the consumer-ist lifestyle that created the shōjo phenomenon" in the first place (Napier 2005, 180) does not address the phenomenal success of this fairy tale film across national boundaries. This film's generic complexity has a multilayered transnational character. The fairy tale genre on which *Spirited Away* draws is grounded not only in a nonhomogeneous Euro-American tradition ("Hansel and Gretel" along with the cinematic *The Wizard of Oz* and Lewis Carroll's *Alice's Adventures in Wonderland*) but in Japanese folktales (Miyazaki's asser-tion in Reider 2005, 7). The fairy tale problem-solving plot combines with topoi of pollution and cannibalism found in older mythic and epic narra-tives from both the West (Proserpina's story as well as *The Odyssey*) and the East (the Japanese mythological story of Izanagi and Izanimi; Ibid., 5–6). Fairy tale fiction and real-world religion, especially Buddhist and Shinto beliefs, are also folded together (Anime and Popular Culture 2007). Here the fairy tale does not link up with the family legend, as in *Ever After*, but with a different kind of belief narrative that imbues specific places and natu-ral forces with spiritual power.

If the mix of fairy tale magic and religious belief is not new (the Brothers Grimm tales are heavily laden with Christian values and dialogue), the reani-mation of the connection between humans and nature that *Spirited Away* embodies has a peculiarly contemporary quality. Both moral and ecologi-cal, this message has at its center the reciprocal bond between Chihiro, the human girl tasked with saving herself, her parents, and others from greed and selfishness, and Haku, a boy who is also a captive white dragon that has forgotten he is a river god. In the English-language version of *Spirited Away*, this relationship is called "love," but it is not romance, and it lacks the sexual overtones of other anime. Rather, this connection energizes dynamics of care, respect, and responsibility that can be restorative, both for perceived social problems in Japan ("the increasing absence of the traditional family"

[Napier 2005, 148]) and the sustainability of life across nations in the face of the horrendous impact of human greed and exploitation on this planet.

In Conclusion

This essay has focused on generic complexity or hybridity to emphasize the competing social uses of the fairy tale in contemporary Western popular culture. Because the films we have considered are based on fairy tale fragments and bypass the retelling of any single tale, they are seeking to participate in the aura of the fairy tale—exploiting, exploring, and renewing the power of the genre. They conceive of that power differently, and the way they use it establishes different relationships between the fairy tale and the "real world." To return to one of our guiding metaphors—the economy of genres—we have tried to understand how choosing to use fairy tale elements invests in the genre: taking a position with respect to the values it entails and the stakes it raises. We have suggested, then, that these films' generic hybridity is symptomatic of the feminist destabilization of the gender ideology historically invested in the genre, with each film mobilizing generic alliances that seek to extend or contain the unsettling of the gender ideology in Disney-dominated fairy tale film.

The films also all intervene in the fairy tale's representational and rhetorical relationship to childhood, and collectively they chronicle a cultural struggle to control the power of the fairy tale to speak to and about the privileges and indulgences granted to childhood as well as the duties and responsibilities expected from maturity. While inevitably participating in the commodification of the fairy tale, each of these films furthers or contests the increasingly common practice of the genre to peddle its franchise byproducts by inculcating the desire to possess their "magic." Finally, the varied dynamics of these films' generic strategies depends upon the historical and cross-cultural hybridity of the fairy tale. "There was never such a thing as a 'pure' folktale or a 'pure' fairy tale" (Zipes 2001, 868–69), and the genre's competing genealogies are very much at work in the narrative and rhetorical construction of fairy tale enchantment in contemporary film.

Drawing on theories of Creole linguistics and his fieldwork in Indian Ocean islands, folklorist Lee Haring writes that hybridization of folktales and fairy tales "most often occurs when cultures converge and clash. Narratives are deterritorialized, decontextualized, combined with other narratives, and recontextualized in different settings and places" (2008, 466).

Such recombining and recontextualizing in recent fairy tale films impacts not just individual narratives but the genre itself. Contemporary hybridization of the fairy tale film reveals a clash of values—a struggle over gender construction and a fight to control the energies of fairy tale wonder—that is far from played out.

2

Building the Perfect Product
The Commodification of Childhood in Contemporary Fairy Tale Film

Naarah Sawers

In the twenty-first century, when genetic manipulation, robotics, organ transplants, and neuropharmaceutical drugs are familiar to most people's worldviews, the story of a little boy who is literally built by a paternal figure continues to engage audiences. The wooden puppet, Pinocchio, written into the cultural imagination by Carlo Collodi in 1883, provides a significantly different representation of childhood than contemporary ones but nonetheless continues to inform current questions about what childhood is, or should be. Collodi's original written text and its screen version, produced by the Disney Corporation in 1940, still speak to cultural analyses of childhood because they reflect a trajectory between the socialization of children and changes in capitalist society.

Collodi's *Pinocchio* provides a metaphor for the social construction of childhood, including what is necessary for the child's successful integration into adult society, and the Disney version offers a dominant model for fairy tale films in the big business of entertainment for children (Zipes 1996). While the ideologies in the book and the film reflect the sociohistoric times when they were created, both texts have important intertextual themes that re-emerge in contemporary films. However, scientific interventions into our bodies have become much more commonplace than they were when these *Pinocchio* texts were produced, and thus this chapter deals with the way films engage the concept of the built child to examine where they position childhood in the growing merger between science and capitalism.

Although they vary in their approach to the physical construction of their protagonists, *AI: Artificial Intelligence* (directed by Steven Spielberg,

2001) and *Robots* (directed by Chris Wedge and Carlos Saldanha, 2005) share with the literary fairy tale *Pinocchio* the notion of a child as manufactured. David (Haley Joel Osment), the protagonist of *AI,* is not only made by humans but is also literally designed for human consumption. As a mechanical, substitute child, he exists as a product in a market of human desire. He is a robot child, programmed to love in a future dystopian world where human capacities for care and responsibilities to others are demonstrably wanting. In *Robots,* however, humans are conspicuously absent in ways that suggest that the robot characters populating the world of the film are metaphorically human in much the same way as anthropomorphized animal characters in films like *The Lion King* (directed by Roger Allers and Rob Minkoff, 1994), *Shark Tale* (directed by Bibo Bergeron, Vicky Jenson, and Rob Letterman, 2004), and *Kung Fu Panda* (directed by Mark Osborne and John Stevenson, 2008). Indeed, using all robot characters as a metaphor for the human condition demonstrates the way that contemporary consumer society now focuses on the alteration of bodies.

Robots ostensibly critiques this new form of consumer capitalism. However, its critical surface is as easily removed as are its characters' external casings. This malleability is partly due to the ways in which it draws on the Disney fairy tale film model without employing the self-reflexivity available through intertextual referencing. Consequently, the film reinforces consumer capitalism primarily through focusing on the body as the center of commodification. *AI,* on the other hand, much more overtly references *Pinocchio* and critically engages the ways in which contemporary filmic stories for children potentially position them as objects for consumption.

While these two films of the new millennium draw on their fairy tale predecessors quite differently and provide alternative cultural perspectives on contemporary childhood, both persistently demonstrate that the manufacturing of childhood in the contemporary Western world is becoming much more literal than symbolic. The role of science in robotics and organ/ tissue distribution and exchange is crucial to new consumer enterprises, and both films point to the commodification of the child/body within these new scientific parameters. Unlike their intertextual ancestor, Pinocchio, the protagonists in the films in this chapter are not rewarded with a biological human form, and this shift away from the original narrative indicates the significance of scientific and technological interventions in human lives within contemporary capitalism.

Pinocchio, Childhood, and Capitalism

Considerable cultural anxiety accompanies the relationship between the child and consumer capitalism. Beryl Langer argues that present-day concepts of childhood, which center on the sacredness of children (where childhood is a time of enchantment), conflict with the ways in which children and childhood have become subjects of corporate greed and exploitation (2002, 71). However, the relationship between children and capitalism is changing, and these alterations are evident in Collodi's story of *Pinocchio,* the Disney version, and, as this chapter demonstrates, contemporary iterations.

The developmental process of Collodi's protagonist results in him becoming a "nice little boy" ([1883] 1973, 214). Niceness here is consistent with the responsibilities of a peasant boy in the nineteenth century and is thus demonstrated by hard work (necessary for capitalist economies) so that it is unsurprising that Pinocchio is principally affirmed when he works tirelessly for his father. The narrative explains that "by his industry, ingenuity and his anxiety to work and to overcome his difficulties, he not only succeeded in maintaining his father . . . but he also contrived to put aside forty pence to buy himself a new coat" (Ibid., 211). However—unlike what boys may do in the shopping-focused present day—Pinocchio doesn't buy himself a new coat. Instead, he gives the money to the fairy, a character who gives him advice about appropriate decision making throughout the narrative. The fairy is sick and impoverished at the time, so Pinocchio returns home and works not just until ten at night but until midnight to make more money for the fairy's well-being (Ibid., 212). This "pull-yourself-up-by-your-own-bootstraps fairytale" (Zipes 1996, 11) describes the position of childhood in an industrial society where children become part of the workforce: their integration into society is marked by their ability to labor for production.

The shift from the child as an industrious worker, who labors primarily for the sustenance of the family, to an individual consumer can be traced through the growth of the Disney empire to which—along with the production of *Snow White and the Seven Dwarfs* (directed by David Hand, 1937)—the film version of *Pinocchio* (directed by Hamilton Luske and Ben Sharpsteen, 1940) was absolutely critical (particularly as a model for future fairy tale films). As has been well documented, Disney made himself fastidiously familiar with Collodi's story but also took huge interpretive license (Zipes 1996).

Disney was concerned with the socialization of American childhood in the 1930s and '40s, a time when America was suffering an economic depression but was also looking toward a future of expansive economic growth during and following World War II. His intention was to capture a mass-culture market (Wasko 2001) and "offer hope in the form of beautifully made films that provide escape from the grim realities of America" at the time (Zipes 1996, 16). To accomplish this goal, the story line is minimized and replaced with enhanced images, songs, and dances that reaffirm the moral lessons. This model has become extremely influential in children's animated and fairy tale film, becoming a new commodity where "the fairy tale film sacrifices art to technical innovation; innovation to tradition; stimulation of the imagination to consumption for distraction" (Ibid., 9). Child audiences of films based on the Disney model are therefore considered primarily consumers, and thus the shift from the written narrative to the film one represents a conflation of pleasure and consumption.

Contemporary children's identities are thus defined by a relationship of desire with consumerism. Children learn not only that they must consume but also that their choices assemble their sense of self in relation to others. The consumer child becomes normalized in contemporary society as "a historically specific product of capitalist market expansion which requires that they learn 'how to want, and in a very particular way'" (Langer 2002, 72). Consumption is increasingly integral to children's sense of self because brands have become signifiers of identity and group affiliation (Bullen 2009, 498.). However, desires for capitalist products can never be satiated because, while consumer societies rest on the "promise to satisfy human desires," this "promise remains seductive . . . only so long as the desire stays ungratified" (Bauman 2007, 80). Therefore, to sustain consumer capitalism, its signifiers into which young people are enculturated must shift so that fulfillment is always deferred and obsolescence guaranteed. Films for children are embedded in this process: not only is the film a product of consumption, but merchandising, cross-selling, and product placement promote a range of brand names with which children identify (Kenway and Bullen 2001). Many authors in this collection note that the primary intention of popular fairy tale film is the creation of a mass commodity. My examination extends this insight to reveal the way the two films I discuss position children as consumers in the diegesis[1] and/or the way the films critique the process of making children into consumable objects.

Both are mainstream movies with big budgets and well-known actors, but *Robots* is an animated production for children, and *AI* is a live-action, dystopian film with a PG-13 rating. *AI* thus speaks more overtly to the way adults perceive childhood in a contemporary consumer-capitalist world. The film marks a specific change in the relationship between childhood and capitalism where the child has literally become the product for consumption. However, this shift from the child as a consumer to the child as a product can also be traced in *Robots* because, although it critiques the construction of children's identities through consumerism, it simultaneously assumes and reinforces the notion that children are consumable. The idea that the child is a commodity primarily comes from the way *Robots* sees the body as a consumable site, where organs and tissues are metaphorically exchangeable. The film thus engages in debates about methods of exchange, either through the economic system or gifts. However, the turn in the relationship between capitalism and childhood initiated by new scientific interventions is a point of contemporary anxiety that is visible in *AI*.

AI: Tales of Perpetual Childhood

If Disney's *Pinocchio* constructs a protagonist who is "almost too perfect to be true" (Zipes 1996, 20), Spielberg's *AI* literally creates the perfect child as a commodity. It depicts a future world where environmental destruction has wreaked so much havoc that it is legally sanctioned for couples "from the developed worlds" to have only one child. Mechanoid robots, or *mechas,* such as the prostitute lover robot, have been built for immediate, but temporary, gratification of human demands. The film thus reflects present-day realities where machines are already used for labor and robot toys are increasingly entering the marketplace.[2] Extending the market for satisfying human desires, the film opens with Professor Hobby (William Hurt), from

---

1   Similarly Linda Pershing and Lisa Gablehouse demonstrate in their chapter in this collection that *Enchanted* (directed by Kevin Lima, 2007) entices its female viewers to consume, not only by showing the main characters shopping but also in Disney's marketing of products, such as dolls and clothing related to the film.

2   The Japanese company Sega, for instance, recently released a robotic girlfriend that kisses on demand. Minako Sakanoue, a spokeswoman for Sega, is quoted as saying, "She's very lovable and though she's not human, she can act like a real girlfriend" (Busty Bot for Lonely Hearts 2008).

the company Cybertronics, proposing to his colleagues/students that they invent a mecha child, a type of "substitute" who will be unique by being programmed to love unconditionally.

In this key scene, the computer scientists and robotics designers gather in a Cybertronics classroom that, reminiscent of a university tutorial, implies an educational institution. But the institute housing this learning is also a multinational robotics company. Consequently, education in this future world is about science thinking creatively to sustain consumer capitalism, and the film foregrounds the growing relationship between the two. The lack of ethical deliberation about the cultural implications of the creative products that result from this merger becomes an ideological center in the film. Though science works to serve capitalism—which perceives cultural criticism and research provided by the humanities as less valuable because they cannot be quantified by market worth—fictional and fairy tale films offer a medium for critical and ethical reflection about where humanity is heading. *AI* addresses this concern by canvassing the social implications a neocapitalist world has for human relationships, particularly when childhood is the focus of new science.

However, the question of ethics is not lost on one of Professor Hobby's female colleagues, who points out that humans may be able to program a mecha child to love its parent(s) but asks, "Can you get a human to love a mecha back?" She wonders aloud "what responsibilities does that person hold to the mecha?" Mechas are used for human services, as the narrator explains, and, except for their initial manufacturing, don't use valuable resources. However, they are a lower order than humans, and the tension between organic and mecha beings is represented in the film by human characters who discuss being taken over by these new others. However, the film does not simply pit humans against mechas in a hierarchy that assumes human superiority; instead, its comments about the human capacity to be responsible to other humans (and organic and inorganic nonhuman entities) in a neocapitalist world are far more compelling.

The question of reciprocal love between humans and robots drives the plot because it also shapes the quest of the mecha-child protagonist, David. The first mecha child built by Cybertronics, he is given to Monica (Frances O'Connor) and Henry Swinton (Sam Robards) as a substitute for their son, Martin (Jake Thomas), who lies in a cryogenic state due to an unexplained accident five years earlier. After David arrives at their home, Monica "imprints" him so that he is programmed to love her unconditionally.

However, shortly after David has been imprinted, Martin miraculously recovers and returns home. Although Martin looks like a cyborg with mechatronic assistance for his legs and a large supply of pills to keep his body functioning, he is very much Monica's real son. David, on the other hand, may "look like someone's ordinary kid" as Martin observes, but is—as Henry reminds Monica—"inside, just like all the rest . . . a hundred miles of fiber."

The ensuing antagonism between Martin and David, and the threat David's love for Monica creates for the family, causes Henry to insist that Monica take David back to Cybertronics to certain death. Instead, she leaves him in the woods—like the children in "Hansel and Gretel" or "Babes in the Woods" (ATU 327A) and "Snow White" (ATU 709)—in what amounts to an aggregate of fairy tale references that preempt childish adventures. Monica tells David she "wishes she had told him more about the world"; for his part, David pleads with her, saying, "If you love me, I'll be so real for you."

In this film, reality or knowing the self as real is therefore intimately connected to relationships with others, specifically, the mother. Even though Teddy, the mecha supertoy (an upgraded, computerized version of the stuffed bear) who is with David throughout the narrative, and Gigolo Joe (Jude Law), the sex robot David befriends on his adventures, prove to be far more caring, David doggedly perseveres in his quest to return to Monica.[3] He traverses the classic three fairy tale adventures of conflict and escape (Zipes 1996, 19) and discovers the brutality of humans who revel in destroying mechas Colosseum style and ultimately obliterate biological life on earth. The end of the film races forward to show audiences that after two thousand years, human civilization has been destroyed. Aliens now inhabit the earth, and David and Teddy are frozen at the bottom of the ocean, having never returned home to Monica and the Swintons. However, after David and Teddy are revived, the aliens recreate Monica at David's request so that he spends a final day with her, and she tells him that she loves him.

Many critics read this ending as Spielberg "sentimentality" (Morrissey 2004, 250). In his discussion of the concluding scenes of the film, Thomas Morrissey writes that Spielberg attempts to "put a happy face on this dismal human self-portrait" and consequently the "classic dystopian theme—the

---

3   Pauline Greenhill and Anne Brydon discuss family relationships in fairy tale film in this volume. Also Sidney Eve Matrix looks at the representation of sexual relationships.

horror of enforced, perpetual childhood—is set adrift" (Ibid., 250). However, happy endings for protagonists are expected in contemporary fairy tale films because of the homogenization of the genre by Disney (Wasko 2001; Artz 2004). Yet, Disney doesn't deserve all the blame; even Collodi acquiesced to the reading public's demand that the puppet become a real boy, thus creating a satisfying and happy conclusion (Zipes 1996, 12).

In drawing upon *Pinocchio,* the film indicates the ways that stories for children construct childhood by socializing their audience. However, because the fairy tale intertext in *AI* is embedded within a dystopian narrative about the relationship between childhood and science in a capitalist world, a tension between the genres results. Indeed, Spielberg harnesses this tension to comment critically on cultural anxieties about the role of new scientific technologies and the function of stories for children by adults in relation to new economic realities.

The crux of the happy ending for contemporary Disneyfied films includes the triumph of the good character (Wasko 2001, 119) and, in line with traditional quest narratives, a return home (Campbell 1968, 246). However, even though the conclusion of *AI* seemingly adapts these conventions because David's quest is successfully completed when he receives his mother's love in the family home, the final scenes do not include the values of "fixed meanings" and "certainties about life" that usually accompany closure in fictional stories for children (Stephens 1992, 41). Instead, the mise-en-scène in the conclusion constructs a counterfeit image because the house (setting) and Monica (character) have been recreated specifically for David by the alien beings. More tellingly, the creation and experience of their loving relationship is constructed as a quasi-theatrical performance where David and Monica are actors—stringless puppets—in an artificial house with the alien audience watching from above.

The element of puppetry crucially invokes the Disney film. Its protagonist, Pinocchio, was considered unique by the evil Stomboli because he was a puppet without strings. Stomboli wanted to use Pinocchio to earn money by performing onstage (made much simpler by the lack of strings). Thus, when Spielberg creates a scene where the characters remind us of stringless puppets, he raises the question of whether the good protagonist, David, in fact triumphs in his quest. He wishes to be a "real live boy," a desire he believes will be granted through his mother's love and the blue fairy. The blue fairy is a direct reference to Collodi's text, which Monica had read to David and Martin, but the fairy only appears in the film as a large Madonna-like statue that David and Teddy find at the bottom of the ocean.

That David's reality is contingent upon the blue fairy—as an intertextual reference to *Pinocchio* and thus to fairy tales—demonstrates the significance of stories for children in constructing childhood. The need for a mother's love and the consequences of its lack are deeply embedded in stories for children and can be connected to myths and fairy tales that frequently include absent and cruel mothers and stepmothers (Warner 1994). But the way the relationship between the mother and child is interpreted has become the foundation of cultural (and scientific) investigation through psychoanalysis.

David's experience of himself and love as real is thus further challenged by the object of his desire. What the audience sees is a primordial (and perverse) scene of the pre-Oedipal relationship between mother and son. Monica and David spend the day together alone, without Henry or Martin. When Monica disposes of her wedding ring, it signifies that their love will be unimpeded. Indeed, the viewer is left with the image of the couple asleep in bed together, holding hands. That David's journey concludes with the son, like Oedipus, actually sleeping with the mother suggests that he does not progress to the symbolic order or through the Oedipal complex to establish his identity and achieve maturity. Rather, unable to separate from his mother, David remains in the unformed state of childhood, and this scene is probably the most abject one in the film.

Viewing audiences both create and consume the concluding scene within the diegesis and, as puppet masters, are integral to the way the relationship plays out. The ending comments about the way contemporary relationships, particularly between adult and child, are subject to capitalist and psychoanalytic influences embedded in stories for children. *AI* is a film predominantly for mature audiences, and adults are thus the creators and consumers of the commodified child (as a perfect entity whose love is unreserved and unrelenting). It is even more telling, then, that in the final scene the audience consumes, fulfillment is satiated; it is the moment of plentitude. Crucial to psychoanalytic models of development is the separation of the mother from the son, just as contemporary consumer capitalism is based on the insistence that people separate from products that previously promised satisfaction. This separation (or obsolescence) is built into consumer societies because "for the expectations [of satisfaction] to be kept alive and for new hopes to promptly fill the void left by hopes already discredited and discarded, the road from shop to garbage bin needs to be short and the passage swift" (Bauman 2007, 82). In this sense, the film marks a critical juncture in the workings of human relationships in a consumer society because it marks the point where consumer capitalism is entirely sidelined: both parties, mother and son, are complete in each other's company.

Consumer capitalism and psychoanalytic models require that real boys displace their mothers for an endless chain of referents. While Monica's biological son, Martin's, normative (human) development progress requires him to replace his mother with love for endless other things and people, David is not (and can never be) absorbed into capitalist culture. He is consumed by love for the mother and needs no material possessions, not even the food, shelter, and other basic necessities that are precursors to the consumer drive. So indelible is this mother love that he cannot be reprogrammed and would have had to be euthanized—making him in some ways the logical conclusion of the humanist belief in an immutable essential self that postmodern and psychoanalytic thinking has challenged.

While science can facilitate the construction of perfect children (or the creation of designer children), where the child becomes a commodified product promising gratification, the nature of the closing scenes in *AI* contests these assurances by affirming the endless repetition of desire that psychoanalytic development models posit as crucial to human subjectivity. That the audience observes the pre-Oedipal scene reinforces fairy tales' role in the socialization of children, particularly the ways in which their interpretations have often been reduced to psychoanalytical narratives (Tatar 1992). This point is significant because it places the blame for any difficulties faced by child protagonists on the children themselves and, in turn, sanctions interventions into childhood. Maria Tatar notes that "if we read myths and fairy tales through the lens of the oedipal drama, we will necessarily see the child as the sole target of therapeutic intervention, for it is children who must work through the feelings of anger expressed through the stories told to them by adults" (1992, xxvi).

AI thus clarifies that the reiteration of the Oedipal drama in cultural contexts and through children's stories and their interpretations results in the wholly manufactured child (intervention in extremis). Furthermore, stories for children that formulaically conclude with happy endings reinforce these promises of self-fulfillment. In the Oedipal drama—and psychoanalytic models that rely on it—human subjectivity is based on lack. Thus, consumer society is sustained because consumption promises to satisfy desire initiated by lack.

David's love for Monica is as fixed as are happy endings in stories for children. However, Monica's love is more flexible, which means that David can be a substitute son with the potential to take Martin's place in her affections. Had Monica bought this toy child, she would be unreflexively emblematic of what is perhaps the most shocking new dimension of consumerism—the purchase of children—and indeed, David is a prototype model who is sold. However, that Monica is an uncertain recipient of this gift (rather like gifted, as opposed to bought, organs, as I will discuss) is one of Spielberg's most critical choices in depicting the relationship (or disjunction) between consumerism and genuine love.

Consuming a child who has been wholly manufactured is the dystopian emphasis of the narrative. That children may become commodifed objects is, in the main, a reprehensible idea.[4] However, there is often a slippage between the consuming child—whose identity is built upon patterns of consumption—and the commodified child, who becomes the product of adult consumption. This gap depends upon new manifestations of consumer society that focus on the body and is exemplified by the heroic narrative writ through Rodney as the youthful protagonist in the animated film for children, *Robots*.

Robots: New Biotechnical Fashions

Robots is a conventional mainstream animated film for children. Though not created by Disney, it nevertheless draws on the children's animation model made famous by Disney's *Pinocchio*. The narrative in *Robots* does the work that *AI* critiques: it presents an Oedipal trajectory as normal and natural, concludes with a happy ending, and is entirely devoid of ethical deliberation or self-reflexivity (favoring instead distraction through consumption). My analysis of *Robots* demonstrates that this film, as emblematic of contemporary films for children, presents the commodification of the child as natural. It thus socializes children to assume that their commodification is not simply a natural process but a culturally sanctioned right. No

---

4   The presence of so-called surrogate motherhood—the medical commercialization of conception—and the advent of "push presents" (expensive gifts from father to mother, often offered during the actual delivery of a child) suggest that the commodified child is a current reality.

longer simply subject to consumer influences, the child's quest is to become a product for consumption.

The shift from the child as consumer to the child as commodity occurs primarily through new scientific discoveries that focus on the body. Manufactured bodies result not just from robotics or cyborgs but also through biotechnical interventions in human bodies. Biotechnologies are the main players in creating designer children. In her analysis of the relationship between children and new science, Elaine Ostry argues that biotechnologies focus on "creating 'improved' children, designer babies, screening foetuses, and as the material site for the administration of neuropharmaceutical drugs" (2004, 222–23). However, in a global capitalist world—the "killer whale inside which we have to live" (Suvin 2003, 193)—biotechnological enhancement is not a philanthropic enterprise.

The ethical dilemma in *AI* centers on the boundaries between the non-human robot and the organic human, and David's nonhuman or manufactured difference remains at the center of the narrative. However, in *Robots,* the characters are all manufactured robots standing in for humans. Using robots as the main characters, rather than anthropomorphized animals, for example, enables the surface story to critique consumer capitalism and thus capitalize on cultural anxieties about children and consumption while, at the same time, promoting the interests of consumer capitalism predominantly through the unquestioned assumption that human beings are enhanced or manufactured. Defining the characters this way means that their mechanical bodies are subject to wear and tear and replacement of parts with newer, better ones is a necessity. Thus, what is particularly telling about this film is the way in which it both critiques the obsolescence and waste in consumer society and simultaneously undermines this criticism by firmly (though metaphorically) reinforcing new biotechnical businesses.

Robots overtly criticizes consumer capitalism by initially marginalizing the protagonist and his family and friends because of their economic status. Rodney and his family, the Copperbottoms, are from the lower socioeconomic class. His father, Herb, is a dishwasher in a restaurant in the small midwestern-style community where they live, Rivet Town. Early in the film, Rodney moves to Robot City, and the friends he makes there are in a similarly dire financial situation. Their lives are threatened because they can neither get new parts for their dysfunctional bodies nor afford the only product available to replace them. It is therefore the Copperbottoms' and Rodney's friends' inability to access all that consumer society offers—and thus the marginalization of the poor in a consumer-driven society—that is the subject of the film.

In addition to aligning viewers with the underclass by directing their sympathies to the potentially obsolete characters, *Robots* appears to critique corporate malpractice and the abuses of today's capitalism by comparing 1950s values to those of the twenty-first century. *Robots* opens with Herb, Rodney's father, running through the streets of Rivet Town telling people that "the baby is being delivered today." The street scenes hark back to an era when children's identities did not depend on their consumer habits. The toys on the streets of Rivet Town include skipping ropes, slinkies, and wind-ups, all long-lasting products compared with those that Beryl Langer calls *commoditoys*. Generic toys, such as building blocks, dolls, toy cars, and train sets, may be handed down through the generations. Commoditoys, on the other hand, "are characterised by their capacity to stimulate rather than satisfy longing"; they have a "short but intense 'shelf life' as objects of desire"; and their essential feature is that "satiation is endlessly postponed" (Langer 2002, 70). The generic toys in the initial scene reflect the community spirit and family atmosphere of Rivet Town, and the film's nostalgia for this environment and its values opposes the speed, waste, and alienation of contemporary consumer society.

The physical appearance of Rodney's dad, Herb, also recalls postwar American values because his chest is a 1950s-style dishwasher. However, he is exploited and exhausted by his work dishwashing so that he regularly tires at night and brings his work home. Rodney, concerned about his father, creates Wonderbot, an (animated) invention to lessen his workload. Rodney takes Wonderbot to Bigweld, the benign CEO/owner of Bigweld Industries, who wants to make the world better by using technological progress to advance human happiness. His slogan, "See a need, fill a need," sums up the good model of technology, that it is designed to make life easier. The message therefore is not that industry and production are bad but that their contemporary manifestations involve wasteful obsolescence, generated by commoditoys and advertising that produce desires in consumers that don't reflect genuine need.

But the robot characters in *Robots* are not supertoys or commoditoys like *AI*'s Teddy. Instead, as metaphorically human, they suggest that people are becoming obsolete and must be repaired or replaced. This process is most obvious from the physical deterioration of Herb. Rodney's quest takes him to Robot City to introduce Wonderbot to Bigweld, but his father gets increasingly sick while he is away. We see this decline when Rodney calls home, and a mechanic/doctor is peering into Herb's open chest, surveying the damage. Herb tells Rodney that they are "having a little trouble finding your old man a spare part." The unavailable spare part (read, heart) is thus parallel to people's access to health services where the boundaries between the cosmetic and noncosmetic, and the life-saving and life-extending medical interventions, are fluid.

According to the anthropological scholarship of Catherine Waldby and Robert Mitchell, the most compelling promises generated by the merger between biotechnologies and capitalism are "the fantasies of immortality" (2006, 17). Bodies are intensely recast in the current era of biotechnologies, especially because they are the site for new science and capitalism's expressions of selfhood. The fact that Herb's anatomy includes a dishwasher emphasizes this fusion by making a consumer product a fundamental part of his being. But related to capitalism's expressions of selfhood through the body, the dishwasher positions Herb within a labor economy, rather than a consumer one, because he is literally defined by his work. However, his relationship to capitalism changes when he receives the spare part to fix his deteriorating body. This development shows that Herb has access to the new consumer economies that center around science and the body.

In contemporary consumer society, the body has become an adjunct to the marketplace; the central significance of new biotechnologies is the "unprecedented possibility of extending life indefinitely with the organs of others" (Waldby and Mitchell 2006, 179). The spare part that Herb has trouble finding thus reflects the perceived lack of body tissues or organs in the current world and the increased demand for them. It marks the body as a consuming site integrated into the trade in body parts and materials, where human flesh becomes fodder for the dynamics of capitalist consumption. However, and most significantly, what underlies these biotechnical practices is the promise that tissue economies will deliver self-regenerating bodies (Ibid.). This development has "created a cultural desire for, and sense of entitlement to, self-regeneration among ageing populations of the wealthy North" (Ibid., 162). This new expectation of longevity also puts pressure on "real-time" therapies, for instance, organ transplants (Ibid.). For these therapies to become accepted as a moral right within a market economy, society needs stories that make the transactions that precede them seem ethically uncomplicated. Unlike *AI*, which draws attention to the way stories for children are implicated in manufacturing bodies as normal, *Robots* sanctions the rise of tissue economies.

These new scientific economies are based on neoliberal ideas, where the body as commodity and exchangeable is accepted as an individual choice or right. As a commodity, the body is also subject to market economies. Whether or not organs should be marketable products is the subject of current bioethical debates, particularly in America (Joralemon 2000). The narrative of *Robots* supports the ideological imperative sustaining the commodifiable body by making the distinction between need and want as a way to correct consumption patterns, and then establishing a tension between the two, beginning with playing off the terminology of delivering goods against delivering babies. Rodney's own construction offers the most profound example. When he is born/built, the film highlights biotechnological interventions into childhood; Rodney's parents, for instance, choose his nose and eyes from his grandparents, they select his sex, and when he cries, they simply turn the sound down. The film doesn't challenge this early (medical) childhood intervention by the parents.

However, as Rodney grows and becomes too big for his external casings, he receives new "parts," which are donated by cousins and humiliate him, particularly those from his cousin Veronica, whose parts are coded feminine. Parts thus function as a metaphor for both clothes and body organs, where the former is identified with desire for fashion and the latter with necessity. However, when Rodney's impoverished street friends in Robot City, the "outmodes," are headed for certain death without access to parts (they are literally falling apart), their parts unquestionably represent organs, rather than clothes. Any potential criticism of want (which consumer capitalism promises to fulfill) is undermined by needs as access to life-saving or regenerating health services (spare parts).

By the end of the film, Herb does not receive just one new part but "enough parts to make two of [him]," including a saxophone to replace his dishwasher. His material (biological) gains are due to Rodney's achievements. The son progresses up the social ladder because his reward is material wealth far beyond his childhood circumstances. Having destroyed the film's antagonist, Ratchet, Bigweld and Rodney return to Rivet Town. In the concluding scenes, Bigweld tells the community, including Rodney's parents, that Rodney is his "right-hand bot" and "eventual successor."

Rodney thus becomes a model for contemporary capitalist success aligned with correct Oedipal development, and this image is reinforced by his love interests. He is initially admired by Piper, one of the street kids who befriends him when he gets to Robot City. Piper is identified in the film as available for romantic conquest, and she is young, spunky, and outspoken. However, Rodney literally outgrows her and thus manifests the capacity for maturation that *AI*'s David can never share. Rodney therefore seeks satisfaction from an upgraded model in Cappy. She works as an executive officer for Bigweld Industries and symbolizes the trophy wife. Unlike Piper, who is made from colorful spare parts, Cappy is a shiny metallic gray, wearing an expensive hegemonic outfit unavailable to the underclass outmodes, and is regularly admired for her physique. In the final scene, Cappy's presence by Rodney's side consolidates his manhood by symbolizing the ultimate reward and thus demonstrating what self-improvement can achieve. Rodney's movement toward this final goal entirely counterpoints David's stasis. He has successfully displaced his desire for a mother to others, and thus his innate lack will be (temporarily) gratified by acquiring them.

Acquiring female others, extensively critiqued in feminist scholarship, becomes increasingly disturbing as society in the global North moves into harvesting body parts from underclasses and the global South. Rodney exists as a consuming body, but the hand-me-down parts he receives during his childhood mean that he has to rely on the generosity of others. Herb's type of body, attached as it is to his labor worth, positions him outside present-day tissue economies. Herb is teetering on the edge of the underclass Zygmunt Bauman observes as emerging in the new consumer economies that focus on the body: those who are "truly and fully useless— redundant, supernumerary leftovers of a society reconstituting itself as a society of consumers" (2007, 101). But he is saved by his son's success and, like the elite, aging, and wealthy of the global North, is now entitled to self-regenerating economies.

In a gesture of material exchange between men that constitutes patriarchy (Sedgwick 1987), Herb's new parts are a gift from Bigweld. However, Herb's receiving them is wholly determined by his son's economic success; Rodney's reward is to become a corporate capitalist just like Bigweld, and in doing so, he can reward his father with a much-needed body part (heart). This singular gift-giving event, which identifies Bigweld as a particularly benevolent character, is entirely underscored by a market economy in parts. There is no question that these acts of giving will be extended to the outmodes or the general population of impoverished robots needing (wanting) new parts. In this case, gifts are the exception to the rule, and the norm is a

market economy; thus this story socializes child audiences into conceptual-
izing the body within a market ethos.

    This new representation of Pinocchio in *Robots*' Rodney is therefore
similar to its predecessors in foregrounding his relationship with his father.
Son provides for father as Collodi's Pinocchio did; Rodney makes his father
happy as Disney's Pinocchio did; he was built obedient, honest, and dili-
gent (and male) and thus was always "easily manipulated for the good of
the country, the good of the corporation," as Zipes argues in the case of
Disney's Pinocchio (1996, 20). But Rodney has become a particularly good
child because he literally embodies the force behind the expansion of global
capitalism into the realm of the body, and he single-handedly enables his
father's access to this new aspect of consumer society. The dystopian world
constructed and critiqued in *AI* is realized through precisely this type of
story, which invites child audiences to aim for successes similar to Rodney's.

Today's Stories of Body Building

Like Pinocchio, Rodney is humanized by his love for his father and his capit-
ulation to ever-changing capitalist systems. Capitalism relies on patriarchal
hierarchies so that the Oedipal boy child, by identifying with the father, can
shift his desires away from the pricelessness of mother love into the space
of continually shifting wants. A female substitute ultimately replaces the
mother but only boys who become men by attaining a successful place as
money earners in the capitalist system can acquire her. In contrast, David
and Monica are consumed by their uncontested love for each other. Thus,
it is Monica's love for a nonhuman child, described on the same level as
her love for her biological son, that destabilizes capitalism. If she genuinely
loves David, he will become—like a real son—irreplaceable. If he can't be
upgraded for a new model, then how will capitalism flourish?

    That *AI* embodies both a threat and a comfort, a happy and disturb-
ing conclusion, indicates the film's criticism of Disney-style fairy tales for
children that avoid the ethical complexities in the modern consumer world.
There remains concern, then, about the tales told to children to civilize
them into ways of being. The use of the metaphor of the built child puppet
in the *Pinocchio* texts has lined up with capitalist changes from socializing
the child into joining a productive labor force to inducing her or him to
shape an identity based on consumption. But modern consumer society has
changed once again; now it has its sights set on human bodies. As Bauman

explains, "The consumer's/consuming body is 'autotelic', its own purpose and a value in its own right; in the society of consumers it also happens to be the ultimate value" (2007, 91). In line with this aim, contemporary films employing the metaphor of the built child do so much more literally than did their predecessors. To civilize contemporary children into hegemonic society through stories, they must understand their bodies as consumers in and of themselves.

3

The Parallelism of the Fantastic and the Real
Guillermo del Toro's *Pan's Labyrinth/El Laberinto del fauno*
and Neomagical Realism

Tracie D. Lukasiewicz

Fairy tales have undergone multiple changes and evolved over the centuries as a result of the prejudices and preferences of authors, folklorists, and film directors, producers, and screenwriters. For example, Cinderella's tale (ATU 510A), replicated in Disney's *Cinderella* (directed by Clyde Geronimi, Wilfred Jackson, and Hamilton Luske, 1950) and *Ever After* (directed by Andy Tennant, 1998), also provided the inspiration for works like *Pretty Woman* (directed by Garry Marshall, 1990) and *Maid in Manhattan* (directed by Wayne Wang, 2002). All share elements commonly associated with fairy tales, such as the phrase "once upon a time," angelic princesses (with or without royal blood), evil stepmothers (or nasty employers), fairy godmothers (or even a helpful male concierge in *Pretty Woman*), and the ultimate triumph of good over evil. These basics lead to the essentially redundant happily-ever-after that the primary characters achieve, allowing hearers, readers, and viewers to feel a certain confidence in the outcome.[1]

Guillermo del Toro's *Pan's Labyrinth/El Laberinto del fauno* (2006), however, presents a much more ominous take on the fairy tale. But despite its lack of the bright colors, comedic characters, and extravagant happiness that mark most well-known fairy tale films—at least those for children—it remains linked to the genre through its use of elements, archetypes, and

---

1 Ming-Hsun Lin, Linda Pershing and Lisa Gablehouse, and Christy Williams discuss and deconstruct these patterns in this volume.

motifs in the original tales. That is—like many of the less familiar stories collected by the Grimm brothers, which contain "graphic descriptions of murder, mutilation, cannibalism, infanticide and incest" (Tatar 2004, 3)—*Pan's Labyrinth* includes violence and betrayal.[2] It juxtaposes a bitter and dark reality with the fantastical world—indeed, one with its own torments—experienced by a little girl.[3]

Writer/director del Toro states that "the one thing that alchemy understands and fairy tale lore understands is that you need the vile matter for magic to flourish. You need lead to turn it into gold. You need the two things for the process. So, when people sanitize fairy tales and homogenize them, they become completely uninteresting for me" (quoted in Roberts 2006). In making *Pan's Labyrinth*, del Toro drew upon events he witnessed while growing up in Mexico, as well as on his own imagination, to create a story that is in itself a labyrinth; "a maze is a place where you get lost, but a labyrinth is essentially a place of transit: an ethical, moral transit to one inevitable center" (del Toro, quoted in Arroyo 2006). Thus, his film fluidly intertwines characters and events to bring them to its concluding cohesion—fundamentally its centralized meeting point. Like its labyrinth, del Toro's film leads the viewer to its moral center with the ultimate death of the corrupt and evil villain. The physical maze on screen interlaces with stories in the film but also with the combination of realism, Grimm brutality, and fairy tale expectations that the narrative weaves together.

Pan's Labyrinth presents a realistic and violent story and parallels it to an equally dark and vicious fairy tale. The two run alongside one another but do not cross paths. The characters and places of each world exist separately, connected only through the character of Ofelia (Ivana Baquero). Del Toro's work draws simultaneously upon magical realism and fairy tales, providing an exemplar for neomagical realism—a hybrid genre, as discussed in Cristina Bacchilega and John Rieder's chapter. In this chapter, I examine, explore, and define the way that magical realism and fairy tales help explain Ofelia's fantasy and real worlds. I thus develop the concept of neomagical realism to

---

2   Cristina Bacchilega and John Rieder, Pauline Greenhill and Anne Brydon, Sidney Eve Matrix, Brian Ray, Naarah Sawers, and Kim Snowden discuss more exceptions to the generalization of the sweet, innocent fairy tale in this collection.

3   As discussed later in greater detail, I use *fantastic* to refer to anything supernatural that occurs for which the reader/viewer (and/or the protagonist) has no commonsensical explanation. Fundamentally similar terms include *magical, extraordinary,* and *wonderful.*

distinguish *Pan's Labyrinth* from the conventional fairy tale's acceptance of magic within its fantasy world, and magical realism's incorporation of magic into the real world.

The Fantastic, the Marvelous, and the Uncanny

Fantasy is derived from the Latin word *"phantasticus,* which means that which is made visible, visionary, unreal. In this general sense, all imaginary activity is fantastic, all literary works are fantasies" (Jackson 1981, 13). However, despite bending the rules and requirements of the real, the world of fantasy has "an obligation to coherence and to the establishment of a relationship with the reader's experience" (Mathews 1997, 3–4). No matter how outlandish a fantasy plot may be, it nonetheless remains tied to the real world. Fantasy "re-combines and inverts the real, but it does not escape it: it exists in a parasitical or symbiotic relation to the real. The fantastic cannot exist independently of that 'real' world which it seems to find so frustratingly finite" (Jackson 1981, 20). The fantastic references "what *could not have happened*; i.e. what *cannot* happen, what *cannot* exist….Fantasy violates the real, contravenes it, denies it, and insists on this denial throughout" (Russ 1973, 52).

For some the fantastic is simply one literary form among many (including horror, fairy tale, and science fiction) within the genre of fantasy "which have similar structural characteristics and which seem to be generated by similar unconscious desires. Through their particular manifestations of desire, they can be associated together" (Jackson 1981, 8). Rosemary Jackson calls fantasy "an enormous and seductive subject. Its association with imagination and with desire has made it an area difficult to articulate or to define, and indeed the 'value' of fantasy has seemed to reside in precisely this resistance to definition, in its 'free-floating' and escapist qualities" (Ibid., 1). For Jackson fantasy is a

> literary mode from which a number of related genres emerge. . . . As a critical term, "fantasy" has been applied rather indiscriminately to any literature which does not give priority to realistic representation: myths, legends, folk and fairy tales . . . all presenting realms "other" than the human. A characteristic most frequently associated with literary fantasy has been its obdurate refusal of prevailing definitions of the "real" or "possible," a refusal amounting at times to violent opposition. (Ibid., 7–14)

However, Tzvetan Todorov specifies and then distinguishes within the concept. To this literary theorist and philosopher, fantastic literature offers "a world which is indeed our world, the one we know, a world without devils, sylphides, or vampires, [where] there occurs an event which cannot be explained by the laws of this same familiar world," producing the "hesitation experienced by a person who knows only the laws of nature, confronting an apparently supernatural event" (1973, 25). Once the story has explained what the supernatural event is, why it has occurred, and its meaning within the person's life, the fantastic then becomes either the "marvelous" or the "uncanny." If the story attributes a rational explanation (such as drug-induced illusions or bad dreams) for the "apparently supernatural event," it instantiates the uncanny. But if the narrative instead accepts the supernatural event as real and magical, it is marvelous (such as in fairy tales). If the narrative does not specify how the actions took place (as in Henry James's *The Turn of the Screw*, which offers no rationale for its supernatural incidents), the story remains simply classified within the fantastic (Ibid., 41–43). Clearly immersed in the fantastic by any definition, *Pan's Labyrinth* often declines to specify whether its supernatural occurrences are actually happening or are simply a product of a little girl's active imagination. Even the film's resolution fails to clarify whether del Toro intends the viewer to understand his film as Todorov's uncanny (the little girl's hallucinations and dreams) or his marvelous (actually magical). However, for the sake of this study, *Pan's Labyrinth* will be regarded as moving into the realm of the marvelous at its conclusion, meaning that the magical events were actually happening. But in its particular uses of out-of-the-ordinary characters and actions, the film also incorporates magic realism.

The Magic-in-Reality of Magical Realism

Most often used primarily to refer to Latin-American writers, the term *magical realism* was originally coined to characterize a movement in the 1920s where visual artists explored "new ways of seeing and depicting the familiar. . . . Subjects most often painted include the city square, the metropolis, still lifes, portraits and landscapes. . . . it was the fastidious depiction of familiar objects, the new way of seeing and rendering the everyday . . . that inspired the style" (Guenther 1995, 33–36). The visual art concept eventually invaded literature. Thus, while magical-realist painting makes the ordinary—the real—unusual and compelling, magical-realist writing incorporates the fantastic into the everyday. A singular aspect of magical-realist stories and novels is the way "the coexistence of magic and realism is presented in a matter-of-fact way as being natural. . . . In the fusion of these two opposite epistemological concepts, the former boundaries between the real and the supernatural fade, and the improbable becomes objectively possible" (Delicka 1997). This cohesion of the real and the fantastic is magical realism's "irreducible element." Something that cannot be explained logically, such as an extraordinary or magical happening, is reported "in the same way in which other, ordinary events are recounted. The narrator's presentation of the irreducible element on the same narrative plane as other, commonplace happenings means that in terms of the text, magical things 'really' do happen" (Faris 1995, 167).

Magical realism's fairy tale (marvelous) happenings are taken out of that genre's world, where they are a normal part of life, and incorporated as ordinary occurrences. Events may float between real and imaginary worlds, facilitating "the fusion, or coexistence, of possible worlds, spaces, systems that would be irreconcilable in other modes of fiction. The propensity of magical-realist texts to admit a plurality of worlds means that they often situate themselves on liminal territory between or among those worlds—in phenomenal and spiritual regions where transformation, metamorphosis, dissolution are common, where magic is a branch of naturalism, or pragmatism" (Zamora and Faris 1995, 6).

Film directors such as Jan Jakub Kolski, Andrei Tarkovsky and Alexander Sokurov have been particularly successful in adapting magical realism to the screen. Ghosts, levitation, and odd events (such as a flying paper butterfly that lands on a wall and suddenly becomes painted there in the 1983 film *Eréndira* [directed by Ruy Guerra]) prevail as natural occurrences in their films, exemplifying the recognizable paradigm for this narrative style. However, even some mainstream American films such as *Field of Dreams* (directed by Phil Alden Robinson, 1989), *Across the Universe* (directed by Julie Taymor, 2007), and *The NeverEnding Story* (directed by Wolfgang Petersen, 1984) employ magical realism in their incorporation of fantastical creatures and/or happenings into the ordinary (Taylor n.d.).

For example, *The NeverEnding Story* primarily takes place in an imaginary world within the book that a young boy named Bastian reads. However, Bastian soon discovers that the events in the story within the story are actually unfolding in the book's fantasy world, with which he becomes involved. By the film's conclusion, viewers witness the boy gaining revenge against a group of bullies, who threaten his daily life, with the help of his new, flying dog/dragon friend, Falkor, from the book's fantasy world. This film consistently establishes and reestablishes its real-world setting by allowing the magical to invade or cross over. Other magical-realist films, such as *Like Water for Chocolate/Como agua para chocolate* (directed by Alfonso Arau, 1992), present odd happenings—such as food incorporating the preparer's emotions—as perfectly normal. Their characters witness and then simply accept extraordinary occurrences. The key to magical realism in films appears to be that although supernatural and strange things may occur, they are nonetheless anchored in and associated with the real (and recognizable) everyday world.

What Is Reality, Anyway?

Despite the rangle of films that play with representing the fantastic and the magical in the context of everyday life, scholars have disputed realism and its part in film virtually since cinema's beginnings. On one level, everything captured by the camera's lens is real. However, especially in this age of computer generated imagery (CGI) graphics and other forms of technology that allow images to be created and/or altered, the filmic reality may be contentious. To develop her argument, Temenuga Trifonova uses theorist Siegfried Kracauer's assertion that "the power of cinema lies in its ability to make us see what normally goes unseen" (2006, 57). Even without manipulation, objects that may be familiar and everyday can become extraordinary in the camera's eye. For example, Kracauer points out that "the close-up reveals new and unsuspected formations of matter; skin textures are reminiscent of aerial photographs, eyes turn into lakes or volcanic craters. Such images blow up our environment in a double sense: they enlarge it literally; and in doing so, they blast the prison of conventional reality, opening up expanses which we have explored at best in dreams before" (1997, 48).

He suggests that filmic special effects can be commonly understood as camera realistic under particular circumstances: "Provided the real and the fantastic are indistinguishable on the screen, the fantastic is cinematic . . . i.e., so long as the fantastic is not represented *as* fantastic but as part of ordinary reality, it is included in camera-reality" (Trifonova 2006, 61). Trifonova applies Kracauer's interpretation of special effects to science-fiction film.[4] She notes that "if alienation [of an everyday object on camera] is essential to the establishment of the real, then an object that is already alienated [one that is not recognizable to the viewer] is more real than an object that depends on the medium of cinema to alienate it" (Ibid., 57). Thus, the unknown and imaginary worlds of science-fiction film—aboard spaceships or strange planets in solar systems or universes that the audience knows nothing about—fundamentally render the fantastical on camera more real to the viewer than the everyday. Consequently, such fantasy may offer a more realistic cinema than, for example, a documentary; there is no alternative, knowable object within the real world against which to compare the imaginary to declare it fake. Magical creatures and marvelous places become increasingly believable as computer graphics, costumes, and makeup techniques continue to advance.

Trifonova's theory introduces new shades of meaning to the terms "magical" and "realism." Thus, if magical-realist literature incorporates and naturalizes the fantastical into the ordinary world, magical-realist film approaches other visual forms in the genre since the camera renders everything real. *Pan's Labyrinth* offers an opportunity to explore these implications. As in magical realism, the creatures in *Pan's Labyrinth* are from a different world—an indistinguishable form of camera reality—and they find themselves interacting with an otherwise real, historic world—the fascist Spain of 1944. In the film's two-layer story—one magical and one real—the two exist independently. There is no incorporation of one space into the other, nor is there a point when they completely converge as in most forms of magical realism. Although at moments the magical makes an appearance in the real world—the chalk door that leads Ofelia to Captain Vidal's (Sergi López) room or the mandrake root that makes Carmen (Ariadna Gil) well—characters other than Ofelia never confirm magic's power; others always deny and ignore it. Only Ofelia experiences the characters and magic of the underworld/otherworld. With the fantastic and the real remaining separate, the only link between them is the little girl herself, who eventually chooses one world over the other. As Jack Zipes notes, Ofelia "has *real* double vision, unique powers that enable her to see two worlds at the same

---

4   Fantasy and science fiction literature and films present "a world different from our own and the differences are apparent against the background of organized bodies of knowledge" (Rabkin 1976, 135). Author Orson Scott Card distinguishes them this way: "If the story is set in a universe that follows the same rules as ours, it's science fiction. If it's set in a universe that doesn't follow our rules, it's fantasy" (1990, 22).

time, and we watch as she tries to navigate through two worlds, trying to use the characters, symbols, and signs of her imaginary world to survive in a social world destitute of dreams and filled with merciless brutality and viciousness" (2008, 236).

Magical realism is undoubtedly influenced by fairy tales.[5] Literary scholar Rawdon Wilson writes that he and his children came to the conclusion—after reading a story by magical-realist author Gabriel Garcia Marquez—that it was "not like a fairy tale nor like a myth. . . . It was not even like, my son observed, 'The Lord of the Rings.' But it had brought to mind all of those other texts they had read" (1995, 209). Wilson goes on to describe a hypothetical pair of brothers and their evolution into magical-realist authors who imagine a world where the sky rains flowers and all human existence is counterfactual. Eventually the brothers begin to tell stories about their invented worlds "with a straight face, without shrugs, secret winks, or other hints that it was, after all, just a tale" (Ibid., 212), a storytelling technique that enables the story to seem natural and real.[6]

Wendy B. Faris relates magical realist narrative style to a story told to an open-minded and curious child instead of a logic-driven adult: "Wonders are recounted largely without comment, in a matter-of-fact way, accepted—presumably—as a child would accept them, without undue questioning or reflection" (1995, 177). While Faris's ideas about age-distinguished thought processes are highly questionable, she describes the essence of magical realism: to make the fantastical appear an ordinary occurrence in the real world. Fairy tales, on the other hand, make the magical a normal part of life but rarely venture into the real world; the normal instead resides fully within the fairy tale world, which does not resemble the everyday one. Consider Jim Henson's film *Labyrinth* (1986). Although there are marked similarities between it and *Pan's Labyrinth*—including not only the labyrinth itself but also a stolen baby and a girl (Sarah [Jennifer Connelly]) who links the fairy tale and real worlds together—they nonetheless fall into different categories.

---

5   In fairy tales, magical and fantastical creatures, objects, and processes are a natural part of life. Seven-league boots may be better than regular ones, but they exist in the same world; humans may transform into birds and birds into humans without narrative notice that such an event is at all unusual. Yet the time and place are not the audience's own. Magical realism, as already indicated, places magic within normal, everyday situations (as fairy tales do), and its location and time are those of everyday life; the reader or viewer recognizes the magical-realist setting as the real world.

6   This style of storytelling is deliberately employed within tall tales, which propose impossible events that the audience takes as real until the narrative's conclusion.

Labyrinth begins in the real world but moves to the fantasy world and remains there. With no parallel between the fantastical and the real, the fairy tale remains disconnected from the real world, just as life for Sarah's parents continues with them both oblivious to and completely absent from the story on-screen.

In *Pan's Labyrinth*, however, each time Ofelia completes one of her errands within the fairy tale underworld/otherworld, she is always among its creatures and in its rooms. Though the faun appears in the real world, only she can see him. No confirmation of the other world's existence comes from any other character in the film. Ofelia's mother could have found temporary remission from pain through the doctor's treatments, not the mandrake root, for example. The magical events are never explicitly incorporated into the real world so that they become natural and everyday as in magical realism. The fantastical layer of *Pan's Labyrinth* is separate and like a fairy tale, in contrast to magical realism. The realistic story told simultaneously with the fairy tale links the film with magical realism, but the film also employs and departs from structures and strategies from more conventional fairy tales.

In *Pan's Labyrinth*, only the viewer and Ofelia experience the creatures and magic of the underworld. However, as Paul J. Smith observes, "although it is tempting to describe [Ofelia's] as the guiding point of view in the film . . . there is a great deal that she does not see" (2007, 8). The story's only true voice and vision rest with the camera—in effect, with del Toro himself. Thus, the viewer experiences "no sense of discontinuity of perspective throughout *Pan's Labyrinth*, seduced by its expert plotting and pacing" (Ibid.). At times in *Pan's Labyrinth*, the fantastical bleeds (sometimes literally, as in the film's opening and closing) into the real; however, it is never an ordinary occurrence as in magical realism. Ofelia remains constantly aware that what she witnesses is unusual. She accepts the creatures and happenings of the underworld as normal in that world, but she recognizes its strangeness in comparison to the boundaries and logical limitations of the real world.

An example of the fantastical infiltrating the real world occurs when the faun gives Ofelia the mandrake root to put under her mother's bed to make her well. Initially the infant-like root remains unseen by any other eyes. Its apparent effectiveness becomes obvious when Carmen begins progressively to get better. When Ofelia displeases the faun by defying his directions and eating from the Pale Man's (Doug Jones) table, the root starts to fail and appears lifeless. Before she can revive it, Captain Vidal pulls her from under the bed. Seeing the smelly root, he angrily shows Carmen and stalks from the room. Carmen also looks at the root in disgust and at her daughter with disappointment. Though Ofelia tries to explain her world of fairies and magic, Carmen throws the mandrake into the fire. A horrifying cry emanating from the writhing creature matches the tremendous pain that causes Carmen to double over. Soon after, she dies in childbirth.

The most memorable incorporation of fantasy into the real world is Ofelia's use of magical chalk to escape her guarded room and enter Captain Vidal's quarters to bring her baby brother to the labyrinth. Soldiers stationed outside her door have been instructed to shoot Ofelia if she tries to leave; thus, the only means of escape is through a door she draws upon the wall with chalk. Because it is apparently seen by others in the film as simply a sign of Ofelia's overactive imagination (although the question of how she manages to escape a locked, guarded room lingers momentarily with the camera on the drawing), no one spends much time thinking about the chalk door. The audience is, of course, aware that the door has magically transported Ofelia to her stepfather's room. But the other characters are apparently too busy with their own problems to wonder about Ofelia's escape. Captain Vidal finds the chalk on the table, but he does not see Ofelia enter the labyrinth through the new door, nor does he see the faun when he reaches its center; he simply sees Ofelia talking to herself because the faun is invisible to his eyes. Only Ofelia and the viewer recognize the other world that runs adjacent to the real one.

The Fairy Tale and Its Heroines

The fairy tale adventures of the young protagonist of *Pan's Labyrinth* begin as she and her pregnant mother, Carmen, are being driven to the home of Ofelia's new stepfather, Captain Vidal. Carmen asks to pull the car over because she feels nauseous. While she tries to regain control over her stomach, Ofelia begins to walk down the road and inadvertently kicks a rock that lies in her path. Upon picking it up, Ofelia notices a mark on its surface that resembles an eye. She eventually locates a large sculpture made of stone—a lone and strange figure among the surrounding trees—and puts the missing piece back into its rightful place. This act initiates her fantastical adventure: immediately a bug resembling a praying mantis emerges from the statue's mouth. It startles Ofelia, but then she smiles, unafraid of this large insect as it seems to flap its wings in greeting.

When Carmen calls her back to the car, Ofelia exclaims, "I saw a fairy!" Her mother ignores this statement (and is apparently oblivious to the rock statue standing alone in the woods as well) and begins to tell Ofelia about Captain Vidal. In fairy tales, the magical is often similarly "depicted as generally unobserved or undervalued by most people . . . they do not see the magic—as is the case in 'Aladdin's Lamp' where the lamp is hidden in a cave and appears rusty and old, or in 'Cinderella' where the fairy godmother appears only to the heroine" (Jones 1993, 13). Yet Aladdin's lamp nevertheless does produce objects in the fairy tale, just as everybody sees the accoutrements the fairy godmother gives Cinderella—both in their original and then transformed shapes. In contrast, neomagical realism prevents the fantastical from crossing over into the real, at least as given conscious validation by other real-world characters. Conversely, some *Pan's Labyrinth*'s fairy tale-world characters seem quite aware of what's going on in both locations and can move between them. Others, like the creepy and dangerous Pale Man, cannot cross the border.

The beings in the underworld/otherworld differ from those in most fairy tale film adaptations for children. The fairies, for example, are not beautiful creatures but instead odd and dark with leaflike wings and bald heads with large ears and eyes.[7] No cute, sparkly dust or glow emanates from the fairy's body as she leads Ofelia down to the labyrinth that first night, and no happy lights or bright colors appear to guide her. These notable differences between the fairies she sees in her books and those in the underworld do not seem to bother Ofelia in the least. She takes everything in stride, as content in this fantastical otherworld as she is out of place in the real one.

From the shadows of the labyrinth emerges a strange figure with horns and legs like a goat, long pointed fingers, ears that stick out, and skin that seems—much like that of the fairies—to be earthlike, made of tree bark or stone. He informs Ofelia that he is a faun (whom the English title names as

---

7   Traditionally two types of fairies populate literature and fairy lore. Nineteenth-century Victorian children's literature presents stories and images of small, beautiful, winged creatures who "flitter about as butterflies and who appear and disappear in the blink of an eye" (Cheadle 2007, 2). In other European fairy lore, fairies were more or less troublesome creatures standing about two feet tall—closer to a leprechaun's size than a butterfly's. These "little people" had a tendency to braid horses' manes to ride them at night (untangling the braids brought punishment); had a penchant for stealing children and leaving in their place a human-looking but evil changeling; and were often blamed for leading people astray with lights and music (Narváez 1991). These fairies were best avoided because the consequences of witnessing their dances or hearing their music were often dire (see Rieti 1991).

Pan) although he, like the fairy, diverges from what audiences may picture in that role.[8] Pan (Doug Jones) explains to Ofelia that she must complete three dangerous tasks to prove her immortality and return to the underworld. Although the viewer may want to believe that Pan is a fairy tale helper sent to assist Ofelia, the "trustworthiness of the faun, who is immense and weird-looking, ancient and sphinxlike, is clearly meant to be ambiguous; he appears to be kind and gentle sometimes and mean and menacing at other times" (Zipes 2008, 238). This consistent contradiction in Ofelia's advisor keeps her and the audience guessing about his intentions until the very end of the film.

Like some other female fairy tale ingenues, Ofelia's independence and strength ill fit her in this new environment. Laura Hubner observes that "in a powerful way, Ofelia disobeys throughout the film: she refuses to call Vidal 'father,' she ventures into the woods and returns to the labyrinth. Finally she disobeys her step-father . . . and disobeys the faun by not handing over the baby and she says 'no' to Vidal after he takes the baby" (2007, 6). Traditional fairy tale princesses were frequently punished for their arrogance and pride. Such a character could be forced to suffer "a humiliating fall that reduces her from princess to peasant, from a privileged daughter to an impoverished menial" (Tatar 1987, 102–3). Ofelia is just such a heroine, temporarily demoted from her royal state. However, she is given an increasing amount of freedom due to her mother's progressing illness and her step-father's utter contempt. While she is reproved for her failure to assimilate to Captain Vidal's world, as with other fairy tale heroines, this reprimand does not force her to abandon her strong attributes. Instead, the indifference of the adults in her life enables her to escape and pursue her adventures virtually unnoticed.

The sequence of events in Ofelia's journey makes her resemble many fairy tale males who consistently receive help and aid despite the fact that they often disregard advice given by the powerful.[9] The three fairies that the faun provides for Ofelia when she journeys to the lair of the Pale Man can easily be associated with fairy tale helpers: creatures or people who guide the fairy tale hero and support his actions. Like Ofelia, the hero continues

---

8   In fact, Paul J. Smith notes that "del Toro's grotesque wooden creature could hardly be further from another recent film faun, the friendly, furry Mr. Tumnus of *The Chronicles of Narnia*" [directed by Andrew Adamson, 2005] (2007).

9   A similar transgendering, but in the opposite direction, is the subject of Ming-Hsun Lin's chapter on Harry Potter as Cinderella.

to receive help and advice in spite of any missteps. Once he "exhibits the virtue of compassion—with its logical concomitant of humility—he can do virtually no wrong, even when he violates interdictions, disregards warnings, and ignores instructions" (Ibid., 97–98). Hubner notes that Ofelia's ease at imperturbably gazing at the creatures of the underworld in their somewhat disturbing states also aligns her with the heroes of fairy tales: "Ofelia confronts head-on her visions of the faun tearing off raw flesh with his teeth . . . the corpse monster whose eyeballs rest on the table . . . the portraits of babies being devoured by monsters on the walls. . . . Her encounter with these decadent, gothic and grotesque images of ageing and decay suggests an awareness of a dark, tangible, mortal side of humans befitting a hero on a quest rather than a passive ethereal princess" (2007, 5).[10]

The paramount example of Ofelia's affinity with the male fairy tale protagonist is her encounter with the Pale Man. Ofelia fails to heed the warnings of those who advise her in the fantasy world, receiving various admonitions before and even as she undertakes this task and getting into near-fatal trouble. The faun tells Ofelia that she must not eat or drink anything from the elaborate feast, emphasizing that her life depends on it. Her magical book similarly advises her. As she enters the Pale Man's cavernous lair, she first sees the delicious banquet spread out on the table and, in her awe at the food, is startled when her eyes discover the grotesque, silent figure seated at its head. A pair of eyeballs sits on a plate before the Pale Man. He does not gaze at the tempting meal before him but—just like the ogre in "Hop O' My Thumb" (ATU 327B) or the witch in "Hansel and Gretel" (ATU 327A)—has other morsels in mind. The murals that adorn the cavern walls depict the Pale Man eating children. Ofelia stares at these paintings in horror and then turns to see a large pile of children's shoes in the corner. All these attempts at cautioning Ofelia, however, fail to give her the strength to resist the temptation of tasting the grapes. Even as she takes the fruit, the fairies try to stop her, and she brushes them away. Ofelia's decision to partake results in the loss of two of her fairy guides and subjects her to Pan's wrath.

---

10   Ofelia resembles the tomboy/transgendered hero/ines in the complex Newfoundland tale "Peg Bearskin" (ATU 327B/328/711) and its relatives "Tatterhood" (ATU 711), "Muncimeg" (ATU 327B/328), and "Kate Crackernuts" (ATU 306/711) (see Greenhill, Anderson-Grégoire, and Best 2010).

The Fairy Tale: Stereotypes and Traditional Tropes

Fairy tale wicked stepparents, like the stepmothers in the stories of "Snow White" (ATU 709) and "Cinderella," are familiar. The traditional fairy tale was often rife with "figures of female evil" (wicked stepmothers, ugly sisters, and witches), yet *Pan's Labyrinth* instead employs a male villain, less common for the genre (Warner 1994, 201–17). As the biological mother who dies, *Pan's Labyrinth*'s Carmen exemplifies a typical female role long established in fairy tales. Generally sympathetic, if somewhat deluded considering Captain Vidal's unsavory attributes, Carmen desires to please her new husband. As independent and strong characters, Captain Vidal's housekeeper, Mercedes (Maribel Verdú), who, unbeknownst to him, is a spy for the Republican guerrillas, and Ofelia have much more in common than do the little girl and her mother. As they lie in bed on their first night in Captain Vidal's home, Ofelia asks her mother why she remarried, and Carmen replies that she was tired of being alone. Like many female characters in both the most popular Grimm fairy tales and Disney features, Carmen yearns for her prince to come and complete her life. Her submissive attitude toward her husband resembles that of many other female characters in the Grimm tales.[11] Life could not have been easy for a single mother in Spain in 1944, but the result of Carmen's marriage—her death and Ofelia's (at least in the real world)—emphasizes the falseness as well as the potentially damaging effects of such a mindset.

In opposition to some traditional fairy tales, as well as many Hollywood films, *Pan's Labyrinth* is free of romance.[12] Carmen finds herself in a relationship where she is essentially a decorative object, exemplified in the dinner scene where Captain Vidal condescendingly remarks that she believes that the story of the way they met is interesting to others, enjoining her to be silent. Where other fairy tales describe a heterosexual couple who come

---

11   Ruth Bottigheimer shows that Wilhelm Grimm often removed direct speech from the good, virtuous female characters and gave it to men or evil female characters. Her examination of the dialogue in "Cinderella" concludes that "it is not an overt curse that condemns her to silence; it is the pattern of discourse in *Grimms' Tales* that discriminates against 'good' girls and produces functionally silent heroines" (1987, 53).

12   As noted in Cristina Bacchilega and John Rieder's chapter, romance remains a significant part of most fairy tale films, even those that attempt to parody Disney's versions of the genre. Romance is similarly absent in Nietzchka Keene's *The Juniper Tree* (1990), where sexual relationships are primarily economic, as discussed in Pauline Greenhill and Anne Brydon's chapter.

together after enduring character-testing hardships, *Pan's Labyrinth* breaks with this pattern to create strong heroines who complete their journeys for themselves and achieve their own advancement. In a more conventional narrative, perhaps the relationship between Mercedes and the good doctor (Álex Angulo) or one of the other Republicans might have developed into romance, but not in the chaotic and dangerous world of *Pan's Labyrinth*.

The film also rejects the long-established happily-ever-after fairy tale ending. Such a conclusion "affirms the moral propriety of the universe. . . . Not only do Snow White, Cinderella . . . and the young hero . . . win their respective mates and hearts' desires [castles and kingdom], their evil adversaries are consistently punished" (Jones 1993, 17). At the film's conclusion, Mercedes fails to save Ofelia from Captain Vidal (such an ending would, of course, have prevented the happy conclusion in the fairy tale world) but succeeds in punishing him (fatally) and rescuing Ofelia's brother. Perhaps in caring for him, Mercedes will obtain her heart's desire because she longs for children. Even so, the film confirms that the Nationalists will simply send another "Captain Vidal" to take his place at the mill, and so the cycle of oppression will continue. While the young Ofelia escapes Captain Vidal's world and returns to the underworld to reclaim her throne, she does so only through death. This dénouement begs the question of whether Ofelia actually achieves her heart's desire—though her reunion with her parents in the otherworld is clearly a happy one.

The Historical

The first indication that *Pan's Labyrinth* is destined to be a story with roots in a grim and dark reality is its introductory sequence. After briefly traveling along a shadowy expanse of cement, the camera stops at Ofelia's face as she lies gasping for life while blood runs from her nose to the ground below. This momentary glimpse of a young girl in a time of suffering is enough to alert the viewer that this film may not have an unequivocally happy ending. The audience then has a brief introduction to the fantasy world as the camera reveals an outline of a young girl running up a circular flight of stairs enclosed in darkness, escaping the underworld and attempting to reach the sunlight of the human world above. The scene changes and the camera begins to follow a car as it drives down a road that leads past ruined, broken buildings, surrounded by forest. It is a beautiful, sunny day, a situation not often seen later in *Pan's Labyrinth*. Ofelia and Carmen are riding in the car, but they will never again be as happy together as they are during this initial sequence. As they become increasingly immersed in life with Captain Vidal, the close relationship between mother and daughter gradually diminishes. (The captain's deleterious impact on everyone involved with him, including himself, is represented by increasing down-pouring rain as the characters approach their generally tragic fates.)

Captain Vidal is no stereotypical fairy tale villain, although he is a typical and easily recognized evil figure. As a member of the Nationalist party—a Fascist political group led by Francisco Franco that received assistance from Nazi Germany and Fascist Italy during the Spanish Civil War—he is an icon of what Hannah Arendt called "the banality of evil" (2006), with no qualms about shooting the innocent and torturing prisoners for the advancement of his political party.[13] He shoots innocent hunters and tortures prisoners but also listens to martial music while he shaves. A symbol of the horror of the Nationalists and their ideology, Vidal is eventually defeated by the Republicans hiding in the surrounding woods, who persistently launch guerilla attacks on his military post at the mill. After Franco's Nationalists won the war in 1939, opposing opinions became nonexistent in Spain. Although the Republicans in Spain did not succeed—arguably until the death of Nationalist dictator Generalissimo Franco in 1975 and the transition to democratic government—del Toro clearly admires their renowned determination to continue fighting for their beliefs and their unwillingness to surrender. Hence, Captain Vidal is at once unredeemable, as in fairy tales, and a character from a historical narrative.

His character is immoral, sadistic, and as a result extremely easy to dislike. Although taking another's life is apparently inconsequential to Captain Vidal, living up to the expectations that he and others have for him as the son of General Vidal progressively weighs upon him as *Pan's Labyrinth* unfolds. The captain is a sociopath, del Toro explains, who "hates himself. He essentially cuts his own throat in the mirror. He's so afraid of his father's legacy that he denies even having the watch his father gave him. But his function, like most fascists in 1944, is that of an absolutely destructive force" (quoted

---

13   In her analysis of Otto Adolf Eichmann's trial in Jerusalem in 1961, Arendt concludes that his willing participation as an S.S. officer during the Holocaust did not result from evil or hatred toward Jews. She argues that Eichmann simply and mindlessly followed instructions to please his superiors. His desire to move up in rank and become a man of importance superseded any personal moral code he may have held. As a result, Eichmann completed tasks efficiently and with no consideration about the consequences for his victims.

in Faye 2009). The larger-than-life father image that the captain contends with—and the fear that he has not reached a position nor made achievements significant enough in comparison—take their toll on Vidal. As the film progresses, time becomes a preoccupation for the captain, and his fear of wasting it increases. The ticking of his watch haunts him. It counts down the seconds as he comes closer to his ultimate and undignified end.

The consequences of underestimating women become clear when Mercedes defeats Captain Vidal. The embodiment of sexism, he "barely acknowledges the existence of the feminine. Welcoming his pregnant wife and stepdaughter to the mill he addresses them in the masculine plural form [*bienvenidos*] on the assumption that the unborn child, his true priority, is a boy" (Paul Smith 2007). He regards women as expendable—he quickly chooses the life of his unborn son over that of his wife—as well as incompetent. Remarkably, he never suspects Mercedes of spying until the evidence literally stares him in the face. Even once he knows she is a Republican and imprisons her in the supply room, he makes the cardinal mistake of turning his back on her. (In a deliberately parallel previous scene, where he tortures a captured male Republican, Vidal consistently turns to smile sadistically at his captive as he describes his plans). The captain unequivocally believes in the strength and superiority of men over women, yet his destruction comes about as a result of the three females—Carmen, Ofelia, and Mercedes—whom he naïvely allows to enter his life.

Neomagical Realism

Siegfried Kracauer asserts that cinema has the ability to make the everyday appear extraordinary. Objects that one encounters on a daily basis can become compelling and exotic when recorded by the camera lens. He and other theorists such as Jean Epstein and Fernand Léger "put forward the argument that the power of cinema lies in its ability to make us see what normally goes unseen" (Trifonova 2006, 57). Alternatively, Duncan Petrie suggests that the "interest in fantasy is related to the belief that fantasy helps to explain the fascination, and so the power, of cinema" (1993, 2). For these theorists, cinema is truly powerful when depicting the imaginary on-screen. Indeed, many Euro-North American audiences seem more attracted to fantasy, science-fiction, and comic-book films than to documentaries or other films with a more serious agenda. An article in *Entertainment Weekly* commented on the ability of "popcorn films" to draw viewers: "This summer's blockbusters (*Iron Man* and *The Dark Knight* for example) have been a mother lode for fans of subtext. And popcorn movies are great vehicles for the transmission of ideas because, unlike overtly political films such as *Rendition* and *Redacted*, people actually go see them" (Nashawaty 2008, 23).

Fantasy films sell tickets not only because they are often visually impressive but also because they superficially appear to offer escapist entertainment. Such works can convey opinions or beliefs in an extremely subtle and nonthreatening way. Much like fairy tales—which were written "for adults who needed to lay bare the real in order to entertain the hope that change might be possible . . . the goal of fairy tales is not a conservative but a Utopian one . . . as if to say 'One day we might be happy, even if it won't last'" (Petrie 1993, 26)—films of fantasy attempt to encourage reform (or like *Pan's Labyrinth,* even revolution) under the guise of visual spectacle.

Conflicts between scholars and filmmakers about whether cinema is a representation of reality or an art form have resulted in "two opposing tendencies: one towards the recording or documenting of external 'reality', the other towards the imaginative use of cinematic illusion" (Ibid., 2). It seems appropriate, then, that this divergence is often placed side by side in a single film, perhaps reaching a culmination in neomagical realism. Although the historicized story of *Pan's Labyrinth* cannot be described as an exact representation or direct recording of reality—the film is by no means a documentary—it is nonetheless based within a specific, historical time period. Yet despite these realist roots, *Pan's Labyrinth* probably attracts its audience through its parallel story of fairy tale fantasy.

As mentioned earlier, Trifonova proposes that a world unlike our own with which the audience is unfamiliar, such as the underworld of *Pan's Labyrinth*, can be perceived as more realistic than recognizable scenery and objects on screen that have a correlative in the real world. The cinema's ability to capture the fantastic, even when filming the everyday, allows it the power to command and thus influence its audience. It is distinct as an art form in this respect.[14] While a superbly performed and filmed realistic story can hold the viewer's attention, a film with fantastical visual effects may find a larger audience. If the aforementioned popcorn films can persuade and affect the viewer, and if—as some film theorists argue—the power of cinema

---

14   Television can also be said to have this influence; however, the medium's smaller screen size limits its impact. Television must rely on its actors and stories more than its visuals to affect the viewer (although the implementation of HDTV may change this situation).

lies in its ability to make the everyday fantastic, *Pan's Labyrinth* accesses both sides of the film-as-art, film-as-reality option and thus manifests some of the most persuasive and engaging attributes of film expression. With its paralleling of real and fantastical worlds using neomagical realism, *Pan's Labyrinth* represents a powerful and innovative new genre.

4

Fitting the Glass Slipper
A Comparative Study of the Princess's Role in the
Harry Potter Novels and Films

Ming-Hsun Lin

THE FAIRY TALE PRINCESS HAS BECOME FAMILIAR to Euro-North Americans through bedtime stories, children's literature, and Disney films. The prolific fairy tale theorist Jack Zipes has gone so far as to claim—possibly exaggerating for effect—that "it is not by chance that the fairy tale film has become the most popular cultural commodity in America, if not the world" (1997, 1). Equally famous—if not more so for children today—is J. K. Rowling's series of Harry Potter novels and the films based on the books. Their phenomenal success has prompted both positive and negative readings of their characters and worldview.

One of the main areas of academic interest in these works has been their portrayal of gender. For example, Ximena Gallardo-C. and C. Jason Smith use a psychoanalytic approach to discuss gender in relation to symbol, the notion of otherness, and narrative in *Harry Potter*, seeing Harry as essentially "a boy caught in a girl's story" (2003, 196). Zipes points out that "the plots of the first four novels thus far resemble the structure of a conventional fairy tale" that "circle around Harry with his phallic wand[,]" but he also describes the series as a phenomenon "driven by commodity consumption" (2002b, 172–80). While some critics share Zipes's view that Rowling's work is essentially sexist and conveys a patriarchal vision of society, Eliza T. Dresang identifies significant feminist traits and praises Hermione in particular for her strong personality and determination. The linking of gender, fairy tales, and modern commodity culture, often seen most clearly in the film adaptations, is my subject.[1]

Though her personal feminism is generally understated, Rowling manipulates gender roles and combines *archetypes* (recognized traditional models) and *stereotypes* (oversimplified ideas following sociocultural conventions) from fairy tales in the Harry Potter series. This chapter focuses on the princess archetype and stereotype and their use in the characters of Ginny Weasley, Hermione Granger, and Harry Potter. Since the emphasis in academic studies of the Harry Potter franchise has remained firmly on the books with the films somewhat neglected, I am extending the focus by providing a comparative study of the first four Harry Potter books and their corresponding film adaptations.[2] Drawing on structuralist and feminist studies of fairy tales, I will show how the princess role shifts from one character to another. Thus, while Rowling applies and subverts the princess stereotype and works through the princess archetype across the three characters, I argue that she positions Harry—not the girls—as the primary fairy tale heroine. This structural transgendering of her main protagonist has arguably been muted in the film versions, which rely much more strongly than do the books on the princess stereotype.[3]

The Fairy Tale Princess and the Fairy Tale Heroine

Who is the fairy tale princess? Vladimir Propp claims that all fairy tales employ two recurrent features: the function of the characters and the type of their roles, which he calls *dramatis personae*. In each fairy tale, Propp finds seven characters—the villain, the donor, the helper, the princess (and her father), the dispatcher, the hero, and the false hero. Each dramatis persona is defined by the specific course of action allocated to her or him. For instance, the hero conquers the obstacles while the false hero tries to take the credit

---

1   The intersection of gender and genre is also the topic of Cristina Bacchilega and John Rieder's chapter in this volume. Naarah Sawers discusses the ways in which childhood itself can become commodified and how films may support or critique such processes.

2   A compelling new development in scholarship is the work of Catherine Tosenberger, which deals with sexuality as expressed in online fan fiction related to the novels and films (2008a and 2008b).

3   A similar exploration of the transgendering of a male-identified character to a female-identified one takes place in Pauline Greenhill, Emilie Anderson-Grégoire, and Anita Best's work on "Peg Bearskin" (a composite of ATU 306, 327B, 328, and 711) (forthcoming).

for the hero's actions. A character may manifest more than one dramatis persona, and the dramatis personae are transferable through different characters in a story. Yet Propp notes that only the princess cannot be clearly defined by her function in the story. Her role in the story appears to be ambiguous. She is usually the "sought-for person" or the "reward" for the hero in the narrative (1968, 64–79). The princess, therefore, is only recognizable by her royal status and relationship to the hero. Though Propp's study fails to define fully the fairy tale princess, her unique feature of lacking a single specific function offers a perspective for examining her role as an archetype. As a dramatis persona, the role of the princess can be transferred to any character—male or female—in a story. Consequently, whoever exhibits the characteristics resembling the fairy tale princess can be identified with her.

What, then, are the characteristic features of the archetypal fairy tale princess and how does the stereotype of the princess emerge from and relate to them? All archetypal princesses possess nobility from social, spiritual, or biological sources. Socially most are of royal birth or obtain royal status by marriage. Spiritually they are often pious and virtuous. Biologically they are usually young and beautiful. Their beauty is an expression of their inner positive qualities—an internalized form of nobility. While nobility is an emblem of princesses, it does not shape all of them with identical characteristics and dispositions. For example, the heroine of "Snow White" (ATU 709)—a story traced to varied oral tales from several countries and possessing more than four hundred versions collected in a span of five hundred years (Jones 2002, 4), can be passive and submissive in some versions but active and subversive in others.[4]

The passive/submissive version of "Snow White" is familiar, but a few examples of her active/subversive counterpart are worth detailing. In Giambattista Basile's "The Young Slave" (1932, 192–96), believed to be the first written version of "Snow White," the heroine, witchlike, casts a spell on her uncle, threatens a doll with a knife, and tries to commit suicide. Christian ethics regards all these actions as rebellious and sinful. In an Italian version called "Maria, the Wicked Stepmother, and the Seven Robbers" (Ashliman 2002), the heroine finds shelter in a house belonging to seven robbers instead of seven dwarfs.[5] This version creates ambiguous

---

4   Unless otherwise stated, all Grimms' fairy tales mentioned in this paper come from Zipes's translation (2003).

5   The only version of this Italian fairy tale I can find is in a German translation (Gonzenbach 1870, 4–7). However, this feature—seven robbers instead of seven

sexual and ethical problems by having the heroine live alone with seven adult men. In another Italian story called "The Crystal Casket" (Crane 1885, 326–31), the heroine gains a stepmother by asking her father to marry her teacher.

In other examples with active/subversive protagonists, like the early version of "Cinderella" (ATU 510) entitled "Catskin" (Jacobs 1975, 268–71), the heroine, escaping from home and an engagement to an old man, finds herself a job as a scullion in a castle and wins the prince's heart in the end. A similar heroine also appears in "Cupid and Psyche," the earliest-known version of "Beauty and the Beast" (ATU 425C). Psyche, who is praised as a "paradigm of female heroism," completes one impossible task after another and ultimately earns her marriage with Cupid (Edwards 1979, 37). But in an Italian "Little Red Riding Hood" (ATU 333), the wolf dupes the heroine into consuming her grandmother's flesh and blood (Dundes 1989, 199). Clearly not all fairy tale heroines are shrewd and resourceful. As Maria Tatar comments, "Cinderella has been reinvented by so many different cultures that it is hardly surprising to find that she is sometimes cruel and vindictive, and in other times compassionate and kind. Even within a single culture, she can appear genteel and self-effacing in one story, clever and enterprising in another, coy and manipulative in a third" (1999, 102).

Similarly, there is no fixed personality for the fairy tale princess. The archetypal fairy tale heroine should be fluid and variable. Unconstrained by her given role, she can act in accordance with it, she can resist it, or she can transform it. However, when her setting and character become predictable—following the culture's expectations more than the narrative's needs—the archetype becomes the stereotype. The stereotyped heroine retains little or no personal autonomy, becoming virtually a prisoner of societal expectations. As relatively unconstrained and variable oral tales become fixed into written literary texts—often by male collectors and anthologists—fairy tale heroines can fall into stereotypical patterns.[6] Some scholars blame Disney's films specifically for their negative effects upon fairy tale princesses. Kay Stone asserts that in them, "Archetype became stereotype and the mystery was gone. This is the problem with all of 'the Disney versions'" (2004, 122).

---

dwarfs—also appears in the fairy tale film *Snow White: A Tale of Terror* (directed by Michael Cohn, 1997).

6   A particularly good example of an oral version's complex archetypal patterns that contrast with more-well-known written versions is Yvonne Verdier's (1980) consideration of "Little Red Riding Hood."

Disney films omit many potentially disturbing or incongruous story elements. For example, in the Grimm version of "Snow White," the prince is first introduced into the story after the main character's sleep/death, and thus he is a stranger when she awakens. In Disney's animation of *Snow White and the Seven Dwarfs* (directed by Hamilton Luske, 1937), Snow White and the prince meet at the very beginning of the story. Their rendezvous authorizes the prince's act of kissing Snow White's corpse and justifies her happily embracing him after waking up instead of running away in fright. Similarly, these films use romance to rationalize the plots. In the Grimm version, Snow White awakens when the prince's servants carrying her coffin stumble, dislodging the piece of poisonous apple from her throat. In Disney's film, however, Snow White is saved from death or eternal sleep by the prince's kiss. While the male protagonist's heroic rescue and masculinity are enhanced in the film, the heroine is depicted as a damsel in distress yearning for romance from the start.

Finding true love therefore becomes the stereotyped desire of all fairy tale princesses in Disney films. Walt Disney is reported to have said, "It's just that people now don't want fairy stories the way they were written. They were too rough. In the end they'll probably remember the story the way we film it anyway" (quoted in Windling 2001). Whether or not this quotation is apocryphal, over time and with increasingly aggressive and far-reaching marketing, the "commodity consumption" (2002b, 172) of princess figures noted by Zipes in Disney films has been remarkably successful. The female protagonist as romantic heroine and damsel in distress in Disney's films has become the stereotyped model for the fairy tale princess into the twenty-first century and is arguably a subliminal reference point for the audience of the Harry Potter films.[7]

Many feminist studies have looked at characteristics of the fairy tale heroine and found that they repeatedly reinforce gender stereotypes. For example, Marcia Lieberman, examining the female images in Andrew Lang's fairy storybooks, declares that the majority of fairy tale heroines conform to the acquiescent stereotype (1972). Simone de Beauvoir also believed that the model for women in fairy tales was limited to overly obedient princesses: "Woman is the Sleeping Beauty, Cinderella, Snow White, she who receives and submits" (1953, 318). Alison Lurie argues that the very passivity of a

---

7   Linda Pershing and Lisa Gablehouse's chapter in this volume argues the resilience of the Disney model in the company's recent offering, *Enchanted* (directed by Kevin Lima, 2007).

fairy tale princess is regarded as her most attractive quality (1971). Sandra M. Gilbert and Susan Gubar further point out that the two extreme images in "Snow White"—the aggressively jealous stepmother and the passively submissive heroine—are both female victims of the mirror, which represents patriarchal approval for women as immobilized aesthetic objects (1979).

Another aspect often identified as problematic by some feminists in these stories is their sadism. Patricia Duncker, for instance, studies the "sadomasochism" in Sara Maitland's (1987) adaptation of the Cinderella story and remarks that "fairy tales allow us to examine and recreate" the "cruelty, brutality, and hatred of woman against woman" (1992, 151–52). Angela Carter further explores and subverts the notion of sadism and women by adapting fairy tales in her work *The Bloody Chamber and Other Stories* (1979).[8]

Troubled by maltreatment at home—from Cinderella's social exclusion to the handless maiden's physical mutilation—a significant number of protagonists of any gender feel isolated and yearn for change to gain a sense of belonging and happiness.[9] The nature of sadism, however, differs in fairy tales with heroines as there is often, as Bruno Bettelheim (1976) argues throughout his psychological analysis of fairy tales, an Oedipal tension. The biological mother's early death is frequently followed by the father's remarriage. The child heroine, at the same time, is recognized as a growing woman, whose desire for her father's attention may transform into Oedipal affection.[10] The heroine, therefore, is viewed by her stepmother as a possible rival for the role of chatelaine in the household. By forcing the heroine to do dirty chores, the stepmother defines her stepdaughter as a maid, rather than the woman of the house. As a result, the maltreatment the heroine receives actually originates from a perceived sexual threat.

Psychological theories argue that fairy tales thus become the vehicle for resolving fears associated with Oedipal tension. Karen E. Rowe comments, "Many tales implicitly acknowledge the potent attraction between females and the father; but, as purveyors of cultural norms, they often mask latent

---

8   In this volume, however, Kim Snowden argues that Carter's stories and the film made from them can both be understood as feminist revisions when examined with a more nuanced vision of both the original texts and feminism.

9   Even as unpromising a figure as the handless maiden can, nevertheless, be recuperated into feminist analysis (see Stone, Jenoff, and Gordon 1997).

10   An extreme example of such story development happens in "Donkeyskin" (ATU 510B), where the father, instructed by his dying wife to remarry only if he can find a woman more beautiful than she, thinks only his daughter fits that description and asks her to marry him.

incest as filial love and displace blatant sexual desires onto a substitute" (1986, 214–15). Many fairy tales work through the heroine's process of transferring her sexual desire for the father onto another male. Thus, many heroines—forced to leave their homes—are separated from their fathers. The sadism overtly constructs the stereotypical image of an obedient heroine who is resigned to adversity. Compared with their male counterparts, who are not afraid of breaking the status quo and venturing out to explore the world, the majority of fairy tale heroines do not set off on a quest voluntarily. These "innocent persecuted heroines" (e.g., Bacchilega 1993; Jones 1993) are taught that, even in the most unbearable situation, as long as they endure and behave well, fate will bring them happiness.[11]

Undergoing humiliation therefore becomes the common experience for fairy tale princesses. Maria Tatar indicates that most of these heroines "rise to or return to the ranks of royalty once they have been humbled and humiliated" (2003, 94). Such abasement occurs in classic tales like "Snow White," "Cinderella," or "The Frog King, or Iron Heinrich" (ATU 440).[12] The purpose of abasement, Carter believes, is to deliver the moral lesson that "being good" is more important than "doing well" (1991, 128). She stresses that fairy tale heroines are expected to accept willingly, or even be grateful for, these degradations. Tatar argues that the virtue heroines obtain through humiliation mirrors patriarchal ideology at its root. Subordinating oneself to male-dominated values is the virtue that fairy tale heroines acquire from the experience of degradation. It is also the quality often found in illustrations of the princess stereotype. Thus, traditional fairy tales can incorporate both stereotypical and archetypal qualities in their heroines.

Princess Harry

When one applies Propp's theory to the Harry Potter series, Ginny—by marrying the hero Harry at the end of the story—appears to be the most promising candidate for the role of princess. Indeed, traces of "Cinderella" are reflected in the transformation of Ginny's appearance throughout the series.

---

11   For a look at the "innocent persecuted heroine" in fairy tales, see Bacchilega (1993) and Jones (1993).

12   The humiliation takes various forms: Snow White needs to clean the dwarfs' house and is choked by the poisoned apple; Cinderella works as a maid in the kitchen and is forbidden to join the ball; and the princess in "The Frog King, or Iron Heinrich" is forced to eat and sleep with the frog.

In the first book, she is described only as a "small girl" who is "red-headed" like the rest of her family (Rowling 1997, 69). Like Cinderella, she has no partner at first and is denied entry to the Yule Ball because of her appearance and status. While she takes a greater role in the fifth book in fighting against the dark force, it is her external transformation in *Harry Potter and the Half-Blood Prince* that establishes her as a suitable companion for Harry. The developing beauty of Ginny hence mirrors Cinderella's transformation and the emblematic glass slipper. While the slipper brings Cinderella marriage with the prince, Ginny's beauty becomes the key unlocking her romantic relationship with the hero.

Ginny's role, however, does not fully correspond to the princess dramatis persona. Despite marrying the hero, she is neither the sought-for person nor the reward. There is no direct link between the conquests Harry makes through the series and his marriage to Ginny. The only passage that positions Ginny as the sought-for person is the rescue scene in *Harry Potter and the Chamber of Secrets*. When Harry finds her on the floor: "face down, lay a small, black-robed figure with flaming red hair. . . . Her face was white as marble, and as cold, yet her eyes were closed" (Rowling 1998, 226). Ginny's condition strikingly mirrors that of Sleeping Beauty. Like this character—in a bewitched sleep to mitigate the curse of death—Ginny remains unconscious while her life is drained away by Tom Riddle's memory, which is preserved in a diary. Just as Sleeping Beauty is wakened by the prince's kiss, Ginny is released from the spell when Harry destroys the diary. The eternal sleep stands for death; both Sleeping Beauty and Ginny become its victims, waiting to be rescued. However, in contrast with Sleeping Beauty, who is the main victim in her tale, it is Harry, rather than Ginny, on whom the diary preys. It confesses, "I have been waiting for you to appear since we arrived here. I knew you'd come" (Ibid., 231). The narrative of the story thus subtly transforms Harry into the sought-for person, while the image it depicts further reduces the importance of Ginny's role as princess.

Princess rescue scenes in fairy tales tend to highlight the nobility of the heroine by displaying her in particular ways, implying her value as the hero's reward. Sleeping Beauty sleeps in a castle surrounded by briars, and Snow White lies in a glass coffin with her name and the title of princess in gold letters. Both princesses' beauty is emphasized in their escape from death. Unlike them, Ginny is found on the floor, low and dirty, her face concealed, her individuality minimized. The princess's sleep in fairy tales symbolizes the suspension of time, while she—with her beauty and virginity intact—awaits the prince to claim her. Ginny, in contrast, is pictured as a wounded prey being hunted to the ground. Her red hair, which becomes the only remnant of her identity, is a symbol of blood. She is there to arouse the hero's compassion more than his desire.

Ginny has a somewhat different appearance in the film. Harry (Daniel Radcliffe) descends a staircase and enters the Chamber of Secrets. He first sees a hall lined with statues of snarling snake's heads. At the end of the passage, on the wall, is a carved stone sculpture of a face, which later opens its mouth and disgorges the monstrous snake Basilisk.[13] The chamber appears spacious and has an atmosphere of Gothic grandiosity. In front of the sculpture lies Ginny (Bonnie Wright). Instead of being face down as in the novel, she lies on her back with one hand holding the diary to her chest. No elements help build the scene into a romantic rescue. On the contrary, the tense music, the giant statues, and the frighteningly somber mood develop an ambience that may remind the audience of adventure or even horror films. Ginny looks ashen and dead, more like a sacrifice fallen into a trap during the quest than an alluring princess put into an enchanted sleep.

The film seems careful to avoid making the rescue scene into a romantic reunion. When Ginny wakes up, she turns away from Harry and does not notice him until he calls her name. They do not have any physical contact. In the novel, Ginny "[draws] a great, shuddering gasp and tears began to pour down her face" when she sees the blood on Harry's robe (Rowling 1998, 237). Compared with the novel, the emotion between the two in the film is rather cold. Ginny sheds no tears when she sees Harry's anguished condition. The scene also shows Harry's physical and metaphorical distance from Ginny. The ink flowing from the diary forms a line and separates the two, socially as well as emotionally. The line may be interpreted as the social boundary that forbids them to get close. It can also be read as the allegorical moral code that condemns Ginny for her indiscretion.[14]

The split between the novel and the film is also clear in the scene where the phoenix, Fawkes, heals Harry with its tears. In the novel, Harry wakes Ginny after Fawkes saves him. In the film, Fawkes saves Harry's life after he

---

13   The face is very like *la Bocca della Verità (The Mouth of Truth)*. It seems more than possible that Rowling is making a visual allusion to this well-known allegorical sculpture in Rome.

14   By confessing her deepest secrets to the diary, Ginny is manipulated by the evil spirit of Tom Riddle (i.e., Voldemort) and thus is unwittingly responsible for the release of the Basilisk.

asks Ginny to escape by herself. The alteration creates different interpretations for Harry's heroic behavior. In the novel, Fawkes's act in curing Harry
is his reward for slaying the monster in the Chamber of Secrets. Killing
the monster is, however, not enough in the film. To prove himself, Harry
has to make a selfless decision—to send Ginny away and die alone. In the
novel, Ginny is not aware that Harry has sacrificed himself to save her. An
unspoken act is intrinsically more heroic than one acknowledged by others. It takes more courage to decide to face one's death alone. Although
bravery is emphasized in both, the novel glorifies humility while the film
praises sacrifice.

The endings of both novel and film avoid the expected fairy tale scene
where the hero triumphantly rescues the princess. In the novel, Harry shows
Ginny the diary and the dead monster, like the hero showing the princess
the slain dragon. Instead of thanking him, Ginny weeps, "I am going to
be expelled!" (Rowling 1998, 238). Her exclamation creates an unexpected
comic effect and subverts the predicted romantic reunion. The film treats
the scene another way. Harry comforts her, "It's all right, Ginny. It's over. It's
just a memory" while a close-up of Harry's face shows his eyes, unfocused,
as if he has just woken from a dream and is trying to remember it. The film
emphasizes Harry's mental reflection on the event and makes it a metaphorical embodiment of his internal experience. The horror and despair of
the Chamber of Secrets are thus construed as the allegorical representations
of the inner fear and anxiety that Harry needs to conquer. The film depicts
the incident as a personal quest for Harry and stresses his role as both hero
and victim.

Hermione can also be compared to the heroines in fairy tales. The scene
where she is attacked by a troll in the bathroom in *Harry Potter and the
Philosopher's Stone* (released in the U.S. as *Harry Potter and the Sorcerer's
Stone*) is crucial as it earns her friendship with Harry and Ron and confirms
her as one of the main protagonists. The scene is also significant because
it exhibits the humiliation required of many female heroines in fairy tales.
Hermione is punished for her pride and vanity. Intelligent and learned, she
is eager to impress and tends to show off, which alienates her classmates.
Escaping Ron's mockery, she cries alone in the girls' toilet, where the troll
attacks her: "Hermione Granger was shrinking against the wall opposite,
looking as if she was about to faint. The troll was advancing on her, knock-
ing the sinks off the walls as it went" (Rowling 1997, 129).

Hermione's helplessness reflects both the physical and mental humiliation she undergoes elsewhere. From the psychical alienation of her peers to the life-threatening attack by the troll, she is literally put down, and her pride is shattered. Saved by Harry and Ron, Hermione surprisingly defends them by lying to Professor McGonagall, saying that it was her arrogance that caused the trouble. Hermione's lie is ironic and persuasive because it is based on her well-known conceitedness. Yet, by inventing a convincing lie, she also acknowledges and repents her vanity.

Maria Tatar notes that fairy tales endorse "the subordination of female desire to male desire" (1999, 27). Hermione's sacrificial act, which positions her in exactly this subordinate role, identifies her with the stereotypical fairy tale princess. Rowling, however, adds an ironic note in the plot that mocks the formulaic portrayal at the same time as it apparently upholds it. In the novel, Harry and Ron try to trap the troll by locking the girl's toilet but discover Hermione is trapped as well. Reluctantly, they are forced to save her from the trouble they have created for her: "It was the last thing they wanted to do, but what choice did they have?" (Rowling 1997, 129).

The rescue scene in the novel thus becomes an ironic inversion of those in many fairy tales. Hermione's position as damsel in distress is no existential gendered trait; instead, it is created by the boys. Harry and Ron are not the traditional heroes who volunteer for the quest but inexperienced children whose bumbling has made their bravery necessary. Also it is only by sheer luck, rather than innate ability, that the boys defeat the troll. While the scene serves as abasement for Hermione, its sarcastic connotation mocks it as stereotypical and predictable at the same time. This twist, however, is diminished in the film, where—when Harry and Ron (Rupert Grint) hear Hermione's (Emma Watson) scream—they head unhesitatingly into the toilet. Omitting the boys' mistake reduces the comic effect, and they come across as more straightforwardly heroic than in the novel. The humor in the film misses the book's subtle sarcasm, and the twist of irony is less evident, which makes the film scene a more stereotypical depiction of prince(s) rescuing a princess.

Hermione also emerges as the princess figure in her physical transformation during the Yule Ball scene in *Harry Potter and the Goblet of Fire*, analogous to the ball scene in "Cinderella." In the first book, Hermione has a "bossy sort of voice, lots of bushy brown hair and rather large front teeth" (Rowling 1997, 79). However, at the ball, Harry fails to recognize Hermione when he first sees her with Viktor Krum: "Krum was at the front of the party, accompanied by a pretty girl in blue robes Harry didn't know" (Rowling 2000, 359). Obvious similarities exist between Hermione and Cinderella. Both girls' appearances change so drastically that their acquaintances do not recognize them. While Cinderella is accompanied by the prince, Hermione is escorted by the prince of Quidditch, desired by almost every girl in the wizard world. Elizabeth E. Heilman thinks a yearning for physical change often occurs in stereotypical female characters and underlines their self-hatred. For Heilman, Hermione "is transformed like Cinderella and, like many tomboys in teen novels, into a 'princess.' She becomes physically acceptable" (2003, 229). The obsession with beauty, linked with the desire for patriarchal approval, identifies Hermione in the scene as the princess stereotype.

The magical spell cast on Cinderella disappears after midnight; Hermione loses grace after quarreling with Ron at the end of the ball. According to the novel, "her hair was coming down out of its elegant bun now, and her face was screwed up in anger" (Rowling 2000, 376). The fight can be seen as a feminist twist on the classic Cinderella story. Unlike Cinderella, Hermione is not bound to leave at the witching hour. Yet, while Cinderella escapes the ball before the spell is broken, Hermione loses the magical charm she possesses in front of everyone. This exposure can be read as the disillusionment of her fairy tale princess dream. Yet unlike Cinderella—in a possible move from stereotype to archetype—Hermione has no wish to continue the fantasy she experienced at the ball. When Harry meets her the next day, "Hermione's hair was bushy again; she confessed to Harry that she had used liberal amounts of Sleekeazy's Hair Potion on it for the ball, 'but it's way too much bother to do every day'" (Ibid., 377).

Hermione's decision can be interpreted in two ways. Her refusal to expend effort on her appearance can be feminist recognition that beauty cannot guarantee happiness as it does for the fairy tale princess. Her act, however, can also be seen as an involuntary retreat from a fantasy world to the reality she cannot avoid. On the one hand, her matter-of-fact tone may indicate that she finally is able to observe rationally the princess fantasy; and on the other, it can be construed as a powerless acceptance of her failed attempt to realize that dream.

The analogy between Hermione and Cinderella grows stronger in the film. Instead of making her first appearance entering the ballroom with Krum (Stanislav Ianevski) and other students, Hermione appears separately at the beginning of the scene. Harry first sees Hermione standing alone at the top of the stairs, which functions to introduce the character. Her position at the top gives Hermione significant status. The act of descending further creates dramatic tension and an atmosphere of expectation. The lighting enhances her beauty. Silver light shines on her back and shoulders, emphasizing the outline of her dress. When she descends, a golden light illuminates her face while the camera gradually zooms in on her smile, all underscored by a soft melody that slowly rises. The mise-en-scène romanticizes Hermione's image and displays her as a traditional fairy tale princess. In the film, Harry is presented as a Prince Charming, rather than as the observer the novel describes. The camera moves from Hermione's smile to a close-up of Harry's face, creating the impression that she is smiling at him. He blinks several times in response, as if dazed by her beauty.

Standing below Hermione, Harry appears to be the prince waiting for his princess. The film, however, offers a small twist by later having Hermione laugh and wave when passing the hallway escorted by Krum. Her gesture implies her vanity and indicates her old tendency to show off. Ironically, this gesture associates her more with characters like the stepsisters than with Cinderella and suggests Hermione is betraying her princess self. After quarreling with Ron, Hermione sits on the stairs, cries, and takes off one of her shoes. The shoe Cinderella accidentally drops on the stair brings her marriage with the prince in the end. Hermione, on the other hand, removes her shoe deliberately with the knowledge that there will be no prince to pick it up. She becomes a false Cinderella, exiled from the ball. In the background, sitting a few steps behind her, are three female students. One is crying while the other two comfort her. By juxtaposing Hermione with the girls in the background, the film suggests that her experience is common to young women. The dream of becoming a princess only exists in fairy tales, and the dreamer eventually wakes. Unlike the novel, the film tends to read the end of Hermione's physical transformation as an inevitable failure, rather than a personal choice.

Yet the novel and the film both endeavor to move away from converting Hermione into a stereotypical fairy tale princess. Though she undergoes humiliation, her epiphany of subservience is only temporary; she and her intelligence remain, as Christine Schoefer notes, "a constant source of irritation" throughout the books (2000). Most importantly, Hermione marries the antihero/sidekick Ron instead of the athlete star Krum or the hero Harry at the end of the series. Fairy tale heroines generally marry a prince, if there is one available, representing the reward of material and social promotion.

Ron, conversely, is neither hero nor royalty in the Harry Potter world. Thus, the lack of radical alteration in Hermione's personality and social status suggests resistance to the ideal image of the fairy tale princess. As a dominant female character, her affection toward Ron—considered the weakest in their circle of three—may seem protective, even maternal. The unconventional opposition to the princess's image, and her predominant position over Ron's in their relationship, creates a strong sense of authority for her. On the one hand, Hermione can be interpreted as a feminist revision of the fairy tale heroine, a role closer to the princess archetype than the stereotype. On the other hand, her domination over others and her role in the narrative place her in a position corresponding to Harry's: closer to the fairy tale hero.

In her study of Grimms' collection, Maria Tatar argues that heroes of tales with more realistic settings have lowly origins, and their trait of naïveté can be interpreted as shrewdness; they are rarely assisted by supernatural force (2003, 96–98). Similarities exist between these heroes and Hermione. Since she comes from a Muggle family, Hermione's parentage is considerably humbler than that of other wizards and witches, especially Harry Potter. Although the element of magic is never far from any of the stories, Hermione's logic and wits are often keys to help her and her companions overcome the danger they encounter. As Tatar stresses, realistic fairy tales are "stories that take advantage of exaggeration, punning, parody, and literalism to produce comic effects" (Ibid., 99). These strategies also appear in Hermione's characterization. The humiliation process and physical transformation develop her into the embodiment of the fairy tale princess. Yet they also serve as an ironic counterpoint, displaying a feminist resistance to the image of the princess based in patriarchal ideology. Hermione's intelligence, which often aids the protagonists, creates a sense of authority and builds her role into an equivalent to the hero in the fairy tale. Yet her brains are sometimes a source of annoyance and are frequently mentioned in jokes to comic and sarcastic effect. Hermione's role is unstable and subtly, but constantly, shifts like that of the princess archetype in fairy tales. Her characterization and the plot of the story, however, frequently associate her with a hero's role, rather than with the princess's. Her complex, self-contradictory qualities make her a foil to Harry and a telling contrast to the stereotypical fairy tale princess.

Despite the presence of female characters who are obvious fairy tale princess candidates, and who indeed at times do embody her, arguably the best manifestation of the princess in the Harry Potter series is Harry himself. The series has developed him into a more profound and complex embodiment of the fairy tale princess than either Ginny or Hermione. The maltreatment Harry receives resembles Cinderella's. She sleeps by the fireplace in the ashes, whereas Harry lives in a cupboard under the stairs. Both protagonists are forced to do domestic chores. Cinderella does the laundry; Harry serves breakfast and cleans the dishes for the Dursleys. Both are forbidden to participate in important activities, unlike other family members. Cinderella is not allowed to attend the ball; the Dursleys try to stop Harry from going to Hogwarts.

Gallardo-C. and Smith point out that Harry is trapped in a continuous cycle of "slavery and liberty, abuse and triumph," more reminiscent of Cinderella than mythical male heroes such as King Arthur (2003, 195).[15] They argue that "appearing within a traditionally feminine narrative structure," Harry's story is essentially a "girl tale," which usually encompasses "feminine themes—abandonment, rape, loss of the protecting mother or father, menses" (2003, 196). Of course, the feminine structure and themes Gallardo-C. and Smith observe in Harry Potter are also found in many other fairy tales with male protagonists. Due to the vast number of these victimized heroes, the Antti Aarne and Stith Thompson tale-type index includes a separate number—AT 511A, "The Little Red Ox"—for versions with male Cinderella-like protagonists (1999, 377).[16] "While there are virtually no male counterparts to Catskin," as Tatar observes, "male Cinderellas abound in the folklore of many cultures" (1999, 106). To identify Harry with the fairy tale princess, I turn to elements that can usually only be found in fairy tale heroines.

As indicated already, Oedipal tension is one distinctive element in fairy tales with heroines, though, as Tatar comments, "mother/son incest seems

---

15   Because Harry rises from obscurity to his rightful place with Dumbledore's help, the two are often compared to King Arthur and Merlin. Gallardo-C. and Smith (2003) argue that most people would identify Harry Potter as a King Arthur figure—the retrieved boy—but for the purpose of their argument, he is Cinderfella. Their allusion is to the film (directed by Frank Tashlin, 1960), where Jerry Lewis plays Fella, whose stepmother (note that this figure is the only one whose gender remains consistent with the original story) and wicked stepbrothers conspire against him but who wins the heart of the princess with the aid of his fairy godfather. For further discussion of the analogy between Harry Potter and King Arthur, see Schafer (2000, 148–49).

16   See Torborg Lundell's critique of gender presumptions in earlier versions of the tale-type index (1986). The most recent edition of *The Types of International Folktales* subsumes the subtypes under ATU 511, which allows for a male or female hero (Uther 2004, 1: 296).

to resist representation in folktales" (1999, 106). The sadism in Harry Potter contains Oedipal tension, which can be unearthed by examining Harry's Aunt Petunia Dursley, and further identifies Harry with fairy tale heroines. As observed by Gallardo-C. and Smith, Petunia's role echoes that of the fairy tale stepmother.[17] As a boy, Harry poses no sexual threat to Petunia. Her resentment toward him, however, stems from her jealousy of her dead sister, Lily Potter, praised by their parents for her gift of magic. Unlike Lily, Petunia has no such talent in her blood and feels edged out by her family. Harry, who has inherited his mother's gift of magic, thus becomes Petunia's scapegoat for Lily. Harry's aunt's bitterness toward his mother puts Petunia in a similar position to the fairy tale heroine's stepsisters. But by taking Harry into her home and becoming his guardian, Petunia's primary role in the story transforms from being Lily's stepsister to Harry's stepmother.

While the cruelty of classic fairy tales is reproduced in the series, Harry's initial attitude toward persecution presents him as the princess stereotype more than the archetype. He does not possess the initiative to improve his life. In the first book, he has never tried to run away nor to fight against the Dursleys. In fact, in spite of the unfair treatment he receives, he quietly complies. Consequently, he undergoes humiliation and is rewarded for his virtues of endurance like the innocent persecuted heroines considered by Cristina Bacchilega (1993) and Steven Swann Jones (1993). Rubeus Hagrid, who knocks at Harry's door one day and tells him he is a wizard, resembles Cinderella's fairy godmother, who waves her magic wand and changes the downtrodden girl's fate by turning her into the image of a princess. The pink umbrella that conceals his wand provides a joke on Hagrid's sensitive and soft personality—maternal and feminine like that of all fairy godmothers.[18] Harry does not attempt to find his own destiny; destiny finds Harry.

Harry's nobility also differs from Ginny's or Hermione's. Unlike Ginny, who becomes beautiful, or Hermione, who chooses not to be, Harry's fundamental nobility is in his blood like the fairy tale heroines born to be beautiful. He is, as Rowling describes him, "the boy who lived" (1997,

---

17   Gallardo-C. and Smith locate this argument in a discussion of conventional gendered categories of labor in the novel, positioning Petunia against the assiduous "good mother," Molly Weasley, and the sacrificial mother, Lily Potter (2003, 192–93).

18   Hagrid may be saved from suspicions about his sexuality that might follow from these characteristics because readers/viewers learn that he has a relationship with Madame Maxime, headmistress of Beauxbatons. However, given his maternal and nurturing personality and the pink umbrella he characteristically carries, Hagrid clearly subverts any easy binary notion of gender. Thanks to Catherine Tosenberger for this insight.

18): the child destined to be the object of admiration in the wizard world. Debasement, however, is necessary because it reconfirms his innate virtue. As Iona and Peter Opie point out, Cinderella "cannot be won until—as in many other fairy tales—she has been recognised by her suitor in her mundane, degraded state" (1992, 121). The motif of Harry's story is restoration. Like Snow White and many other innocent persecuted heroines, Harry must regain the position and life that have been taken from him.

Harry's bond with Lily is the most important element that identifies him as the fairy tale princess. The close link with the mother, found more often in fairy tale heroines than heroes, appears in various ways. Typically the heroine inherits the biological mother's beauty and virtue. Though the mother may die, help comes to her daughter from natural forces or magic used by a good fairy or godmother who can be regarded as an avatar for the absent biological mother.[19] Harry's connection with his own dead mother is repeatedly emphasized throughout the series. As Dumbledore explains to Harry, "Your mother's sacrifice made the bond of blood the strongest shield I could give you" (Rowling 2003, 737). In *Harry Potter and the Philosopher's Stone,* Professor Quirrell, within whom Voldemort lives as a parasite, feels great pain when touching Harry, for Lily's love has imprinted the protection spell on his skin. When Harry meets Voldemort in *Harry Potter and the Goblet of Fire,* the shadow of Lily merges with others from the wand and stalls Voldemort so Harry has time to escape. Also it is the blood relationship of Lily and Petunia that creates the defense for Harry during his first seventeen years of life. As long as Harry lives under his aunt's roof, he is protected from the Dark Lord. Moreover, because of his affection for Lily, Professor Snape devotes his life to guarding her son.

The conspicuous resemblance between Harry and Lily is repeatedly stressed. Harry's parents' acquaintances agree that though Harry looks like his father, James Potter, importantly he has his mother's eyes. Having Lily's eyes signifies that Harry has inherited his mother's soul. Through the proceeding story, Harry gradually learns that James used to bully Snape when they were studying at Hogwarts and Lily was the only one who stood up against his bullying. The snobbish feudal-prince role played by James at Hogwarts parallels that of Draco Malfoy (the biggest bully and Harry's foe in school) in his son's time, while Lily's role resembles Harry's. Like

19   See also Gallardo-C. and Smith on the relationship of dead mother and the protagonist in "Aschenputtel" and Harry Potter (2003, 195).

his mother, Harry shows great compassion for the poor and the weak. His characteristics are closer to his mother's than his father's and are associated with qualities understood in Euro-North America as feminine. To a certain degree, Lily not only protects Harry through their blood bond but also lives on through him.

Like Lily, Harry possesses the virtue of self-sacrifice, a characteristic almost unique to heroines in fairy tales. Selfless sacrifice is rare for heroes; they are the dominators in the patriarchal world of the fairy tale. The motivation for their stories is usually justice and revenge. Tales from "Faithful Johannes" (ATU 516) to "The Juniper Tree" (ATU 720) offer examples of this pattern in male characters. Notwithstanding being a gifted wizard, when facing a crisis, Harry frequently displays self-sacrificing behavior instead of using the force of magic as a resource. He defeats Quirrell by clutching him with his arms, suffering extreme pain. He also rescues Ginny while he is bitten by the deadly poisonous snake.

Another example of Harry's self-sacrificing, nurturing, and compassionate nature occurs in the Triwizard Tournament, where the second task is to recover one's most precious possession from the bottom of the lake. The passage parallels the story of "The Little Mermaid" (Andersen 1846, 44–82). Just as the Little Mermaid is transformed by love into a human, Harry is changed into a merman. With their lives at stake, both choose to sacrifice themselves. Refusing to kill the prince to save herself, the Little Mermaid throws herself into the sea, where her body dissolves into foam. Harry, determined to return all the hostages safely, gives up his chance of winning the task and nearly drowns in the lake. Like the Little Mermaid, who is rewarded with a soul, Harry's sacrifice is recognized with full marks from most of the judges in the tournament.

The film adaptations tend to enhance Harry's heroic image by highlighting his masculinity or overromanticizing scenes that have a different weight in the books. In addition to the scene at the Yule Ball already discussed, the film version of *Harry Potter and the Goblet of Fire* has Hermione throw herself into Harry's arms and embrace him before he performs the first task in the tournament. A pure creation of the film, this scene portrays Harry as a potential patriarchal hero in a solemn, yet romantic, atmosphere. Yet the scene gives a false impression of Harry and Hermione's relationship to the audience. It is clear from the novel, published long before the release of the corresponding film (2000 and 2005), that Hermione is most likely to partner with Ron at the end of the series. Director Mike Newell probably saw Hermione and Harry as a more suitable couple to represent the conventional princess and prince. Alongside the other changes in the adaptation, the power and familiarity of this image of romance may influence the reading of the film. The audience is led to identify the characters' gender with the sexes of the actors and ignore more connotative or nuanced concepts of gender.

The resemblance between Harry and the princess figure, however, is not completely diminished by the alterations in the film. The elements that identify Harry as the innocent persecuted heroine lie not only in the lines he delivers or the acts he undertakes. They are deeply rooted in the stories' characterizations, plot structure, and motifs. These are at the heart of the stories and cannot be easily removed through adaptation. Surface changes or audiovisual elements do create a different emphasis, but the films' adherence to the books' essential narrative mean that these alterations cannot wholly transform Rowling's approach to her characters. At times the films may even enhance Harry's contrast to other male characters, implicitly feminizing him. For instance, Krum is described as "thin, dark and sallow-skinned" in the book (Rowling 2000, 95). In casting Stanislav Ianevski, a hypermasculine and heavily built actor, the film emphasises Krum's identity as athlete hero and, perhaps unintentionally, enhances Harry's divergent and arguably feminine qualities. As I have already discussed, the film version of the rescue scene in the Chamber of Secrets reinforces Harry's role as the victimized protagonist by portraying his experience as a reflection of his mental journey. With this "Sleeping Beauty" (ATU 410) scenario, the film's analogy between Harry and a fairy tale persecuted princess becomes both more prominent and more sophisticated than in the novel.

Rowling has applied both the archetype and stereotype of the fairy tale princess to the Harry Potter books in an unconventional way. The series possesses structures and scenarios like those of classic fairy tales, yet the characters offer the possibility of reading gender in a different way. The traits of the princess are present in Ginny and Hermione. Yet the feminist twists in the story, and the complexity of Hermione's character particularly, subvert patriarchal expectations that dominate too many well-known fairy tales, making her a female version of the hero. Harry, on the other hand, is the metaphorical embodiment of a male Cinderella. The glass slipper may appear to fit all three, but it actually belongs to Harry alone.

In contrast to Rowling's novels, the films strengthen the patriarchal concepts of gender so that stereotype predominates over archetype. The subversive ideology adapted from the novels to the films, however, is not completely obliterated and is sometimes even reinforced. Evidence from readership studies shows that having a boy, rather than a girl, as the protagonist makes the story more acceptable for both male and female readers and audiences.[20] In their research on adolescent reading preference, Karen C. Beyard-Tyler and Howard J. Sullivan report, "Boys' preferences for male protagonists became significantly stronger as grade level increased, whereas girls' preferences for female protagonists decreased significantly as grade level increased" (1980, 104). Terri Doughty examines the success of *Harry Potter* in the boys' book market, commenting that it shows "the continued appeal of a certain brand of masculine fantasy of empowerment for boy readers" and emphasizing that readers "*would* read the Potter books differently if they were about Harriet Potter" (2004, 257).

However, perhaps more than the primary character's sex, it is the application of fairy tales that makes the series such a phenomenal success. Containing the familiar sadism and formulaic pattern leading to happiness in fairy tales, the story gives readers and audiences a nostalgic feeling along with the pleasure of reading and viewing. Both avoiding and manipulating popular cliché, Rowling subverts fairy tale stereotypes and gives a new generation a fresh experience of gender roles, one that employs fairy tale archetypes to imaginative advantage. Perhaps too predictably, the film versions are less bold and transgressive.

---

20   Gallardo-C. and Smith give a slightly different emphasis to the narrative shifts between the Cinderella story and *Harry Potter,* arguing that the series resembles a "girl tale" and "feminizes Harry in ways that allow female readers to identify strongly with a male protagonist" (2003, 191).

5

The Shoe Still Fits
Ever After and the Pursuit of a Feminist Cinderella

Christy Williams

T HE 1998 FILM *EVER AFTER: A CINDERELLA STORY*, directed by Andy Tennant and starring Drew Barrymore, is a delightful retelling of "Cinderella" (ATU 510A) for a contemporary audience that has grown up with second-wave feminism and its arguments about the problematically sexist representation of women. Unlike other popular literary and cinematic Cinderellas, who need the help of birds (Grimms and Disney), mice (Disney), or fairies (Perrault and Disney) to accomplish chores and prove themselves worthy of respect and love, Danielle (Drew Barrymore) wins the affection and esteem of her prince (Dougray Scott) by being -smart, caring, strong, and assertive. She does not rely on the prince to save her or on others to solve her problems. What sets Danielle apart from her fictional and cinematic predecessors, as well as from the other women in the film, is her self-confidence and lack of interest in material wealth, social status, and prince hunting. However, like her predecessors, she does not completely break from tradition, and the film fails to question the patriarchal structures of the "Cinderella" story.

Some critics and reviewers have labeled *Ever After* a feminist film due to Danielle's strength in contrast to the expected passivity of heroines of popularizedfairy tales. Despite disagreements as to the merits of the film, popular

An earlier version of this article was presented at the eighth annual New Voices Graduate Student Conference at Georgia State University in September 2007. I thank Cristina Bacchilega and Jennifer Orme for their guidance in revising the article and the Graduate Student Organization at the University of Hawai'i, Mānoa, for its support.

reviewers have often labeled it "feminist," or even "postfeminist,"[1] calling
attention to its "girl-positive" (Schwarzbaum 1998) and "female empowerment" (Burr 1999) qualities. While academic critics have been more resistant to calling *Ever After* a feminist film, their analyses emphasize characteristics that generally fit feminist ideology, and they praise the film for its
efforts at representing a strong heroine. Elisabeth Rose Gruner claims that
the film "rewrit[es] Cinderella for a feminist, perhaps even a post-feminist,
future" (2003, 146). John Stephens and Robyn McCallum recognize it
as "a story of female resistance within a dominating patriarchy" (2002,
206). And Cathy Lynn Preston argues that *Ever After* attempts to "redefine
gender boundaries" and "respond to the last thirty years of feminist critique of gender construction" in popular fairy tales (2004, 206 and 203).
These critics' careful wording situates the film firmly in feminist territory
by recognizing how it attempts to represent gender without stating directly
whether or not it succeeds. Their resistance to making an explicit "feminist" claim for the film—as many of their popular counterparts do—indicates a tenuous relationship between the pro-girl posturing of the film and
contemporary feminism.

Resistance against calling a popular fairy tale feminist is not new to
fairy tale studies. In the early 1970s, Alison Lurie and Marcia R. Lieberman
began the debate about whether traditional fairy tales could be feminist.
The problem Lurie outlined (1970 and 1971) was that though there were
strong female heroines in the classic tales, the male-dominated publishing
industry had hidden them from view.[2] Fairy tales—even the traditional
ones—she argued, have strong female characters and are indeed feminist.
Lieberman (1972) responded that the Disney versions created the primary
image of fairy tales and their passive heroines superseded lesser-known ones
who might have had some pluck. The *popular* fairy tales—the ones actually affecting mass culture—she argued, were not feminist. They reinforced
limiting notions of femininity and worked to acculturate girls into passive
roles under patriarchy.

---

1   For a sampling of reviews that describe the film as feminist, see the *New York Times*
     (Holden 1998) and *People* (Rozen and Gliatto 1998); for post-feminist references, see
     the *Los Angeles Times* (Turan 1998) and *Chicago Tribune* (Wilmington 1998).

2   Classic refers to the widely popular collections of traditional tales by Charles Perrault
     and the Brothers Grimm, as well as literary tales by Hans Christian Andersen and
     Oscar Wilde.

As the heroine of a popular retelling of a traditional fairy tale, Danielle's 1998 appearance seems to suggest that the debate over feminist/antifeminist fairy tales has been settled. Not only is she a strong female lead who represents the ideals of girl power and liberal feminism, but she recaptures the strength of the older heroines Lurie described. Preston suggests that *Ever After* "plays off of what both folklorists and feminists have asked for: an acknowledgment that there have been many versions of 'Cinderella' and that there is a need to return, as it were, to a Cinderella figure who is a 'shrewd and practical girl persevering and winning a share of the power'" (2004, 204). Danielle, according to the impressed prince, "swims alone, climbs rocks, and rescues servants," suggesting a turn in American cinema toward a strong fairy tale heroine.

Though certainly a strong heroine, Danielle is concerned with her immediate world, and her actions belong to a personal and individually centered type of feminism. Stephens and McCallum explain that "Danielle's free-spirited behavior overturns social hierarchy, codes governing female conduct, and dress regulations" (2002, 208); however, all of these changes affect only Danielle. In their discussion of agency in the film, these same critics note the inadequacy of Danielle's shift from a "vision of a just society . . . to the more private well-being envisaged within the schema of romantic love" (Ibid.). I agree that containing Danielle's utopian ideology within the framework of heterosexual romance is problematic; however, my criticism does not focus on the film's romantic vision of utopia but, instead, its narrow depiction of feminism.

Ever After assumes a feminist stance but offers a mass-mediated idea of feminism where individual women can be strong and achieve equality through personal actions that do not, however, challenge or change the underlying patriarchal structure of society.[3] And these heroines can still be (sexually) desirable and marriageable in doing so. The problems identified by second-wave feminism are simplified, emptied of their radical critiques of systemic gender inequality, and marketed to young women.[4] This limited perspective, which draws on girl power and liberal feminism, reinforces patriarchal authority by emphasizing individual achievements and isolating one woman, the heroine, as an exception to standard feminine behavior. To

---

3   Linda Pershing and Lisa Gablehouse aptly refer to this idea as "faux feminism" in their analysis of *Enchanted* in this collection.

4   For a discussion of the marketing of *Ever After* to teenage girls, see Moira McCormick (1999).

counter the idea of feminism *Ever After* projects, I will focus on the limited power of Danielle's action within the film's dynamic of narrative authority, her highly gendered representations, the reversal of the damsel-in-distress plot, and the regendering of the fairy godmother as male. The fragments of the "Cinderella" tale that are manipulated most consistently in *Ever After*— the phrase "once upon a time," the dress, the rescue, and the godmother— placate a late-twentieth- and early-twenty-first-century audience's expectations of popular feminism but fail to move the "Cinderella" story beyond the structural misogyny knit into the tale's plot.

Framing Danielle's Feminism

Ever After opens with a frame narrative where her elderly great-great granddaughter tells the Brothers Grimm about Danielle, the "real" Cinderella. This storytelling scene then shifts into the embedded tale that reclaims the Cinderella story for Danielle and a contemporary, mainly female, audience before returning to close the frame at the end of the film. In the final scene of Danielle's story, after she has wed her prince, she chides Prince Henry, "You, sir, are supposed to be charming." He replies, "And we, princess, are supposed to live happily ever after." "Says who?" she challenges, and he replies, "You know? I don't know." The two are in the center of the screen, framed by the window behind them, and they kiss. This scene has been cited for its genre-establishing (Gruner 2003, 150), transitionary (Preston 2004, 200), and metanarrative (Stephens and McCallum 2002, 204) work. It also questions the authority of fairy tale formulas. The characters recognize the pattern but not the authority that gives it power. As the scene ends and the film returns to the frame story, the audience is prompted to ask why the Grimms (or other fairy tale collectors) get to establish the authoritative version of this fairy tale. While the visual framing of the couple and the closing kiss in Danielle's story place the film into fairy tale and romance genres, the dialogue opens up questions of agency.

In positing Danielle's story as an alternative to the Grimms', the frame explores the struggle of who gets to tell stories and whose versions become most authoritative. Preston suggests that the film questions male authority: "In the case of *Ever After* the appeal to authority is multivocal. The film invokes the historical authority of male tradition (Perrault, Brothers Grimm, da Vinci), which it then contests through a performance of gendered genre. . . . By disrupting genre boundaries, she [the Grande Dame] is able to tell a different story, one that played to the competing authority of a popularized 1990s film" (2004, 211). Similarly Gruner argues that *Ever After* "finally privileges the story of woman over the history of men, the passion of women over the rational rulings of men" (2003, 146). Stephens and McCallum add that the frame "asserts that the story is told by a woman and therefore presents a female point of view, and that this view is reliable. As Marina Warner suggests about other female narrated folktales, it authenticates the tale's misogynistic attitudes" (2002, 203). While I agree that the film cultivates the privileging of female voice and desire and certainly questions male authority, the way *Ever After* is constructed and told undermines the girl power and liberal feminist stance it claims to make by qualifying and containing feminist action and speech within patriarchal structures and frames. The female narrator and overtures to feminism conceal, as Warner suggests, the male authority behind the female voice (1994, 208–9).

While the film seems to offer an alternative to the authority of the Grimms, Perrault, and Disney by presenting a superficially feminist heroine (who despite her displays of independence still needs a happily-ever-after with a charming prince to be satisfied) in a female-narrated story, the frame ultimately undercuts the film's representation of a strong heroine and female narrative authority. The film begins and ends with a crane shot of the carriage of the Brothers Grimm (Joerg Stadler and Andy Henderson), which has brought them to an unnamed Grande Dame (Jeanne Moreau) they address as "your majesty." The Grande Dame has sent for the Grimm brothers to "set the story straight." Their version of "Cinderella" is not correct, and due to her heritage, *she* possesses the painting, the shoe, and therefore, the true tale. However, *Ever After* negates the power of the Grande Dame's version by positioning her story against the Grimms' and limiting it since the audience knows that the Grimms did not change their text.

The Grande Dame mimics the narrative patterns of classic fairy tales in telling her story but, at the same time, grants authority to them. She begins her story with "once upon a time, there lived a young girl who loved her father very much," a phrase that immediately establishes Danielle in relationship to a patriarchal figure. The Grande Dame recognizes that her opening is an allusion to the Grimms, but her use of the phrase is ironic. As explained by Elizabeth Wanning Harries, a fairy tale opening is usually meant to distance the audience from the time and place of the tale and denote the creation of a fictional space (2001, 104). However for her claim of authenticity to work, the Grand Dame clearly requires her audience to recognize the historical setting of her story. This claim of truth suggests a blurring of genre identified by Preston as "legend" (2004, 201) and Stephens and McCallum as "historical narrative" (2002, 206).[5]

The legend status offers a narrative validity to the Grande Dame's version of "Cinderella" that other storytellers cannot claim. Preston argues that the shift from fairy tale to legend "provid[es] a fictionalized historical precedent" for the assertive and independent young women viewing the film, thus validating their own transgressive behavior (2004, 202). For the young female audience members who identify with Danielle's assertive behavior, the fairy tale-cum-legend, which blurs truth and fiction, authorizes their own ways of acting. Thus, by using the formula, the Grande Dame mocks the Grimms for not believing that the story can be true. However, because the formula "once upon a time" denotes a fairy tale, not legend or history, she undercuts her own assertion of truth.

In closing her story (and the film), the Grande Dame declares that "the point, gentlemen, is that they lived." As Gruner, Preston, and Stephens and McCallum have shown, the film conflates fairy tale with legend and history, thus allowing the Grande Dame's assertion "that they lived" to make an argument for the validity of her version of the tale, which seemingly trumps all other versions. However, her use of "gentlemen" reminds the film's audience that without the Grimms and their authority, there would be no situation requiring Danielle's story to be told. The setting of the Grande Dame's storytelling and her narrative patterns are reactionary and framed by male authority.

The film does not give the Grimms the possibility of revising their "Cinderella" to mirror the authentic tale provided by the Grande Dame or acknowledge its authority. They come, they listen to the nice old lady tell her story, and then they leave, taking her story with them. The brothers acknowledge other versions of the story (Perrault's glass slipper), but it is not those versions that the Grande Dame wants to correct. Though she claims higher social status, wealth, corroborating evidence, and a historical setting for her version, the power remains with the Grimms. While her narrating the story provides a context for the film, it does not alter the most authoritative version of the text. The Grimms' carriage, which begins and ends the movie, remains a closed vessel, containing Danielle and the Grande

---

5   See Cristina Bacchilega and John Rieder's essay in this volume for a discussion of the
     "generic complexity" of films like *Ever After*.

Dame's story. Though the film offers an alternative version of "Cinderella" more amenable to contemporary audiences and points to problems with the Grimms' story, the narrative and visual framing implicitly validates the authority of their version, thus undermining the feminist ideology of the entire film.

Danielle's Masque

In the establishing scenes of her happy childhood, a young Danielle (Anna Maguire) is portrayed as a typical tomboy who nevertheless attempts and fails to act like a girl in her stepfamily's presence. In the first scene of the embedded tale, an exchange between the eight-year-old Danielle and her male, peasant playmate Gustave (Ricki Cuttell) establishes the underlying problem. When he sees his tomboy friend clean and in a dress, Gustave exclaims, "You look like a girl!" Danielle replies, "That's what I am, half-wit." Danielle's problem is that she is a girl who does not act or look like a girl.

Judith Butler argues that gender is performative. Rather than expressing an essential quality, it is constructed by the repetition of bodily "acts and gestures" "within established political contexts" ([1990] 1999, 173, 189). Repeated behaviors are assigned gender labels within a regulating social structure, which Butler identifies as "reproductive heterosexuality" (Ibid., 173). Danielle is not shown on camera deciding to be a boy or a girl and then acting accordingly. Instead, she responds to other characters and situations and assumes a male or female approach to solve problems. Though it seems her own choice would be a potentially androgynous tomboy way of acting, her behavior is gendered by the characters in the film and the viewing audience. Danielle is identified as female by the romance plot that ultimately results in her marriage to a male, but her behavior in the film is a mix of gendered responses ranging from hyperfeminine to tomboy. Mary Ann Doane describes hyperfemininity as a masquerade that distances the female spectator from the on-screen, amplified expression of femininity, thus constituting "an acknowledgement that it is femininity itself which is constructed as a mask—a decorative layer which conceals a non-identity" (2000, 426). The masquerade "flaunt[s] femininity," showing that "womanliness is a mask which can be worn or removed" (Ibid., 427). Like Butler, Doane notes that "femininity is produced very precisely as a position within a network of power relations" (Ibid., 434).

Though gender performance is not as simple as changing clothes, Danielle's feminine and masculine behavior is often signaled by her change in wardrobe (from her blue and white servant ensemble to a variety of fancier dresses). Danielle's masquerade—her donning of the costume, mannerisms, and behavior of a lady—contrasts with her masculine behavior. Judith Halberstam describes socially accepted forms of female masculinity, such as those Danielle demonstrates: "Tomboyism tends to be associated with a 'natural' desire for the greater freedoms and mobilities enjoyed by boys. Very often it is read as a sign of independence and self-motivation, and tomboyism may even be encouraged to the extent that it remains comfortably linked to a stable sense of girl identity" (1998, 6). Though the characters in the film tolerate Danielle's masculine behavior, and the audience applauds it, her heterofemininity is never truly at risk. The balance of female masculinity with feminine masquerade ensures that though Danielle may act like a boy, she is still recognizable as a girl. Halberstam argues that female masculinity becomes less transgressive when coupled with easily identifiable heterosexual behavior. Thus, Danielle's masculine behavior as an adult is rendered unthreatening because she is playing a part in a heterosexual romance, and her masculine behavior as a child is naturalized as a phase to outgrow.

Danielle is quickly identified as a tomboy in this first scene of her story. Later, when she is dressed in nice, clean clothes to meet her new stepfamily and Gustave recognizes her as a girl, Danielle responds, "Boy or girl, I can still whip you." The two children engage in an off-screen mud fight, and when approached by the now-muddy Danielle, her father (Jeroen Krabbé) says, "I had hoped to present a little lady, but I suppose you'll have to do." Because she presents herself as a tomboy, Danielle's femininity is called into question by the authority figures in the film: her father and her new stepfamily. Danielle's father recognizes that she behaves in a way more masculine than feminine and points to that disjunction as a problem. While her father hugs Danielle and laughs when speaking the chastising line, the words denote disapproval of her unladylike appearance and behavior. Danielle's gender is being negotiated, and she cannot conform to either expectation presented in this early scene. Resolving this lack of sex-gender coherence is a task that she accomplishes as the film progresses.

The term *lady* also suggests class behavior. Danielle is the daughter of a merchant landowner and becomes the stepdaughter of a baroness. The scene where she meets her new stepfamily foregrounds Danielle's gender as a product of social negotiation and demonstrates the way these negotiations relate to class. It establishes a pairing of gender and class mobility that Danielle continues to practice throughout the film because her occasions to assume a more intense femininity also require her to act like nobility.[6] Halberstam has noted a greater gender fluidity available to those with lower class expectations (1998, 57–58) as Danielle's adoption of more masculine masks while in servant dress demonstrates.[7]

The remainder of the film, which focuses on Danielle's adult life, reflects her ability to alternate differing degrees of feminine and masculine behavior in a way that, to contemporary audiences, still falls comfortably within her role as a female heroine. Her stepmother acts predictably as the female villain who cannot accept Danielle's new or feminist behavior. Much later in the story, Rodmilla (Anjelica Huston) blames what she calls Danielle's "masculine" behavior on her masculine features and status as an only child raised by a man. Indeed, Drew Barrymore, the actor playing the adult Danielle, while certainly pretty, is not Western-idealized, supermodel skinny. Though she is hyperfeminine (curves, long hair, soft edges), her film roles and the public discourse on her life have reinforced a childlike image that suggests a nonthreatening female sexuality (perhaps due to Barrymore's child-star status and the film's family audience). The scene where Rodmilla accuses Danielle of being masculine begins as a touching investigation of the possibility of mother-daughter bonding as Rodmilla gazes fondly on Danielle, recalling her similarities to her father. However, any possibility of a reconciliation is harshly cut short when Rodmilla reidentifies Danielle as a rival for her husband's (Danielle's father) affection and her biological daughters' future. The stepmother acts as a female agent of patriarchy, ensuring that patriarchal ideals of gender behavior and hierarchy are not solely perpetuated through male figures. It is clear from Rodmilla's comparison of Danielle to her father that masculine traits in a female body/mind are unacceptable.

As an adult—knowing that dressing above her station is a crime—Danielle masquerades as a courtier to rescue a male servant from being transported to

---

6   Danielle's dismissal of class differences reflects American ideology rather than the historical truth the frame implies. The American myth of a classless society, demonstrated by Danielle's ease in moving from merchant's daughter to servant to courtier to princess, is reinforced by Prince Henry's desire to open a free university, suggesting the possibility of upward mobility through education.

7   Though she is not originally from the servant class, this is the most common descriptor used about Danielle.

the Americas. When she demands his release, her assertive behavior attracts the attention of the court, including the prince. The man with whom she is disputing responds to her forcefulness by shouting, and Prince Henry chastises him, "You dare raise your voice to a lady?" Danielle's behavior is masculine, though her dress is feminine. The man she is arguing with responds to the masculine behavior, the prince to the feminine and class-inflected dress. The film seemingly offers flexibility in defining femininity. Danielle can act out of character for a woman by communicating with men on equal terms and taking direct and aggressive action to solve problems she encounters. She is, however, the only woman in the film given this opportunity, and it is explicitly linked to a masquerade as a person of higher class. Danielle's transgressive behavior is always enabled by men, in reaction to men, or framed by men and is thereby safely contained in a clearly patriarchal structure.

Danielle's many masks represent both gender and class positions, and their identifying markers are easily assumed or dropped. Her trouble arises in choosing the correct mask for the situation. Danielle must wear the mask preferable to the powerful men whose gazes frame her life: her father in her childhood and Prince Henry in her adult life. The audience is led to identify with the prince's point of view through shots that align the camera with his perspective in several scenes (such as when Danielle climbs the rock face) so that we fall in love with her spirit, just as he does. The narrative supports this framing gaze of men. Once Danielle's story has started, the narrator breaks in after the death of her father to say, "It would be ten years before another man would enter her life." The elision of ten years not only suggests that nothing important happens but completely ignores the plethora of servants, neighbors, courtiers, and other males whom she must inevitably have encountered during that time. The only men who matter are patriarchs or potential ones. Danielle's story centers on the way two men influenced her—one raised her to be like him, the other raised her to his position in society. Though she appears to have gender fluidity, the gazes of Danielle's father and the prince are validated throughout the film so she appears to have gender coherence. The tomboy behavior is naturalized as a phase, and the hyperfemininity of masquerade is expected behavior for a princess.

Girl Power to the Rescue

More like young women of today than those of the time frame of the film, Danielle, as well as the actress who plays her, is a symbol of the girl power culture that began in the 1990s, most famously embodied (and marketed) by the Spice Girls. Though it had more radical roots, aspects of girl power have become a socially acceptable form of feminism, emphasizing individual strength and independence while remaining sexually attractive over working toward social or systemic change. While not calling it girl power, Jack Zipes takes issue with this representation of feminism in contemporary fairy tales, claiming that "the majority of fairy tales produced for children and adults pay lip service to feminism by showing how necessary it is for young and old women alike to become independent without challenging the structural embodiment of women in all the institutions that support the present socio-economic system" (2009, 129). In an earlier work, he argues that "the significance of the feminist fairy tales lies in their Utopian functions to criticize current shifts in psychic and social structures and to point the way toward new possibilities for individual development and social interaction" (1986, 32). Tales that "pay lip service to feminism"—often by relying on the popularity of girl power as in *Ever After*—but do not challenge systemic sexism fail to make social criticisms that mark many feminist fairy tales as potentially transformative.[8]

A common strategy in feminist fairy tale retellings is to empower a traditionally passive heroine, popularized in tales of the innocent persecuted heroine like "Cinderella," "Sleeping Beauty" (ATU 410), and "Snow White" (ATU 709).[9] The value systems within the tale that privilege certain behaviors—bravery, cleverness, dedication, attention to beauty—remain consistent. While certainly a feminist move that accounts for some of the girl power heroines popular in the late-twentieth century, this reversal from passivity to activity does not necessarily challenge the systemic misogyny in fairy tales, thus failing to meet Zipes's criteria for a feminist fairy tale. Donald Haase argues that "some feminist fairy tale analyses remain stuck in a mode of interpretation able to do no more than reconfirm stereotypical generalizations about the fairy tale's sexist stereotypes" (2004a, ix). I argue that his critique is also valid for fairy tale retellings like *Ever After* that remain focused solely on reversing the representation of the traditionally passive heroine. An exclusive focus on

---

8   Kim Snowden discusses both antifeminist postfeminism and girl power as defined in the undergraduate classroom in her consideration of literary and film versions of Angela Carter's retold fairy tales.

9   See Cristina Bacchilega (1993) and Steven Swann Jones (1993) for a discussion of the innocent persecuted heroine.

this reversal merely reconfirms sexist stereotypical generalizations of the way fairy tale heroines are supposed to behave.[10]

The themes of rescue and role reversal are first associated with Prince Henry. He is shown escaping from his tower room down a rope of bed-sheets, a scene visually reminiscent of "Rapunzel" (ATU 310). As a reversal of the princess-locked-in-a-tower motif, this is a visual cue to the viewer that it is not the prince who will be doing the rescuing in *Ever After*. In two separate scenes, Danielle subverts the damsel-in-distress trope when the prince attempts to rescue her. The first occurs when they encounter Gypsies in the forest and Danielle rescues the prince; the second happens at the film's conclusion, when she has been sold into slavery and extricates herself from danger before the prince can save her. In both cases, however, her subversion is undercut. Danielle's decisive action is transformed into a joke and explained away.

In the first scene when Danielle rescues the prince from Gypsies in the wood, she and Henry are lost. Danielle climbs to the top of a tree-covered rock to get a better sense of their location when Gypsies arrive and attack the prince. They steal her dress, which she has cleverly removed as it would have made it impossible for her to climb, and Danielle enters the fray by jumping on a Gypsy's back, fists flying. The prince barters for her release because two people are no match for a band of Gypsies. Danielle asks for her dress and a horse, and the Gypsy leader tells her she can have anything she can carry, expecting her to take the dress. Instead, she lifts the prince over her shoulders in a firefighter's hold and begins to carry him off. Plot-wise, this creates a light moment in the film where everyone can laugh at Danielle's pluck, but it also undermines her courage and resourcefulness by turning them into a joke. The humor only works if the audience and the characters in the film recognize that Danielle is acting out of character for a woman. She is bold and strong and is rewarded for those characteristics by the Gypsies with the return of her dress, the use of a horse, the freedom of the prince, and a night of revelry. In fairy tale tradition, there are many heroines who succeed by being clever and strong, so this is not an original move on the part of the filmmakers. However, in many of these tales—like "Molly Whuppie" (ATU

---

10   Ming-Hsun Lin describes many of the fairy tale princess/heroine stereotypes that *Ever After* engages at length in her discussion of the princess's role in this collection.

327B) and "Kate Crackernuts" (ATU 306, 711)—the heroine's actions do not inspire laughter in every witness to her cleverness.[11]

Significantly, Danielle's feminism and strength are superfluous when it comes to being assertive with the prince about who she is. The day after the Gypsy revelry, Danielle has been beaten for her insolence at punching her stepsister (the punch is a popular example of the film's girl power). She attempts to tell the prince she is not a noble woman, but he refuses to hear her because he is too excited by his own plan to create a university. She tries to correct his misconception more than once, but he silences her, a silence she accepts as they kiss. While in terms of plotting, this is an effective way of postponing her revelation to the climax of the film, rhetorically this scene demonstrates Danielle's inability to speak when confronted by male authority; rather, she is seduced. She is only allowed to act outside of gender norms when the men in her life—the prince, her father, Gustave, and her (fairy) godfather Leonardo da Vinci—permit it.

The second scene when Danielle defies the damsel-in-distress stereotype is also disappointing. After the prince rejects her for lying about her identity, but before the requisite happily-ever-after, Rodmilla sells Danielle to Pierre Le Pieu (Richard O'Brien), a lascivious neighbor who, dressed in black, is a walking stereotype of male villainy. Despite variations in the way the two men are presented, Le Pieu and Prince Henry differ little in their attitudes: both wish to claim Danielle for their beds. At the masque, Henry intended to announce their betrothal without her consent or foreknowledge. Then, after she has been sold, Danielle is shown in shackles, and the unnamed threat of rape lingers in the exchange between her and Le Pieu. Danielle's restriction and immobility, however, are the primary danger; she is clearly denied her freedom because she is a woman and therefore can be possessed—either as a servant or wife. Danielle has no say in either case.

When told that she belongs to Le Pieu, Danielle responds, "I belong to no one." Then she skillfully takes his weapon when he least expects it. Using sword and dagger, she defends herself and threatens Le Pieu with death. He hands over the key to her shackles, and all is well. Even in this moment of triumph, when Danielle is subverting the princess-rescue-story pattern by rescuing herself, however, the whole action is qualified and framed by men. Not only are Le Pieu and Henry depicted as polarized forces, but

---

11   See Pauline Greenhill, Emilie Anderson-Grégoire, and Anita Best (forthcoming) for a
      discussion of these tales as explorations of androgyny and transgender.

Danielle says to Le Pieu, "My father was an excellent swordsman, monsieur. He taught me well. Now hand me that key or I swear on his grave I will slit you from navel to nose." Her swordplay and courage are attributed to her father: she is not allowed to have this moment of strength herself. It is not Danielle who learned well but her father who was a good teacher. Her ability to defend herself is explained away by her father's everlasting influence, just as is her utopian philosophy of social equality.[12] When Danielle tells Prince Henry that Thomas More's *Utopia* is the lasting connection she has to her father, he exclaims, "That explains it."

Once Danielle has left the home of Le Pieu, the prince rides up to rescue her and is surprised that she has escaped so expeditiously. He recovers enough to propose to her, sliding her lost shoe on her foot in the defining "Cinderella" scene. In their exchange before the shoe is returned to its rightful owner, Danielle is struck—not by the prince's apology for his rejection of her but his use of her name. Up until this point in the film, Henry has called Danielle "Nicole," the pseudonym (her mother's name) she gave him while dressed as a courtier. A romantic might argue that in this moment, he sees her for who she truly is and loves her for being Danielle, not a courtier who reads Thomas More. However, the romance depends upon Danielle's abandonment of her earlier commitment to protect her father's land and property. She marries Henry, neglecting her previous desires to run her father's property, and goes on to be the princess and live in the castle. She leaves everything she has been fighting for when marriage is offered.

The Absence of Female Power

The only undeniable location of female power in the classic versions of "Cinderella" is the fairy godmother in Perrault's version and the dead mother's spirit in the Grimms' tale. The most potent figures in both stories are women in maternal roles who provide Cinderella with the material goods she needs to win the prince. Warner explains that both the godmother figure and the mother's spirit wield a great deal of power and influence the

---

12   Danielle's demonstrations of strength (the girl power and feminist moments cited by reviewers) are enacted out of her sense of morality, formed by her schooling in socialism at the foot of her father and Thomas More. She dresses above her station and lies to the prince about her identity to save a servant sold into slavery. Despite her selfless motivation, she does not take any action to better society (other than chastise the prince).

success of the tale (1994, 48, 205). Jeana Jorgensen notes that fairy godmothers are notably absent from many traditional versions of "Cinderella,"
but "later literary incarnations of fairy tales often feature fairy godmothers
whose appearances erase Cinderella's initial efficacy" (2007, 219, 217). In
helping Cinderella, the fairy godmother displaces the heroine's independence. In *Ever After*, this character and all of the power associated with
her becomes male. The role of the fairy godmother is split between two
men—Leonardo da Vinci (Patrick Godfrey), who builds Danielle wings
for the masque and breaks her out of her cell; and the adult Gustave (Lee
Ingleby), who finds Leonardo when he is needed and creates Danielle's first
makeover when she goes to court to save a servant. In both cases, men provide Danielle with what she needs to win the prince. Implicitly, then, power
is denied to women, but its removal is less noticeable because these acts are
performed by modern men who do not threaten heterosexual romance.[13]
By reversing the gender of the godmother, this supposedly feminist version
reinforces male authority and removes the main locus of female power from
the story entirely.

The magic situated with the maternal figures in the classic tales is
replaced by logic and science—or "forward thinking," as the prince would
say—in this modernization of the "Cinderella" story. Elisabeth Rose Gruner
argues that because Leonardo (and not the prince) frees Danielle from the
cellar, "art, not love, is her true salvation" (2003, 149). However, it is not
just Leonardo's art but also his logic and science that free Danielle. Rodmilla
has locked Danielle in the cellar to prevent her from attending the royal
ball, and Leonardo breaks her out by removing the door's hinges. Gruner
argues that rational thought replacing magic implies that as "Cinderella's
situation is realistic, her solution might be as well" (Ibid., 147). But with
that realism, female power is erased. To deny female authority further, when
her stepfamily forces Danielle to choose between her father's book and her
mother's dress, she chooses her father. Her stepfamily, of course, denies her
both of them, and the book is burned. The dress resurfaces as the one she
wears to the masque, but that, too, is not just her mother's dress anymore;
Leonardo has transformed it into a costume that marks Danielle's metamorphosis. Adorned by wings, her costume is symbolic of both butterfly

---

13   Both Leonardo and Gustave hint at a different kind of masculinity: neither is presented
     as a sexualized figure—one is a father figure, and the other is queered—and both are
     artists, a feminized career choice in present-day opinion. While powerful, they are no
     threat to the prince.

and angel: the heroine is changed from the tomboy of her childhood into a virtuous woman worthy of being a princess. Leonardo's wings—not her mother's dress—make Danielle's appearance at the masque spectacular. The mother—the woman—in fairy godmother is erased, and her erstwhile power is firmly resituated in the hands of men.

The Obligatory Happily-Ever-After

The problem with *Ever After* is not that it fails as a feminist revision of "Cinderella." Rather, the popularized, restricted, and simplified version of feminism it presents masks the elements of the film that reinforce social and patriarchal structures that determine the plot and limit Danielle's possibilities as a character. The reversal of the passive-heroine trope—while certainly offering an alternative to the weak-minded Cinderellas of the past—actually naturalizes gender expectations and the idea that demonstrations of female strength are akin to gender equality. Danielle's power surfaces in reaction to and is enabled by heteropatriarchal ideology. Her independence and self-reliance become possible because of the liberal, sensitive, forward-thinking men who *allow* her to step outside of gender boundaries, not because she has fought for and won equality in society. Female power in *Ever After* is contained, undermined, and erased. The men are still in control, and despite Danielle's strength, she has no more options than the passive Cinderellas from whom she supposedly differs.

Masking its reliance on the patriarchal structure of the romance plot by dressing its heroine in the mass images of girl power, *Ever After* offers no real critique of gender oppression and creates in Danielle a Cinderella who may be more outspoken, literate, and active than her predecessors but is ultimately sucked back into the trap of heterosexual romance. She is so embedded in the naturalized complex of gender, class, political power, and upward mobility that any power she may wield as a strong feminist is restricted by the patriarchal authority demonstrated throughout the film. Danielle is ultimately limited by the stereotypical girl power and liberal feminism popular in today's media. Her feminism is thus distilled into a manner of representation: show a strong woman standing up for herself and working for equal relationships with the men in her life, and a film can be called feminist. This perspective on feminism suggests that, as a social movement, it is no longer viable because women *are* strong; the simplified standard of feminist goals has already been met. Its logical conclusion is that there used to be something wrong with women—they were weak and passive—but now that they are stronger, everything is okay. Such a view not only does nothing to critique social structures, but it suggests that feminism is only about women, not about gender and society.

Furthermore, the feminist idea of gender as socially constructed is restricted in *Ever After* to create the tension between Danielle's hyperfeminine masquerade and her inherent androgyny or masculinity. The multiplicity of her masks reaffirms for an audience familiar with basic concepts of feminism that girls can be physically and intellectually strong without undermining their femininity. The characters in the film may take issue with Danielle's masculinity, but today's young female audiences should embrace it. Gender stereotypes are reaffirmed, as are their association with heterosexuality. Although initially skeptical about her eventual partner, Danielle never challenges the romantic myth of heterosexuality, embracing the soulmate wedding and happily-ever-after ending when it is presented to her. As an audience, we suspect that Danielle would be fine if she did not marry the prince, but the film does not allow that possibility. In his review, Michael Wilmington states that the film "might have ended more logically and congenially if Danielle had run off to organize and care for country peasants with the good stepsister. . . . But you don't want to mess with fairy tales too much. Especially when everybody knows the ending" (1998). Danielle believes in and enacts upward mobility through the American ethic of hard work but reaffirms the notion that for women, upward mobility is still best attained by marrying a prince. Danielle, though a stronger and more independent heroine than her foresisters, has yet to outgrow the glass slipper worn by the classic, passive Cinderellas of Charles Perrault, the Brothers Grimm, and Walt Disney.

6

Mourning Mothers and Seeing Siblings
Feminism and Place in *The Juniper Tree*

Pauline Greenhill and Anne Brydon

> *Narrators are free to vary or extemporize on the elements of the tales, which nevertheless constantly reassert themselves.*

A. S. Byatt, 2004 (xxii)

Folklorists contend that some stories can be traced through time and space yet retain their fundamental form even in the face of different tellers' cultural and symbolic inflections. Indeed, a few fairy tales, like "The Juniper Tree" (ATU 720), have been extensively told and retold in genres other than their primary oral and written forms. They contain multiple messages, explicit or tacit, for tellers and audiences, which can refer to individual psychology, performance context, and/or underlying cultural patterns, among many possibilities. Given the extreme variability within the genre, what light can a filmed interpretation shed on this story and its meaning?

The two authors explore this terrain. We examine "The Juniper Tree," most famously documented by the Grimm brothers, using the 1990 film version by the late American director Nietzchka Keene as our fulcrum.[1] How does a telling by an American woman writer, director, editor, and producer who chose to film a German version of this international tale in

We thank Dorinda Hartmann of the film and photo archive at the Wisconsin Center for Film and Theater Research for assistance with Nietzchka's Keene's papers and Juliette Loewen for locating relevant materials from M2005-051/WCFTR, boxes 4 and 5. Lára Jónsdóttir made relevant portions of Keene's Fulbright application available to us; Ingunn Ásdísardóttir, Bryndís Petra Bragadóttir, Jesse Byock, Valdimar Örn Flygenring, Robert Guillemette, and Dominique Poulain graciously offered their memories of Keene and the film's creation.

Iceland with Icelandic actors speaking English elaborate the narrative? What does this telling make of the story? Anne considers the film's geographic location in terms of social history and cultural interpretation, and Pauline focuses upon feminist analysis. Each perspective opens to the other, but neither fully encapsulates the film nor the filmmaker's intentions.

Nietzchka Keene (1952–2004) received her BA (1975) in Germanic linguistics from the University of Massachusetts, Amherst, and her MFA in film production (1989) from the University of California at Los Angeles (UCLA), though she began her graduate work there in folklore, specializing in the folktale. While at UCLA, she completed three short films but also continued her involvement with old Icelandic language and literature, which she developed while working as a research assistant for archeologist and saga scholar Jesse Byock. Although her successful application for a 1985–86 Fulbright Fellowship to Iceland describes a less ambitious short film of a legend from Jón Árnason's nineteenth-century collection of Icelandic tales (1993, 2: 274–76), Keene apparently already intended to shoot a film based on the Grimms' "The Juniper Tree." According to production manager Ingunn Ásdísardóttir and others, film shooting took place during the summer of 1986, with a return trip to record additional sound. The editing was completed in 1989, and the film was released in 1990. Keene described her work as "focused on the enduring power of folklore in modern life" (Memorial Resolution). Her concern to represent folklore in film is evident, for example, in her script for a "Sleeping Beauty" film and her plan to make a movie of the legend of nineteenth-century American female serial killer Belle Gunness.[2] Keene taught at the University of Miami and then at the University of Wisconsin at Madison. Tragically, she died of pancreatic cancer on October 20, 2004, at the age of fifty-two.

Keene's film is only one of many interpretations of this tale outside oral and written traditions. Barbara Comyns's contemporary novel *The Juniper Tree* (1985) eschews all but the realistic elements. Micheline Lanctôt's Canadian/Quebeçois film version, *Le Piège d'Issoudun* (*The Issoudun Exit/ Trap* [*Juniper Tree*]) (2003) is likewise present-day realist but includes the tale's marvelous aspects in a play within the film. The story has spawned two

---

1   Keene's Wisconsin archive files contain reviews from local newspapers and trade periodicals, generally without full citations. We provide the information available in the text.

2   On Gunness, see Langlois (1985). Keene's TV film *Heroine of Hell* was released in 1996; her feature film *Barefoot to Jerusalem* was released posthumously in 2008.

operas, one composed in 1984 with libretto by Arthur Yorinks and music by Robert Moran and Philip Glass (Glass n.d.), and another by Rodney Watkins and Patricia Debney (see Meph 1997, 42). T. S. Eliot's poem "Ash Wednesday" riffs on "The Juniper Tree," and a quotation from that poem forms the prologue for Keene's film (see Traversi 1976). Performance and video artist Joan Jonas aims for "reinterpreting Grimm's fairy tales" in her 1976 *The Juniper Tree* (see Hanhardt 1990, 439) as does writer/director Wendy Kesselman in her 1983 *The Juniper Tree: A Tragic Household Tale* (see Mankin 1988, 50). This is a narrative that many find compelling.

Distinguished Grimm scholar Maria Tatar calls "The Juniper Tree" "probably the most shocking of all fairy tales" (2004, 209). But one wonders why she singles it out, given her oft-quoted inventory of the genre's "murder, mutilation, cannibalism, infanticide, and incest" (1987, 3). The problem can't be the murderous mother; lots of fairy tale (step)mothers practice bad behavior toward their (step)children. Is it the father's greedy, unknowing, incestuous cannibalism that takes this one over the top? Is it the almost campy horror of the stepmother decapitating her stepson by smashing the lid of a chest on his neck, then persuading her daughter that she's literally knocked his head off, combined with the boy's revenge by dropping a millstone on her? Whatever prompted Tatar to make this claim, tellers and theorists alike have found "The Juniper Tree" extremely tractable.

Unlike the majority of their tales, the Grimms collected "The Juniper Tree" from a male teller, Romantic artist Philipp Otto Runge (1777–1810).[3] Perhaps not surprisingly, then, male characters prevail, and the two female protagonists are polarized as nearly literal angel and devil. The Grimm version allies a young boy, his father, and his stepsister against his stepmother, and the story closes with their mother-absent, nuclear family. Tale scholar Hans-Jörg Uther summarizes the traditional narrative:

> A childless couple wishes for a child. A boy is born but his mother dies. The little boy is slain by his cruel stepmother who closes the lid of an apple chest on him. . . . She cooks him and serves him to his father who eats him unwittingly. . . . The boy's stepsister [Marlene

---

3   Many Grimm tales were collected from women (Zipes 2002a, xxix). Though its traditional credentials have been questioned (Byatt 2004, xxii), "reviewers and friends [of the Grimms] repeatedly singled out 'The Juniper Tree' . . . as . . . a quintessential *Märchenstil*, or fairy tale style, that captured the vitality of a poetry of the people even as it conformed to highbrow aesthetic standards. . . . [It] became the gold standard by which other tales in the collection came to be measured" (Tatar 2004, xxxix).

in the Grimms' version] gathers up his bones and puts them under a
juniper tree. . . . A bird comes forth and sings about what happened.
It brings presents to the father and the sister and drops a millstone on
the stepmother, killing her. . . . The boy is resuscitated. (2004, 1: 389)

In Keene's film, two sisters, Katla (Bryndís Petra Bragadóttir) and
Margit (pop singer Björk Guðmundsdóttir in her feature-film debut), flee
the region where their mother has just been burned for witchcraft. The
elder, Katla, plans to find a man to take care of them, intending to bind him
with spells. Her choice is a widower, Jóhann (Valdimar Örn Flygenring),
whose son, Jónas (played by a girl, Geirlaug Sunna Þormar), is immediately suspicious. But the younger sister, Margit, bonds with Jónas over their
shared grief at the loss of their mothers. Margit has regular visions of her
mother (Guðrún Gísladóttir).[4] She convinces Jónas that a feather on his
mother's grave was placed there by her as a charm. But all Katla's attempts to
get along with Jónas fail. He repeatedly calls her a witch—not without cause
since he witnesses her casting a spell to ensure pregnancy and wonders at his
father's seeming enchantment. Jónas resists all his stepmother's attempts to
gain power in her relationships with him and his father.

Eventually a pregnant Katla taunts Jónas to show how his mother will
protect him if he leaps from a cliff. He falls and dies. Katla sews one finger from Jónas's body into his mouth and puts another into a stew for the
family. Margit finds it and does not eat any stew, though Jóhann and Katla
do. When a raven appears on a tree that grows from the mother's grave,
where Margit buried Jónas's finger, she tells Jóhann that Katla killed his son.
Katla flees, but at the film's end, Jóhann has gone in search of her with the
apparent intention of resuming their relationship. The final scene focuses
on Margit. Her voice-over tells the haunting tale of two children whose
mother was a bird, and whose human father fails to recognize them when
they return from the land of the birds. "And so they stayed behind, and they
knew what the birds know."

Keene's version emphasizes women's experiences far more sympathetically and with greater nuance than does the original tale. The film's art director, Dominique Poulain,[5] noted women's perceptions as central to the film.
In Keene's hands, *The Juniper Tree* examines the fraught relationships within

---

4   The story described in Keene's Fulbright application was about the *draugar*, whom she
     described as "actual corpses risen from their grave . . . walking dead [who] must be laid
     to rest in order to give peace to an individual or a region" (n.d., 3).

5   Dominique Poulain's name is mispelled in the film's credit as "Polain."

a family awkwardly patched together by grim circumstances. But she also included historical experiences of women in situations of social need and strife. Shooting in various museums and farms in Iceland, Keene aimed for a mood of melancholia and loneliness, rather than a specific interpretation of the tale. As Poulain pointed out, the ending is deliberately ambiguous; whatever follows only deepens the damage that has already rocked the characters' lives. Though interpersonal pain informs all its relationships, the film offers a commentary on the tenuousness of social connections and the enduring succor derived from the imagination's links to the spirit.

Keene confessed to a longstanding fascination with the gory horror of "The Juniper Tree," explaining that it "had been one of my favorite stories as a child. One of the things I really like about it, it's really gruesome" (2002). Her version is simultaneously distinctive and traditional. She sticks quite closely to the Grimms' narrative, and yet she chose to film in Iceland, where no version of the tale was found by the collectors' contemporary, Jón Árnason, or other gatherers of folk narrative. Elements of the film and its context resist the interpretation that it is an Icelandic version of "The Juniper Tree." In Keene's telling, the characters' motivations cannot easily be read; the acting looks flat and emotionless. In one reviewer's interpretation, "the actors are playing archetypes, not characters" (Fred Haeseker, *Calgary Herald*, 1991), and indeed their lack of expression gives the film an archetypal quality it shares with many folktales. Another commented, "Ignoring conventional storytelling niceties, [Keene] concentrates on moments of abject despair, brutal confrontation, intense privation and mystical insights" (McCarthy 1991, 70).[6]

The lack of overt psychological definition and focus on narrative highlights are consistent with the Grimm tales, where "schematic characterization leaves a gap into which the [audience] may step" (Warner 1994, 23). Robert Guillemette, the film's still photographer, commented that Keene first and foremost wanted to tell a story. Thus, the film's viewers, like the tale's hearers, are implicitly invited to attribute meanings on the basis of their own concepts, ideology, or psychology and fill in inchoate elements. Such moves fit well with feminist theorist Teresa de Lauretis's notion that women's cinema is moving toward "an aesthetic of reception, where the spectator is the film's primary concern" (1987, 141). Nonetheless, not all

---

6   Consider Tatar's evaluation of the Grimm version as "evocation of sheer dread" (1999, 183).

viewers find the film's lack of inflection compelling; it subverts audiences' expectations that they can rely on clues of character and motivation to interpret behavior that otherwise appears obscure or ambiguous.

Somewhat surprisingly, fairy tale and film scholars have overlooked Keene's film, despite its 1995 release on VHS and 2002 reissue on DVD. Moreover, it won several awards and was screened at festivals in Canada, the United States, and Great Britain, attesting to its merits as an art film. However, now dropped from the art-house circuit, it primarily attracts younger viewers who are fans of Björk.[7] Reading their online discussions reveals clashing views of its merits, primarily due to the writers' lack of familiarity with the demands of non-Hollywood cinema and (with a few exceptions) the traditional tale on which it is modeled. While some are receptive to the film's alternative aesthetic, others dismiss what they view as bad acting and storytelling and express impatience with its deliberate pace (*The Juniper Tree*, 1990).

Reviewers were also ambivalent. Some described *The Juniper Tree* primarily in terms of atmosphere and mood, citing its "ascetic style and eerie subject matter" and "gothic quality" (*Boston Globe*, March 31, 1991); "psychological and spiritual suggestiveness" (Fred Haeseker, *Calgary Herald*, 1991); and "stoic purity" (*Deadlock*, St. Louis, 1991). Many linked Keene with her acknowledged northern influences—directors Carl Dreyer (Denmark), Ingmar Bergman (Sweden), and Andrei Tarkovsky (Russia)—suggesting that her aesthetic invoked the high-art seriousness of European cinema. Indeed, Peter Birnie (in the tabloid *Vancouver Sun*) cynically deflated what he saw as West Coast therapy-speak masquerading as high art. In his reading of the film as a parable of blended families gone wrong, he sarcastically questioned Jónas's motivation for his hatred of Katla: "Is it because she's a witch, or because he's a 14th-century latchkey kid who failed to undergo ego separation from his dead mother?" (December 2, 1992). While displaying his animus toward film-school graduates, Birnie nonetheless touched on an issue that at least one other reviewer noted, namely the problems arising when a film "transplants contemporary tensions—sexual tensions and family tensions—into a medieval setting" (*Boston Globe*, March 31, 1991). Most, however, sympathetically acknowledged the patience required from viewers of this "bravely counter-hip" film with its stark black-and-white visuals and formalist, restrained camerawork reliant on the medium shot.

---

7   Her involvement probably explains the film's continuing availability on DVD.

This last reviewer, Johanna Steinmetz, commented that Keene uses "the movie's desolate Icelandic location to develop sinister tension. This turns its stiff presentation into something more choreographed than directed, possessing all the formal grace of a Japanese No tragedy" (American Originals).

Reviewer Angela Baldassarre—rather unusually among her colleagues—interviewed Keene, providing vital clues to the director's vision. Her deliberate aesthetic suggests a personal and psychical expressiveness: "I like bleak. I really wanted to use cinema as an art form, that's very important to me. I made what was in my heart, essentially." Keene's feminism was manifest: "I'm also very interested in bringing people into a very female state of mind. Particularly Margit—she's going through something very mystical and visionary. I put her through a particular age, puberty, where things are more possible" (Baldassare 1993). Elsewhere, Keene articulated her concern with the persistence of folk beliefs and magical influences during times ideologically construed as secular and rational. She understood stories as malleable: their telling is a function where, as anthropologist Albert Doja puts it, the "contents of thought are always subject to being transformed into signifiers" (2006, 20).

Films by women who serve simultaneously as producer, writer, director, and editor are rare. In the U.S. and Britain, only 7 percent of film directors are female (Krum 2006). Feminist film theorists have argued that women directors' works undermine the expected economy of film creation and viewership in which the male voyeur consumes the female object.[8] A female auteur like Keene may create alternative perspectives that speak to female desires, both sexual and gendered. As feminist film theorist Anneke Smelik suggests, "Many feminist directors self-consciously play on the tradition that has made women into a visual object" (1998, 23). Keene accepts this challenge by turning the men-and-mothers focus of the Grimm tale into a portrait of women and siblings. But her location of the tale in Iceland encapsulates her deliberate effort to dislocate it from any readily apprehended time or place and render it, paradoxically, more universal.

Icelandic Connections

The reason I think it fit in so well with Iceland is partly the going back and forth between the world of the dead and the world of the living. One of the places we shot . . . the people

---

8   We refer to Laura Mulvey's (1975) classic discussion of the male perspective in cinema and acknowledge extensive critiques of the concept (including Mulvey 1981; Doane 1991; hooks 1992; and Clover 1992).

who owned the farm said . . . "we had a film that shot here about six years ago but they
shot over two weeks and it rained every day. So the spirits in the rock must really like you
because you have great weather.". . . . Just sort of a dreamy quality which for me works in
terms of Icelandic folklore. . . . I wanted to create another world, which is one of the reasons
I shot in black and white. I looked at it as a film of texture, which the Icelandic landscape
plays very well in the black and white.

Nietzchka Keene, 2002

Given Iceland's recent popularity as a fashionable tourist destination and home to pop-music innovation (the country's 2008 bankruptcy tarnished that fashionableness but not the popularity since exchange rates have benefited foreign visitors), it would be an easy, but mistaken, leap to characterize Keene's choice of film location as an attempt to capitalize on this trend. However, that image of Iceland is a more recent creation (see Brydon 2005). When Keene first traveled there in 1985, it was still an insular and homogeneous society of 225,000, with an economy based on fishing and farming and an urban life that was yet to experience the excesses of wealth wrought by market liberalizations in the early 1990s and bank privatization in 2002, or the more recent economic collapse. Not until a decade later did the effects of tourism, immigration, and new media turn the country's stark, dramatic landscape into a familiar backdrop for TV commercials and fashion shoots. Instead, Keene encountered a challenging locale. For example, no cameras or lights could be rented on location, so Keene had to ship what she needed from the United States at considerable expense. Given her nearly nonexistent budget—Keene herself largely financed *The Juniper Tree,* and those involved often joked that it was not "low budget" but "no budget"—that the film was produced at all remains a remarkable achievement.

Nevertheless, Iceland offered advantages to the filmmaker. She benefited from the sheer eccentricity of a foreign woman embarking on such an unlikely adventure. Those who knew and worked with Keene declared their admiration for her focus, determination, and passionate commitment to the film. That Icelanders recognized her drive—a trait that they considered propelled their own society—further suggests a need to shift any thinking about the film's local connections away from cultural associations and toward the social relationships that surrounded its making, shaped by the particularities of the performing arts in Reykjavík in the mid-1980s.

The best example of the film's distinctive development is casting Björk as the central character. The director met the singer through Robert Guillemette, an immigrant from Normandy whom her UCLA contact Jesse Byock knew, and French national Dominque Poulain, then working in theater. Björk was patching together a livelihood after the breakup of her first band, Tappi Tíkarrass, and had yet to achieve popular success at home, much less abroad. She was eager for the novelty of participating in a film project, despite the token amount it paid.[9] Initially a younger girl cast to play Margit cut her hair in disobedience to the director's explicit instructions. Keene realized that actor would be too difficult to work with and began searching for an alternative. Although Björk was about eight years older than the character she played, her postpartum plumpness suggested the fullness of a girl entering puberty.[10]

Keene also benefited from the regulations governing actors' union membership. Bryndís Petra Bragadóttir and Valdimar Örn Flygenring had just finished acting school. They had both achieved recognition in the theater, but to gain union membership, they needed to appear in three productions following graduation. Despite the low pay and difficult conditions of the shoot, both actors are adamant that making the film was a career highlight for them. Close bonds formed among the crew and actors, and Keene generated a sense of creative adventure.

Both Guillemette and Poulain make clear that Keene did not want *The Juniper Tree* interpreted as a historicized Icelandic story. In Guillemette's words, she sought a sense of "always and never," a mythical nowhere that conveyed the transhistoric truths of human existence. For example, though Keene used a reconstructed premodern house in the national museum as a shooting locale, she removed all but the most minimal props to avoid too many intrusive historical details. Further, using actors with another first language to speak English dislocates their speech for the Euro-North American viewer. Keene repeatedly rehearsed the cast's lines until the disparities in their accents were smoothed over. In an interview in the Icelandic press when the film screened there in 1993, she also admitted that using Icelandic actors speaking English was a means to create a mood of cultural difference and distance *(Morgunblaðið,* February 12, 1993, 42–43).

---

9   Her honorarium of $2,673 was the largest in the cast, slightly higher than Bryndís Petra Bragadóttir's at $2,263. Valdimar Örn Flygenring got $1,458.

10   Björk's son, Sindri, was born a few months before shooting began.

Non-Icelandic viewers' lack of familiarity with the landscape—at least at the time when the film was shot—also ensured that this primary audience would be unable to place the setting. The unpopulated starkness of the lava fields conveys little information about season, heightening the disorientation. Despite her notion of the location as unrecognizable, it's clear that Keene conceptualized the Icelandic landscape in her screenplay. Specifically noted are rocks, hills, small lakes, ducks rising from the water, ravens wheeling overhead, glaciers, rivers, and caves. Though by no means unique to Iceland, their presence is explicit in instructions like "Margit is walking by the seashore, gathering seaweed by the basalt columns"; "she is walking by a glacier. The wall of the glacier is formed of dripping black crags"; "it is very windy and she walks along the basalt columns"; "she . . . pulls some seaweed over herself for a cover"; "Margit walks through a stony field"; "they disappear into a waterfall"; "Margit goes back to the lava-field"; "Jonas runs down to the water at twilight. He wades through, slashing at the reeds (grass) with his arms"; or "a pink light crosses through the northern lights" (undated script). Keene uses the Icelandic landscape to underscore the mood of melancholia and otherness. The treeless expanse dwarfs the characters. For European and North American viewers, the absence of a middistant wood emphasizes the difference between the vastness of sky and land and the isolation and frailty of the individuals who bridge the space between. The film's black-and-white images reinforce this melancholic aspect.

Keene was also attracted to Iceland as a logical continuation of her interests in mythology and folklore. Her familiarity with Old Norse literature drew her, as it has other scholars. The sparse population and continuity of place names allow an imaginative entry into events described in the sagas, written down as early as the thirteenth and fourteenth centuries.[11] The persistent—but by no means naïve—beliefs among Icelanders about stories of magical nonhuman beings from elves and trolls to witches and ghosts also compelled her. Keene could draw upon archival records of magical practices and rhymes, and the historicized costumes also gave the film a certain mood.

In Keene's treatment, "The Juniper Tree" transforms into a dark meditation upon the loss of connection to others in an era of persecution. Keene quoted actor Guðrún Gísladóttir, who plays the ghost of Katla and Margit's

---

11   Interested non-Icelandic-speaking readers can begin exploration of the sagas and the vast literature on them through *The Complete Sagas of Icelanders* (Hreinsson et al. 1997). Selections from these five volumes appear with an excellent introduction by Robert Kellogg and suggestions for further reading in *The Sagas of Icelanders* (2000).

mother, as saying "that she thought that it was one of the most Icelandic film topics she had seen when she agreed to be in it. . . . But she just felt it was very true to the spirit of Icelandic folklore" (2002).[12] Nonetheless, the film's depiction of witches particularly suggests that it is not intended to be understood—particularly by Icelanders—as an Icelandic story but instead as a general/universal narrative. Given her academic background and extensive research, Keene was undoubtedly aware of the marked differences between the documented persecution of women in continental Europe and the witchcraft craze in Iceland. There, as elsewhere, the witchcraft trials between 1554 and 1720 and executions between 1625 and 1685 occurred in an era of considerable danger from religious and legal authorities. Murder, incest, adultery, theft were all subject to capital punishment. To be caught with a piece of vellum inscribed with runes—a bit of magic to protect one's life when rowing at sea to fish—could lead to an accusation and conviction for witchcraft (Flowers 1989). Yet during the Catholic era, church authorities tolerated pagan folk beliefs and practices, including the myths of Ásatrú, the old religion of the Norse gods. Indeed, many practitioners were members of the clergy.[13] Nevertheless, about 350 witchcraft trials took place, but in the 125 surviving trial records, only 9 record accusations directed at women, and only one of twenty-six individuals burned was a woman.

Literary scholar Matthías Viðar Sæmundsson (1992) notes that in Iceland, as distinct from elsewhere in Europe and North America, solitary poor women were unlikely to be accused of witchcraft. The majority of Icelanders lived in isolation on farms, and poverty was ubiquitous. Further, the practice of using runes and magical symbols, which could lead to witchcraft charges, was dominated by men because it related to their gendered control of language and knowledge. Yet other aspects of Keene's film resemble Icelandic belief systems more closely. While white magic protected you and your property from hostile forces or restored the natural order of life, black magic usually destroyed and attacked, although it could both harm

12   Those translated into English show that Icelandic traditional narratives include material about ghosts and child murder (Hallmundsson 1987; Simpson 1972), but not all stereotype women as negatively manipulative (Waters 2002; Simpson 1972).

13   In about 1536, a small-scale religious war took place in Iceland between Catholics and Protestants. The popular conversion of all Icelanders to Protestantism took more than a hundred years, hastened by the privations exacted by the Danish trade monopoly established in 1602. For further information on this era of Icelandic social history, see Gunnarsson (1983).

and save, repair and demolish. In *The Juniper Tree*, Katla crosses the line from white to black magic as her relationship with Jónas deteriorates.

The rhymes that Keene composed for Katla and Margit are typical of Icelandic magical songs blended with saints' blessings. Further, Icelanders do distinguish between the conscious practice of spells and magic (Katla's activities) and the ability to *see*—perceive supernatural beings and ghosts (as Margit does). That ability runs in families, something you are born with and cannot learn; hence, Katla's hopeless envy of her younger sister's powers. Margit, for her part, is at first fearful of her gift of sight but learns to take comfort in it. Keene herself noted that whether the magic has efficacy or not, people's beliefs or fears make it a socially powerful force (2002).

Also true to the film's cultural historical location is the need for the two sisters to ally themselves physically and economically with Jóhann. In an exchange between the two children, Jónas attempts to establish the identity of the place from whence Margit and Katla came:

Jónas: Where are you and your sister from?

Margit: It's not there anymore.

Jónas: It disappeared?

Margit: No, there aren't any people there anymore. They're all gone.

Jónas: Will . . . you ever go back?

Margit: Katla says we'll stay here. That we're from here now.

Jónas: But you can't change where you're from.

Margit: But what if where you're from isn't there anymore?

In the scene that follows, as Katla prompts Margit to recall her experience of second sightedness (that is, seeing the shadows or spirits of the dead),[14] she comments that Jónas's mother wishes them to go away. Keene thus indicates something of an old-world politics of place, where identity and locality are inextricably linked. The viewer senses a battle between Jónas's dead mother and the usurper Katla, or, in a different interpretive register, within Katla's own psyche as she projects onto her predecessor her own sense of vulnerability and tenuous hold on the farm.

Katla and Jóhann manage a scrap of rented land, eking out a bare subsistence. Their mutual need is not so much emotional as a matter of survival. The alternative—servitude on a wealthier farm—would be risky

---

14   For more information on northern European (including Icelandic) concepts of second sight, see Flowers (1989, 55).

for both genders but particularly so for young women, who faced rape and unwanted pregnancy, which would further a downward social spiral. The social historical reality is echoed psychologically. As feminist Nancy Chodorow argues, "Men love and fall in love romantically, women sensibly and rationally.... On the societal level, given especially economic inequality, men are exceedingly important to women" (1976, 462). Thus, the film is grounded in the material reality of women's lives, allowing the viewer to understand how Katla could be driven to battle a child to the death as a matter of her own and her sister's survival. Both psychologically and economically, to be without place or kin is a powerful punishment. The viewer understands the desperation behind Katla's spells since—without the skills and labor a man provides—she and her sister will likely perish or be forced into abusive servitude. With magic she tries to control those forces of chance and society that have already ostracized them.

The Grimms—Men and Mothers

Fairy tales are by nature very matriarchal worlds in which fathers are traditionally irresponsible or absent.

James Lapine, 1988 (54)

If *The Juniper Tree* is not a tale from Icelandic tradition about Icelandic experience, what are its meanings? Without suggesting that ours parallels Keene's, we offer an understanding of the film's feminist implications in keeping with the filmmaker's clear intention that the viewer interpellate her own vision. Until the burgeoning of feminist analysis of fairy tales, theorists tended to ignore salient aspects of gender in them.[15] In contrast, most feminist analyses of this narrative make family and gender relations central. Thus, for example, "stories such as . . . 'Juniper Tree' retain transformative power because they function both literally and figuratively. . . . When real violence is treated at a comfortable distance, as in a seemingly unrealistic folktale, both teller and listeners create their own space for making personal connections. These stories also function as an emotional release for

---

15   For example, because Bruno Bettelheim (1976) assumes essential human problems are genderless (implicitly male), his analysis cannot address the family dynamics in "The Juniper Tree."

the stresses of ordinary day-to-day parenting or from childhood fantasies of feared abuse and abandonment" (Stone 1998, 192).

Folklorist Kay Stone pays attention to the son, noting that "this is one of the very few Grimm tales in which a victimized protagonist . . . avenges himself directly rather than having the villain punished obliquely" (Ibid., 69).[16] Teller Susan Gordon, who uses the story in "therapeutic, educational, and religious settings" (quoted in Stone, Jenoff, and Gordon 1997, 257), focuses upon the crucially absent father—the mother is the sole active parent. Maria Tatar says the tale "demonizes mothers in a powerful way and represents fathers as passive and detached" (2004, 210). Indeed, in the Grimms' "The Juniper Tree," the mother gets the final blame. Her death has no negative consequences for anyone, though the story repeatedly attributes her actions to the devil: "The devil got hold of her so that she began to hate the little boy . . . it was as if the devil had taken hold of her . . . the devil got her to speak sweetly to him . . . the devil prompted her" (Ibid., 191). The piggy father not only greedily eats the stew made of his son but also hoards it: "'Give me some more,' he said. 'No one else will get any. Somehow I feel as if it's all mine.' And he kept eating and threw the bones under the table until he had eaten everything" (Ibid., 192). He is rewarded with a gold chain.

Marina Warner links the father's incestuous cannibalism to that of mythic patriarchs like Kronos, who devour their children and then vomit them up whole: a motif of male parturition or, in effect, of male biological motherhood. She argues that

> the nameless father is portrayed as innocent, ignorant of his act of cannibal incest—or has he been shielded by the story from complicity in the dark events, as other fathers are in other tales in the Grimms' versions? However it may be, in "The Juniper Tree," incorporation into the father—when the little boy is unwittingly eaten for dinner—does not spell death for him. . . . Paternity, in this fairy tale as well as in the Greek myth of divine origin, can bring forth the whole child again. (1998, 63)

Warner links the parents' specific roles: "the sequence of fatal foods climaxes with the millstone for a murder weapon. The instrument for grinding good bread ends the life of a woman who put bad food before her family; only after she is dead can the family regroup around the restored, disinfected

---

16   Joseph Falaky Nagy also references kinship and family (1979; 1984).

table in a scene of domestic—and patriarchal—stability" (Ibid., 65). Tatar says the Grimms' version of "The Juniper Tree" invokes "two alternative, mutually exclusive scenarios"—either that it exaggerates "a child's very real fears about parental aggression and engulfment"; or that it responds "to the distress felt by a child grown up under the weight of guilt . . . produced by the death of a mother during childbirth, or even by the symbolic 'psychic' death of a mother when she gives birth" (1992, 223); that is, immediately on becoming a mother, a woman's life is no longer her own, but subsumed to her child's.[17]

Scapegoating mothers, as the Grimm tale does, is a common technique not only in traditional folklore but also in popular cultural and hegemonic media narratives. Feminist film theorist E. Ann Kaplan argues that "the Mother as a complex person in her own right, with multiple roles to fill and conflicting needs and desires, is absent from patriarchal representations" (2000, 467). She is replaced by one-dimensional characters: "The Good Mother; who is all-nurturing and self-abnegating. . . . The Bad Mother . . . sadistic, hurtful, and jealous. . . .The Heroic Mother, who suffers and endures for the sake of her husband and children, [and] . . . The Silly, Weak, or Vain Mother . . . generally scorned and disparaged" (Ibid., 468). Similarly, folklorist Janet Langlois discusses the contemporary legend of "The Inept Mother," who can't deal with multiple, simultaneous, life-threatening crises and thus becomes the scapegoat for the consequences. Langlois argues, in mothers' defense, that "mothering is a domestic task in which both competence and incompetence are double-edged swords" (1993, 94) because the children must be trained for both closeness and independence, both obedience and the ability to think through their own solutions to problems. Thus, a competent mother trains her child for her own obsolescence.

Incompetence at mothering can prompt the heavy hand of the law. But alternatively, it can allow women space to be human within a role that expects them to be (always balanced and appropriately) all knowing, all nurturing, and all giving. Keene's film, unlike its Grimm precursor, recognizes

---

17 Warner, again citing Greek mythology, finds that unlike fathers, mothers "do not eat their own offspring on purpose, nor are they duped into feasting off their own children. This can hardly be because they are soft-hearted, given the extreme mayhem they perpetrate. Mothers in classical myth are infanticidal, but not incestuously cannibalistic, because the stories deal with the question of parental relations to nature and to generation. The act of eating represents an inverted birthing: biological ownership through incorporation" (1998, 56).

this paradox. Mothers who fail at their impossible task—as they always must because it is impossible—face accusations that they have mutilated their children. Thus, Katla literally cuts up her stepson, but their mother mutilates Margit by binding her so closely that the daughter is unable to relinquish the relationship. That Euro-North American popular-culture representations of mothers paradoxically tend to view social (nonbiological) mothers as ideals and biological mothers as inadequate to utterly abjected (see Karpin 1997, 2000; Kaplan 1997; Ashe 1997) further complicates the love/hate relationship in these representations.[18] Indeed, the "dialectic between the maternal unrepresentable and the paternal already-represented" (Williams 2000, 489) forms a central tension in *The Juniper Tree*. Yet while motherhood is a concern for Keene, it's not the only primary relationship in her version; siblings, and particularly sisters, are also a focus.

Keene—Women and Sisters

You look like our mother did when she saw. Your eyes look the same. She could tell every-thing by what she saw. But I can't see.

Katla to Margit

The Juniper Tree presumes the centrality of women's relationships—(dead) mother to daughters; sisters to each other. The arguably male-centered tale becomes an unabashedly female-centered film. Teresa de Lauretis contends that feminist film focuses upon "both self-expression and communication with other women" (1987, 135), and Keene's work fits her description well. In the action that opens the story, the community has broken the triad of a mother and two daughters by burning the mother as a witch. There is no mention of the husband/father.[19] The film's men (son and father) are catalytic but also emotional and capricious, conflicted. The adult has dif-

---

18   Shuli Barzilai analyzes "Snow White" as a story of mothers (1990). In another genre, the film *Aliens* (directed by James Cameron, 1986) dramatizes the conflict between the Alien—a biomother whose oozing orifices and acid blood epitomize what Barbara Creed (1993) calls the "monstrous feminine"—and the capable, sensible, and resourceful Ripley (Signourney Weaver)—whose biological daughter dies of old age before her return and who becomes social mother to the child Newt (Carrie Henn).

19   His utter absence underlines Tatar's assertion that "The Juniper Tree" "eliminates both stepmother and biological mother in the end, yet it is . . . *matricentric* from beginning to end" (emphasis in original 1992, 221).

ficulty reconciling the roles of father and husband; the child, of son and quasi-brother.

Folklorist Joseph Nagy suggests a theme of sibling rivalry in the tale, noting that although "the victim in 'The Juniper Tree' is slain by a step-mother . . . in the Grimm version the stepmother actually makes the vic-tim's half-sister, her daughter, an unwitting accomplice in the act of murder" (1984, 188). The film focuses particularly on the often ambivalent relation-ship between the two sisters. Several scenes suggest that Margit is sexually compelled by her sister's husband. In one she stands by Katla and Jóhann's bed and touches first her sister and then the husband. In another, having searched for and found Margit who has wandered away from the house, Jóhann tells her a possibly cautionary tale about a wife who is stolen by trolls, who put her in "a glass box, asleep as if dead" (undated script). The viewer sees Margit envisioning herself in the glass box—as the story's inac-cessible wife. Her attraction to Jóhann may involve a wish to replace her sister in his affections. However, given the absence of a father figure, it may equally refer to her wish for one and the extension of that desire onto the most available object.

The closest—though ambivalent—links in the film are between women. The males are alternately loving and violent to their female age mates (Jóhann slaps Katla, Jónas throws a stone at Margit), though the inter-generational relationships are consistently complex. As Nancy Chodorow explains, "male-female relationships seem to become strained in regularized ways . . . often taken to be accidental or due to the psychological peculiari-ties of particular women and men" (1976, 454). She thinks this pattern—as well as the potential rivalry between women—is a result of a patriarchal model that makes women as mothers primarily responsible for their chil-dren's care. In particular, since "her first love object is a woman, a girl, in order to attain her proper heterosexual orientation, must transfer her pri-mary object choice to her father and men" (Ibid., 457) while retaining a close identification with her mother. Men must become erotic objects but remain secondary because they follow mothers and women as emotional objects. Boys, on the other hand, understand their father as a rival for their mothers' affections. Chodorow argues that "a daughter turns to her father looking for . . . confirmation and a sense of separateness from her mother, and cares especially about being loved. She (and the woman she becomes) is willing to deny her father's limitations (and those of her lovers or husband) as long as she feels loved, and she is . . . able to do this because his distance means that she does not really know him" (Ibid., 460).

Margit isn't sister only to Katla; she is simultaneously Jónas's nonbiological half sister (and his stepaunt) and his father, Jóhann's, sister-in-law. Culturally as well as personally, such relationships can be difficult, but Keene adds not only the problem of sisters and brothers who live together and are not biologically related but also that of husband to wife's sister.[20] Margit seems torn between her relationship to her sister and her quasi-brothers. Her role conflicts drive the plot—does she want to be Jóhann's sister, daughter, or wife? Does she want to be Jónas's sister or mother? Is she Katla's sister or her rival? The questions, more than the answers, texture *The Juniper Tree*.

The result of this complex web of relationships is a "triangular affective constellation" (Ibid., 461), complicated in both tale and film versions of "The Juniper Tree" by the presence of a stepmother, and in the film version by the relationships of sisters, and sister to brother-in-law and stepnephew, within the apparent nuclear family. Both tale and film explore ideas surrounding the composition of the heterosexual family. But Keene—by ridding the story of the boy's act of vengeance—bypasses a simplistic moral closure that eliminates the evil stepmother. Thus, the distribution of good and evil becomes more ambivalent, and motherhood is neither romanticized nor excoriated.

Hollywood woman's films—rarely made *by* women—were and are made *for* women. Linda Williams argues that "the device of devaluing and debasing the actual figure of the mother while sanctifying the institution of motherhood is typical of the 'woman's film' in general" (2000, 479). Not a woman's film in the latter, conventional sense, *The Juniper Tree* refuses either alternative. Those characters who worship the mother (Margit and Jónas) fall victim to their convictions that she is eternal or immortal. But the actual mother figures—the manifest ghost of Margit and Katla's mother and Katla herself as stepmother—are each, in her own way, problematic and imperfect. Quite literally, Margit embodies the psychological maturation of women because she "develops her feminine gender identity in the *presence* of an ongoing relationship with the specific person of her mother" (Williams 2000, 485; emphasis in original).

---

20 Marriage to a deceased wife's sister but, significantly, not to a deceased husband's brother was illegal for a time in parts of Britain and Europe (Brown 2004).

Melancholia

I wanted to leave the little girl as the main character still because it's her experience in the new world that she goes into after they flee their home. But I wanted to make it more of a spiritual experience, more of a deeper personal experience for her than it was in the original tale.

Nietzchka Keene, 2002

In making Margit the central protagonist—especially because the viewer exegetically shares her gift of second sight—Keene creates an additional focal point of the film: death, mourning, and the transition between childhood and womanhood. Sigmund Freud's early descriptions of the concept of melancholia called it an inability to grieve properly, where the melancholic "repudiates the finite process of mourning, languishing instead in the refusal to grieve. . . . [T]he lost object is finally incorporated into the self, turned into the shelter of the ego, and preserved as a form of ghostly identification. In this refusal to sever any attachment to the lost object, the melancholic becomes instead haunted by it" (Eng 2000, 1276). This process is literally embodied in Margit, who regularly sees her mother's ghost; and ambivalently in Jónas, who accepts Margit's assertions that his real mother is present, watching over him and giving him a gift.

The film addresses the ambivalence of motherhood and its relationship to mourning. Even when mothers do not literally die—Jónas's in childbirth and Katla and Margit's by execution/murder—becoming one means the loss of ego because the child's interests are expected to become primary (Barzilai 1990). Katla has difficulty mothering Jónas because she retains self-interest. She and Margit grieve the death of their mother. Katla also grieves her lack of the gift of seeing, which her dead mother possessed and Margit has inherited. Jónas mourns his mother's death, and his own death prevents closure of that experience.

The conflict between Katla and Jónas is particularly sad because of their common experience of melancholia, of "unspeakable loss and inexorable suffering . . . a pathological form of mourning [in which they are] unable 'properly' to grieve the loss" (Eng 2000, 1276). Freud eventually repudiated his pathological evaluation of melancholia, seeing it instead "as a constitutive psychic mechanism engendering subjectivity itself" (Ibid., 1277). However, Julia Kristeva links melancholia, depression, and mourning, saying that they conceal "an aggression toward the lost object, thus revealing the ambivalence of the depressed person with respect to the object of mourning" (1989, 11). She sees women's and men's (heterosexual) development as melancholic particularly because of the need to sacrifice the relationship with the mother (see also Butler [1990] 1999).

Jónas's uncontrollable anger against his stepmother may be an expression of his actual anger against his (biological) mother for leaving him, thus dividing the mother figure into an object of worship and one of abhorrence.[21] His explosive reaction to Katla—"she's a witch! she's a witch! she's a witch! she's a witch!"—is reminiscent of Kristeva's description of the melancholic's language: "I cannot inscribe my violence in 'no,' nor in any other sign. I can expel it only by means of gestures, spasms, or shouts. I impel it, I project it. My necessary Thing is also and absolutely my enemy, my foil, the delightful focus of my hatred" (1989, 15). Because Jónas's mother has actually died, "the . . . violence of matricidal drive . . . entails, when it is hindered, its inversion on the self; the maternal object having been introjected, the depressive or melancholic putting to death of the self is what follows" (Ibid., 28). But in their common mourning for their mothers, Jónas refuses to give her up, and Katla's fear of the discovery that her mother was considered a witch prevents her from making him an ally. Their common repression of anger against their mothers for leaving them creates murderous intentions in Katla and suicidal ones in Jónas, though each mistakes that fury as directed against the other.

Keene represents Margit's ambivalence to her mother more graphically. The girl twice encounters her mother as hole, not whole. The most striking image in *The Juniper Tree* is the ghost with "a hole where her heart should be" (undated script). Dori Laub sees the black hole as an indication of trauma (1992, 64-65), potentially linking the mother's ghost to Margit's actual experience of loss. Keene provides a powerful image of the physical experience of grief. Margit is befriending Jónas and telling of the way she sees her own mother. After the girl helps him perform magic beside his mother's grave—using threads to protect him—he leaves, and her mother appears. Margit inserts her hand into a black hole in her mother's chest, accompanied by what the script calls "vision music." This image resonates

---

21   Nancy Chodorow might differ that the mother and stepmother have fundamentally different roles, explaining that "the boy's 'normal contempt' for women . . . is a pathological and defensive reaction to the . . . sense of inescapable maternal omnipotence" (1976, 463–64).

because the hole in the diaphragm coincides with the frequent location of the sensation of grief: below the ribs. Julia Kristeva describes the black hole as a manifestation of female depression: "A nothingness that is neither repression nor simply the mark of the affect, but condenses into a *black hole*—like invisible, crushing, cosmic antimatter—the sensory, sexual, fantasy-provoking ill-being of abandonment and disappointments" (1989, 87). The image also critically evokes the notion of women as simultaneously visual object and absence explored extensively in both poststructuralist feminism and film theory.

Telling Tales

Every telling of a story is a fragment and a transformation; it stimulates emotions and perceptions and, in so doing, connects the teller to social context. As there are many interpretations of any fairy tale—and of "The Juniper Tree" in particular—there seem to have been many Nietzchka Keenes. Her colleagues and students praised her knowledge and dedication. Those Anne interviewed in Iceland, who worked on *The Juniper Tree,* spoke of her ebullience, talents, drive, and individuality. But her friend, the film's associate producer, Patrick Moyroud, commented that "to people who met Nietzchka the first time, she could seem eccentric, stubborn and hard to know, except on her own terms" (quoted in Liedl 2004). His insight oddly echoes the impressions of many, ourselves included, who have approached *The Juniper Tree.* Keene's wish to dislocate the tale from any particular location or time and her obvious feminist perspective give us permission to construe her film in our own ways. Yet throughout, we have experienced what has proven to be a creative tension. On the one hand, viewing the film has unleashed the pleasures of interpretation, speculating about possible meanings. On the other hand, we wish to respect the filmmaker's intention that her work be experienced first and foremost as a story in its own right and not as metaphor—or object of analysis! Indeed, however univocal our final result may seem, it is the result of considerable disagreement among the two authors about what the film and filmmaker (allow us to) say. But given the generic and archetypal quality of fairy tales, an openness echoed in this film—as it is in no other that we know—that's probably as it should be.

7

Disney's *Enchanted*
Patriarchal Backlash and Nostalgia in a Fairy Tale Film

Linda Pershing with Lisa Gablehouse

> *Everything still encourages the young girl to expect fortune and happiness from some Prince*
> *Charming, rather than to attempt by herself their difficult and uncertain conquest.*

Simone de Beauvoir, 1953 (126)

WALT DISNEY STUDIOS PROMOTED THEIR MOVIE *ENCHANTED* (directed by Kevin Lima, 2007) as a celebratory self-parody of their classic fairy tale films, including *Snow White and the Seven Dwarfs* (directed by David Hand, 1937), *Cinderella* (directed by Clyde Geronimi, Wilfred Jackson, and Hamilton Luske, 1950), and *Sleeping Beauty* (directed by Clyde Geronimi, 1959). Extensive advertising touted *Enchanted* as a musical comedy that pokes fun at the conventional damsels in distress, the villains seeking to destroy them, and their manly rescuers, all presented in the context of a contemporary story line.[1] We contend that the film reinforces previous Disney fairy tale ideologies, including attitudes critiqued by Simone de Beauvoir more than fifty years ago. Rather than offering an updated perspective, *Enchanted* appropriates and reworks folk and fairy tale motifs to support a conventional Euro-North American worldview that both obfuscates and reinforces patriarchal ideologies. Like other Disney movies, *Enchanted* is

---

1   Cristina Bacchilega and John Rieder, in this volume, draw attention to the film's structuring of "a passage between a fairy tale world and a realistic one" and explore the way it "exploits the two worlds' differences to comic effect as a kind of metacommentary on the suppression of realism in earlier Disney productions."

not just a vehicle for generating corporate profits; it sustains the cultural ideology that has shaped Disney fairy tale films from the beginning.

Enchanted typifies Disney fairy tale films in at least two ways—its representation of women, and its sociocultural perspective. Thus, in this film, the female protagonist seeks personal fulfillment through romance. The outcome—a happy ending in marriage—follows the heroine being subjected to a threat or danger, rendered vulnerable, and finally rescued. By no means a self-actualized feminist, *Enchanted*'s main character Giselle (Amy Adams) finds her one true love and becomes a heteronormative role model for her future stepdaughter. Nancy (Idina Menzel), her hitherto feminist counterpart and rival for the affections of the lawyerly—if not princely—Robert (Patrick Dempsey), retreats at the film's end from the real world to the make-believe realm of Andalasia, giving up her professional career to become a fairy tale princess and bride. Her enemy, Narissa (Susan Sarandon), is her prospective mother-in-law, an evil witch lusting for power. Further, the film offers a worldview built on patriarchal, capitalistic, heterosexist, and racist assumptions.[2] Two scenarios set the stage for our analysis.

Scenario one comes from *Enchanted*. It is morning, and a beautiful young woman named Giselle awakens in a Manhattan apartment. Robert, a handsome divorcé, and his six-year-old daughter, Morgan (Rachel Covey), gave her lodging the previous night, when they found her lost and wandering in New York City. Having fallen through a magical portal in her fairy tale homeland of Andalasia, she has no idea where she is or how to function in the "real world." Nevertheless, Giselle notices that the apartment is a mess; clothes and newspapers are scattered everywhere, and dirty dishes fill the kitchen sink and counters. In a parody of Disney's heroines Snow White and Cinderella, who call on their animal friends to assist with chores, Giselle summons hundreds of city animals (pigeons, rats, and cockroaches) to come to the rescue. While dancing and singing the (Oscar-nominated) "Happy Working Song"—with lyrics that include "We adore each filthy chore"—Giselle and the animals scrub the place from top to bottom. When everything is spotless, she rhetorically questions, "Now, wasn't this fun?" The scenario raises a number of issues. Giselle cleans the apartment of a complete stranger, a man she met in the streets of New York City and in whose home she slept without any concern for her safety. Apparently he is

---

2   To the list of problems and exclusions offered by Robyn McCallum and John Stephens (n.d.), we have added heterosexism and racism.

unable to do his own cleaning, and despite being an attorney employed by a major Manhattan law firm, he cannot manage to hire a housekeeper.

Scenario two occurs on November 23, 2007, in Hollywood, California. We join the crowd of a thousand people leaving the El Capitan, a classic theatre that has been purchased by the Disney Corporation. After shelling out eighteen dollars each for a ticket (the good seats were thirty dollars) and watching the movie, we are herded into "Disney's *Enchanted* Experience," an enormous white tent behind the theater where a banner tells viewers to "meet all your favorite Disney Princesses together under one roof" (El Capitan Theatre 2007).[3] The place is awash with pink and pastels, Disney music, and twinkling lights. We encounter a regal ballroom movie set, complete with young women dressed like Sleeping Beauty, Belle, and Cinderella, who smile while posing for photos. On another stage, we see Snow White, Ariel from *The Little Mermaid* (directed by Ron Clements and John Musker, 1989), and Jasmine from *Aladdin* (directed by Ron Clements and John Musker, 1992), wearing slightly darker makeup than the other princesses. Mulan and Pocahontas are nowhere to be found. But dressed in her big white wedding gown, a Giselle look-alike draws an especially long line of young girls, who wait to have their photos taken with her. One precious three-year-old wears a silver tiara and oversized white wedding dress. Her mother appears to be Asian, perhaps Filipina. When it's her daughter's turn to meet Giselle, the woman coaxes the child to pose and smile. The tiny bride's brown skin and dark eyes contrast sharply with the light complexions of the Disney royal court.

Princess land is all consuming. In one area, girls sit in front of mirrors and have "princess makeup" applied. The five young women of color who staff the booth have full figures that do not conform to those of the princess images surrounding them. Another area offers fancy gowns in varying colors and sizes. Girls try them on and pose in front of blue screens so that computers can superimpose background scenes from Disney movies, literally embedding them as consumers. One employee photographer says she has taken a thousand photos in a single session. The sessions follow five screenings per day. Our heads ache by the time we leave, overcome by the pink chiffon and refrains of "someday my prince will come."

---

3   For a discussion of the conventional depiction of fairy tale princesses, see Ming-Hsun Lin's chapter in this volume.

Dis-Enchanting Disney's Corporate Capitalism

We have no obligation to make art. We have no obligation to make a statement. To make money is our only objective.

Michael Eisner, CEO of Walt Disney Corporation,

1981 staff memo (quoted in Wasko 2001, 29)

Although Eisner clearly expressed Disney's capitalist mandate, numerous scholars have gone further by examining the company's pervasive, multi-billion-dollar brand name and exploring the dimensions of Disney's capitalist ideology.[4] Like so many of its predecessors, *Enchanted* quickly became a box-office success. With few exceptions, critics reviewed the movie positively (Reviews of *Enchanted* 2007). It was nominated for eighteen awards, including two Golden Globes and three Academy Awards, and it received the prize for best family film at the Critics Choice Awards.[5] Ticket sales over the Thanksgiving 2007 holiday, shortly after it was released in the U.S., were $49.1 million, $7 million more than even Disney projected (Bowles 2007). Distributed to more than fifty countries and territories around the world, by April 2008, *Enchanted* had earned a total of more than $127 million in the U.S. and $340 million globally, making it the fifteenth-highest-grossing film released in 2007 (*Enchanted* Box Office Earnings 2007).

Princesses have been the fastest-growing product brand for Disney in recent years, with marketing strategies to attract females—infants to adults—as consumers of its merchandise.[6] Gary Strauss comments, "Disney,

---

4   See, for example, Ayres (2003b); Eliot (1993); Fjellman (1992); Giroux (1999 and 2009); Grover (1991); Schickel (1968); Smoodin (1994); Wasko (2001); and Watts (1997).

5   A list of awards that *Enchanted* received, or for which it was nominated, is available at http://en.wikipedia.org/wiki/Enchanted_%28film%29#Awards. These include winning the best live-action family film award from the Phoenix Film Critics Society; being named best family film at the thirteenth Critics Choice Awards; and garnering three Saturn Awards (best fantasy film, best actress for Amy Adams, and best music for Alan Menken).

6   For a discussion of this phenomenon, see Marr (2007). In their chapter in this collection, Bacchilega and Rieder note that Disney has successfully used the fairy tale genre to "peddle its franchise byproducts by inculcating the desire to possess their 'magic'" on women and little girls especially. Naarah Sawers in this volume suggests that "child audiences of films based on the Disney model are . . . considered primarily consumers, and thus the . . . filmic [narrative] represents a conflation of pleasure and consumption."

the undisputed leader in princess merchandising, made a major move on the market in 2000, when it decided to package 'princesses' Snow White, Sleeping Beauty, Ariel, Belle, Cinderella, Jasmine, Mulan and Pocahontas under the same marketing umbrella. The move spawned a sales juggernaut. Disney and 300 licensees sell 25,000 princess-themed products" (2004). By 2007 Disney's princess franchise was bringing in $4.6 billion. According to Dick Cook, chair of Walt Disney Studios, one goal in developing *Enchanted* was to create a new franchise by adding Giselle to the inventory of Disney princesses and reinvigorating the sales of her earlier counterparts. However, when company executives realized the cost of securing lifelong rights to the image of Amy Adams, who plays Giselle, they abandoned the plan. As a result, although Giselle is not officially marketed as one of the Disney princesses, *Enchanted* merchandise is available in a variety of venues, with Giselle's animated (rather than actor Amy Adams's) likeness on all the products (Marr 2007).[7]

Toys and movies are only part of Disney's marketing strategy. In their essay in this collection, Cristina Bacchilega and John Rieder suggest that "the ball, the wedding, and the other make-believe scenarios naturalize the appeal of fantasy and display the power of magic for sale in the contemporary world." Thus, for example, Chrys Ingraham notes that, beginning in 1997, Disney became a key player in the wedding industry by selling the idea of "fairy tale weddings" through its media and merchandising and later producing actual weddings at its theme parks and properties (2008, 87–89; see also Jacobs 2001).[8] Ingraham focuses specifically on Disney in her analysis of "the wedding-industrial complex," the social and economic systems

7   A Giselle look-alike led the 2007 Hollywood Holly-Day Parade at Disney's Hollywood Studios *(Enchanted's* Princess Giselle Debuts 2007). She was also featured, along with Cinderella, Snow White, Belle, and other Disney princesses, in the 2007 Walt Disney World Christmas Day Parade in the Magic Kingdom. Its unwillingness to pay Adams for the rights to her image has not stopped Disney from marketing *Enchanted* products. On Disneyshopping.com, consumers can purchase clothing, tiaras, Game Boy products, and figurines (including an Armani rendition of Giselle for $450) marketed under the *Enchanted* label. Products relating to the other Disney princesses are listed under their names.

8   Rana Dogar reports that Disney's "ultimate fairy tale wedding," which allows couples to reserve time in the Magic Kingdom, became available to purchase in 1997. For a hundred thousand dollars, the bride could buy the opportunity to ride down Main Street in a glass carriage drawn by six white horses, greeted by uniformed trumpeters. Her prince—the groom—would ride to the wedding on a white stallion (1997; see also Ingraham 2008, 87–89).

through which the massive wedding industry reasserts heterosexual dominance and promotes women's oppression in capitalist societies.[9] Examining
the ways in which Disney movies, television shows, toys, and theme parks
promote weddings, Ingraham observes that the prevailing standard represents the bride as a princess—white, thin, rich, privileged, and heterosexual—who uses cultural consumption to demonstrate her marital status.

Parody, Fantasy, and Reality

*Disney wasn't passively or innocently reflecting anything; he was actively emphasizing and
exaggerating certain assumptions about women and girls while clearly ignoring others.*

                                                        Susan Douglas, 1994 (31)

The initial scenes in *Enchanted* humorously exaggerate familiar tropes in
Disney fairy tale films: a maiden sings joyfully to a chorus of forest animals about her one true love, the young man who tries to win her heart is
brawny and brainless (a takeoff on Gaston in *Beauty and the Beast* [directed
by Gary Trousdale and Kirk Wise, 1991]), a wicked witch/hag/queen inter-
cepts the young maiden before she can marry the prince. Giselle's character is intentionally over the top, always giddy, naïve, ever so sweet. One
reviewer described her as "a Strawberry Shortcake version" of a fairy tale
princess (Seymour 2007). At first the movie seems to poke fun at itself and
all that is Disney. Designed by director Kevin Lima as a "playful homage"
and a "giant love letter to Disney classics," *Enchanted* is highly self-referential, incorporating hundreds of allusions to earlier Disney movies as well
as motifs from the literary fairy tales on which they were based (especially
Snow White, Cinderella, and *Sleeping Beauty)* (Adler 2007). Lima became
obsessed with embedding Disney references in *Enchanted* through the visual
imagery, plot, actors, voices, camerawork, costumes, music, dialogue, and
sets (Wood 2008). Poison apples (from *Snow White)* and the "true love's

9   There has been some criticism of Ingraham's analysis for being too totalizing, including
     Freeman (2002) and Otnes and Pleck (2003). Yet even well-known feminist Naomi
     Wolf ([1995] 1999) wrestled with conventional and sexist stereotypes and cultural
     expectations about weddings. Sidney Eve Matrix notes the way advertising and
     wedding registrations give "modern I-Do Feminist brides permission to indulge in the
     guilty pleasures of romantic, nostalgic, fetishized housewifery" (2006, 66).

kiss" (from *Snow White* and *Sleeping Beauty*) are just two of the more obvious examples.[10]

However, the parody suggested in the initial scenes—seemingly a good-natured spoof of the outdated gender relations represented in earlier Disney fairy tale films—dissipates soon after Giselle finds herself in New York City.[11] *Enchanted* deteriorates into a pretext for retelling the familiar narrative: a beautiful (motherless) maiden seeks her true love; she encounters trials and tribulations; a handsome young man appears; and they marry and live happily ever after.[12] *Enchanted* discards its metacommentary and is absorbed into the story line it supposedly parodies, using iconic, self-referential humor and imagery to reinforce Disney products and values. Rather than providing an alternative to the male-identified and single-minded Disney princess whose mantra is "one day my prince will come," *Enchanted* simply proves her right.

Enchanted is a romantic comedy, combining hand-drawn animation, computer-generated imagery (CGI), and live action. With thirteen minutes of animation, it is Disney's first feature-length, live-action/traditional-cell-animation hybrid since *Who Framed Roger Rabbit?* (directed by Robert Zemeckis, 1988). Film critic Tim Ryan aptly described it as "sort of a *Wizard of Oz* in reverse" (2007). The first ten minutes are classic Disney animation, then the narrative switches to live action, and finally the movie ends with a short, animated scene back in Andalasia. The relationship between fantasy and reality is a prominent motif. Advertisements for *Enchanted* proclaim, "The real world and the animated world collide." While they are in New York, fairy tale characters fail to distinguish between what is real and what is fantasy: Giselle spots a big pink castle on an advertising billboard and tries to enter it; Prince Edward (James Marsden) sees a television screen and assumes it is a magic mirror. Giselle's changing appearance reveals her transition between the two realms. Her hairstyle progresses from loads of curls

---

10   Ardent fans have devoted Web sites to identifying all of the Disney elements from earlier films (see List of Disney References n.d.).

11   An expressive form created to comment on, mock, or poke fun at its referent, usually by means of exaggerated imitation or humor, *parody* differs from satire's sarcastic critique. Unlike satire, parody may also convey admiration for its subject. Literary theorist Linda Hutcheon comments that "parody . . . is not always at the expense of the parodied text" (2000, 7).

12   Like *Snow White, Cinderella, Sleeping Beauty,* and *The Little Mermaid, Enchanted* offers a fairy tale in the subgenre of innocent persecuted heroines, who suffer abuse and seek relief or rescue to remedy their situations (Bacchilega 1993).

and bows to a contemporary, long, straight coiffure; her costume shifts from a fairy tale wedding dress to a sleek, modern gown.[13] Robert, the New York attorney who falls in love with Giselle, is pragmatic and disillusioned, decrying people who engage in fantasy, until she turns his world upside down and teaches him to believe in the fairy tale version of "true love." In her analysis of the seductive and omnipresent character of the "Disney spell," Justyna Deszcz argues that "the Disney fairytale is no longer confined to the sphere of the imaginary, but enjoys an alternative world, continually spilling from the fantastic fairytale realm into the real one" (2002, 83). *Enchanted* rhetorically raises the question, can a fairy tale romance survive in the real world?—and then answers with a resounding yes!

Reinscribing Disney Ideology—Enchantment or Antifeminist Backlash?

Perhaps this is the greatest of Disney's achievements: to render harmless that which is harmful.

Mark Axelrod, 2003 (29)

Henry Giroux suggests that Disney's strategy in cultural production involves masking its ideological constructions with claims of "innocence," rendering "it unaccountable for the diverse ways in which it shapes the sense of reality it provides for children [and adults] as they take up particular and often sanitized notions of identity, culture, and history in the seemingly apolitical cultural universe of 'the Magic Kingdom'" (1997, 56). His recent work implicates Disney in formulating notions about public life and civic responsibility:

> As citizenship becomes increasingly privatized and youth are increasingly educated to become consuming subjects rather than civic minded and critical citizens, it becomes all the more imperative for

---

13   Her enormous wedding gown amplifies Giselle's frivolity and femininity. The sleeves are extremely puffy to make her waist look even smaller. The skirt includes a metal hoop designed to support twenty layers of ruffles and petticoats (Kam 2007). It took more than two hundred yards of silk and satin to make each gown (the dressmakers created eleven of them for various scenes), and the finished product weighed approximately forty-five pounds (Washington 2007). "Grueling" was the word Amy Adams used to describe the experience of wearing it, noting that "the entire weight was on my hips, so occasionally it felt like I was in traction" (Murray n.d.).

people everywhere to develop a critical language in which notions of the public good, public issues and public life become central to overcoming the privatizing and depoliticizing language of the market. Disney, like many corporations, trades in sound bytes and the result is that the choices, exclusions and values that inform its narratives about joy, pleasure, living and existing in a global world are often difficult to discern. (2009)

Stressing the ways in which "Disney's commercial carpet bombing of children" tends to shut down popular critique and critical engagement, Giroux contends that "as one of the most influential corporations in the world, Disney does more than provide entertainment, it also shapes in very powerful ways how young people understand themselves, relate to others and experience the larger society" (Ibid.).

Thus, *Enchanted* prompts analysis of its contemporary U.S. social and historical contexts. The film was in various stages of development for ten years, most of that time concurrent with the regressive administration of U.S. President George W. Bush. In this period of rising anxiety came a push by governmental, corporate, and religious leaders to reinvigorate conservatism and return to the "traditional family values" of male dominance, female domesticity, and heteronormativity. The era was shaped by debates about the Iraq War, cuts in government spending for education and social programs, a growing divide between the rich and working classes, pervasive struggles of blended and single-parent families, attempts to legalize same-sex marriage, and debates about a white woman (Hillary Clinton) and an African American man (Barack Obama) hoping to become the next president of the United States. *Enchanted* offers a conventional, patriarchal worldview as a remedy for the alienation of modern life, providing what feminist Hortense Powdermaker, as long ago as 1950, called "filmic fantasies . . . about a peaceful and virtuous society" and, with them, the possibility for the restoration of the male-dominated, nuclear family and a resurgence of repressive gender roles (quoted in O'Brien 1996, 160).

Although the parochial worldview in Disney fairy tale films can be traced to Walt himself, the movies created by Walt Disney Studios after his death have continued to reflect his biases.[14] Numerous scholars have documented the Disney Studios' patriarchal, homophobic, and xenophobic

---

14   See Watts (1995) for a critical biography of Disney. See also Ayres (2003b); Bell, Haas, and Sells (1995); Eliot (1993); Giroux (1999); Grover (1991); and Smoodin (1994).

characterizations.[15] This perspective is no accident; it is based on "conscious decisions made by management and creative forces, and influenced by social and financial contexts" (O'Brien 1996, 180). Predictably, then, conventional and mainstream Euro-North American assumptions about gender, sexuality, race, class, and culture shape *Enchanted* and influence the ways in which Walt Disney Studios formulates the fairy tale.[16]

Disney cultural expression attempts to naturalize social and political hierarchies of race (Giroux 1999, 106). *Enchanted*'s ideology endorses white privilege with its racialized use of color. Its light-equals-good versus dark-equals-bad symbolism is consistent with earlier Disney animated films (Ibid., 225).[17] The prince has blue eyes and rides a white horse; Giselle's blue eyes, fair skin, and light auburn hair contrast sharply with the black/blue costumes and makeup of the evil Narissa (Susan Sarandon). The primary characters are white. The few people of color who do appear are peripheral or secondary to the New York story line.[18] Cultural diversity and national identity are trivialized and marginalized by using racial and ethnic stereotypes. For example, Latinos appear as mariachi band members, and a black male in a Caribbean steel-drum musical group wears an African dashiki.

Enchanted further assumes a middle-to-upper-class lifestyle. Money is never an issue for any of the main characters, even those who fall through the portal into New York and somehow manage to rent hotel rooms, ride

---

15 See, for example, Bell, Haas, and Sells (1995); Berland (1982); Do Rozario (2004); Henke, Umble, and Smith (1996); Hoerrner (1996); Maio (1998); Mosley (1990); O'Brien (1996); and especially Haase (2004a); and Zipes (1997).

16 In this volume, Kim Snowden also draws attention to the "conventional and stereotyped idea of the way gender is constructed" and perpetuated in Disney versions of fairy tales.

17 For analyses of racism in Disney fairy tale films, see also Giroux (1997, 60–63); Macleod (2003); Robertson (1998); Wasko (2001, 139–43); and Wise (2003). Dorothy Hurley investigates the way children of color conceptualize Disney princesses and Disney's binary color symbolism (2005, 224–25). She observes, "The problem of pervasive, internalized privileging of Whiteness has been intensified by the Disney representation of fairy tale princesses which consistently reinforces an ideology of White supremacy" (Ibid., 223).

18 This selective racialization contradicts New York's own Department of City Planning, which lauds the city's "unique level of diversity: 43 percent of the city's 2.9 million foreign-born residents arrived in the U.S. in the previous ten years; 46 percent of the population speaks a language other than English at home; in just 30 years, what was primarily a European population has now become a place with no dominant race/ ethnic or nationality group. Indeed, New York epitomizes the world city" (http:// www.nyc.gov/html/dcp/html/census/nny_overview.shtml).

ferries, and purchase food and souvenirs.[19] A diamond necklace, tiara, and earrings that Giselle wears on her wedding day symbolize her social status. Robert's young daughter, Morgan, takes a credit card from her father's dresser drawer and goes on a shopping spree with Giselle, buying bags of clothing and shoes at exclusive Manhattan boutiques. A homeless man who encounters Giselle on the streets is the only character who struggles with financial hardship. He turns out to be a thief; indifferent to her predicament of being lost in New York City, he robs her.

Heterosexuality is presumed in the narrative of *Enchanted;* viewers see no same-sex couples or alternative gender depictions. Two quick gags in the story line question if the prince and squire are gay, but viewers are quickly assured they are not.[20] When Giselle first meets a female client at the law offices where Robert is an attorney, Giselle presumes that the client is heterosexual, proclaiming, "You are beautiful. The man who holds your heart is a very lucky fellow indeed." Romance and love exist exclusively within a heterosexual framework. The narrative assumes that women are attracted to men and promotes the idea that women's problems are solved when they fall in love with men (see Stone 1985, 143). It also portrays as the norm girls and women who relish the idea of becoming socially elite and have no apparent desire to be self-sufficient.

Nancy, whose character represents the contemporary career woman, is no exception to this pattern. Even she, in the end, relinquishes her job and the real world for a fantasyland marriage in Andalasia. She exemplifies

---

19   Consider, in contrast, the statistics provided on the city's own Web site, estimating that 16.3 percent of New York families lived below the poverty line in 2008 (http://home2. nyc.gov/html/dcp/pdf/census/acs_pov_stat_family_2006.pdf)

20   After Prince Edward comes through the portal onto the streets of Manhattan, his squire, Nathaniel (Timothy Spall), follows him in pursuit. Sanitation workers at the opening of the portal ask Nathaniel if he, too, is looking for a "beautiful girl," and he replies, "No, I'm looking for a prince, actually." They raise their eyebrows, assuming he is gay, and the audience laughs. In another scene, Prince Edward is searching for Giselle and knocks on the door of an apartment, thinking she is inside. A large, burly, middle-aged, white male, wearing a bandana and black leather vest, opens the door and smiles coyly, insinuating that he would be happy to have male companionship. Edward winces.

An alternative reading of Queen Narissa (Susan Sarandon) as a drag queen—in her black leather; heavy blue/purple/black eye makeup; and tall, black platform heels—is never explored in the film. She seduces the squire Nathaniel to go after Giselle, but Narissa's attraction to Nathaniel is never intended to be convincing. Though the queen is highly sexualized, the audience never sees Narissa involved in a sexual or romantic relationship.

Enchanted's presentation of competition among women as they struggle to snare the prince. And the men for whom Nancy and Giselle vie are an insensitive hunk (the prince) and a bewildered male completely immobilized by women's liberation and changing gender roles (Robert). Consistent with Disney's worldview, both Giselle's future husband, Robert, and prospective mother-in-law, Narissa, refer to Giselle as a "girl." Of course, sexist gender roles are nothing new for Disney, but in light of the pervasive influence of feminist and other social change movements, *Enchanted* offers a distinctly anachronistic tale.

Because advertisements represented the film as a deconstruction of the traditional fairy tale, the outdated representations of gender are especially troubling. Feminist social critic Susan Faludi labels this phenomenon *backlash*, which she defines as "a powerful counter-assault on women's rights, . . . an attempt to retract the handful of small and hard-won victories that the feminist movement did manage to win for women. This counterassault is largely insidious: in a kind of pop-culture version of the Big Lie, it stands the truth boldly on its head and proclaims that the very steps that have elevated women's position have actually led to their downfall" (1991, xviii). Faludi's concept exemplifies the ways in which the main characters in *Enchanted* perform gender, revealing an underlying ideology that is sexist and patriarchal.

Gender stereotypes reach beyond the main character, Giselle, or her age mate and rival, Nancy. In a glamorous version of *Sleeping Beauty*'s Maleficent or Cruella De Vil in *101 Dalmatians* (directed by Stephen Herek, 1996), Susan Sarandon's performance as Queen Narissa—powerful, seductive, slinky, conniving, and sexual—provides a sharp contrast to Amy Adams's Giselle. Narissa, who is Prince Edward's stepmother, is depicted as reptilian by her costumes (scales on a long, slinky, black dress and cape), dialogue (Prince Edward refers to her as "you viper!"), and mannerisms (flicking her tongue). In the finale, this characterization is confirmed when she turns into a dragon. However, despite her cunning and power, even she is vulnerable, dependent on men for her status and survival. For reasons never explained to the viewer, Narissa believes that Prince Edward's future marriage will endanger her claim to the throne. She thus sees Giselle as a threat, and the primary tension in the plot revolves around one woman trying to eliminate the other.

Twice during her efforts to get rid of her competition, Narissa transforms into an old and disfigured hag or witch, the opposite of the lovely Giselle.

In this guise, she fits the profile of Disney's female villains as Laura Sells observes: "Within Disney's patriarchal ideology, any woman with power has to be represented as a castrating bitch" (1995, 181). While the king is absent (he is never mentioned in the story), Narissa struggles for legitimacy.[21] The crone versus the virgin, she sees Giselle solely as a competitor for social position and male validation. Thus, for Giselle to find fulfillment, she must kill her prospective mother-in-law—the only untamed, liberated female character in the story.[22] Indeed, to fulfill this symbolic requirement, the story line requires the audience to suspend its need for consistency within the plot. After Giselle pursues her to the top of the Woolworth Building, Narissa falls to her death on the streets below. Given her prodigious magical powers, why can't she save herself? The possibility of Narissa's survival is never explored because it would undermine the younger-innocent-woman-kills-older-wicked-woman motif.

Giselle is Narissa's opposite. Sweet, trustworthy, cheerful, caring, and selfless, she has never experienced anger before she arrives in the real world. She is simple minded and seems to lack any critical sensibility about what she encounters. After Giselle is pushed through the portal, she makes no attempt to return but instead passively waits for the prince to rescue her. She is lost—literally and metaphorically—and the only way she thinks she can get home is for the prince to come and get her. Like other recent Disney female protagonists (including Ariel, Belle, Jasmine, and Pocahontas), Giselle is simultaneously innocent and sexualized. Rebecca-Anne Do Rozario observes this dynamic in the portrayal of earlier Disney princesses: "The sexuality of the princess appears incongruous in features deemed suitable for young children, but the princesses of Team Disney [Eisner era], including Ariel, Jasmine, and Pocahontas, have all been read through sexual thematics" (2004, 51). While they are both getting a makeover at a beauty salon, Morgan tells Giselle that "boys are only interested in one thing." When Giselle looks puzzled and asks Morgan what that means, she confesses that she has no idea, and both females acknowledge their ignorance about sex.

However, mixed messages abound: the plunging necklines of Giselle's dresses are cut low and tight, revealing bare shoulders and cleavage. While Giselle is in Robert's apartment, he accidentally walks into the bathroom as

21 See Craven (2002, 128) for a discussion of the struggles of Disney heroines.

22 Narissa is also a stepmother; see Axelrod (2003) and Haas (1995) for discussions of representations of these figures in Disney films.

she is taking a shower. She is nude but undaunted by his presence. During the resulting confusion, Robert and Giselle trip over one another and fall to the floor while Giselle is wearing nothing but a towel. Robert's partner, Nancy, walks in and sees them, then storms out of the apartment, assuming they are having an affair. Giselle is mystified by Nancy's reaction. The dynamic changes toward the end of the movie, when Giselle first experiences sexual desire. She wears a pair of men's blue pajamas; Robert seems to be wearing nothing under his bathrobe, suggesting he has given his pajamas to Giselle. She touches his bare chest, and they stop just short of acting upon this moment of intimacy.

Giselle's other female counterpart, Nancy, Robert's partner, is portrayed as an outspoken, "modern" woman. Yet she has nonetheless been waiting five years for Robert to propose to her, evidently unable to take the initiative herself. She is a savvy entrepreneur who runs her own business—Nancy Tremaine's Design Studio—and the dialogue suggests that she and Robert have a sexual relationship. In a scene that producers later cut, Nancy tells a coworker, "It's not like I'm one of those women, you know, who sit around their entire lives waiting for some perfect prince in shining armor to take me off to his castle in the Hamptons. I got over that fantasy a long time ago" (*Enchanted* DVD 2008). Perhaps the dialogue was removed because viewers soon learn this isn't true; what Nancy really wants is to be "swept off her feet" by her Prince Charming.

Loving the romance of it all, she is ecstatic when Robert uncharacteristically invites her to the Kings and Queens Costume Ball. When Giselle and Robert fall in love, Nancy quickly abandons her cosmopolitan sensibilities by jumping through the portal back to Andalasia with Prince Edward, marrying him, and literally turning into a two-dimensional character. During the animated wedding ceremony at the end of the film, Nancy's cell phone rings. She giggles, snatches the phone, and throws it to the ground, where it shatters, symbolically leaving behind her modern life. When the Andalasian priest declares Prince Edward and Nancy "husband and wife," Nancy upends convention, taking the lead and tilting Edward backward to deliver a powerful kiss. However, she has left her life as a cosmopolitan businesswoman behind, preferring to marry the shallow and half-witted prince. Nancy becomes the princess she (and, by inference, other women who profess independence) really wants to be. Like many female characters in Disney tales once they find their true loves, Nancy loses her "mildly feminist attributes" to become "merely [a] blushing bride" (Bean 2003, 58).

Faux Feminism: Disney's Response to the Women's Movement

In a scene from *Enchanted,* while rushing into the lobby of the Time Warner Center in Manhattan, Giselle and Robert pass Fernando Botero's twenty-foot nude statue entitled *Eve.* The figure is dark brown and rotund, with enormous hips and thighs. Giselle, taken with the sculpture, pauses and exclaims in a sweet voice, "She's beautiful!" Annoyed with Giselle's delays, Robert replies, "She's fat." Given the very-white-and-very-slender appearance of all the female lead characters, Giselle's comment creates a kind of cognitive dissonance. The only woman in the film who looks anything like the statue is a bus driver. She is overweight, loud, aggressive, and speaks in black vernacular; her character perpetuates stereotypes about African American women, and the portrayal is anything but flattering.

Feminism seeks to disrupt conventional masculine/feminine polarities, see other positions and identifications, and raise significant questions about issues of power and privilege, not only with regard to gender and sexuality but also race, ethnicity, class, culture, dis/ability, religion, and nationality. And indeed, as Giselle struggles to become a three-dimensional character in the real world, she begins to think (however minimally) for the first time, questioning—if only in a superficial way—the narrowly defined script for her life in Andalasia. In the process of her transformation, however, she also loses her own voice, no longer singing the songs that signal plot development. Prior to falling in love with Robert, Giselle sings about her life and dreams. Robert instructs her to stop singing in public because she embarrasses him. When the prince finally locates Giselle in New York and starts singing to her, she can no longer think of lyrics to sing back to him. Beginning at the Kings and Queens Costume Ball, other characters sing the tunes that structure the story line: a male soloist takes the spotlight, vocalizing "So Close," the song that brings Giselle and Robert together.[23] Giselle literally gives up her singing voice to find love, much as Ariel does in *The Little Mermaid.*

---

23   Vocalist Jon McLaughlin performs "So Close" while Giselle and Robert share an intimate dance and finally recognize they are in love. With music composed by Alan Menken and lyrics by Stephen Schwartz, the number was nominated for best original song at the eightieth Academy Awards. At the end of the movie, Carrie Underwood sings "Ever Ever After," the only original number in the film not sung by someone on-screen.

The characterization of Morgan, Robert's young daughter, is one of
the most disturbing aspects of *Enchanted,* however. Robert wants Morgan
to be able to protect herself (he insists she take karate lessons), read a book
entitled *Important Women of Our Time* (she grimaces and protests), and, as
he says, "face the world for what it is." Yet his daughter really wants to be a
princess, symbolized by the pink crown on her bedroom door, her princess
canopy bed, her adoration of Giselle, and her fondness for wearing pink and
princess/fairy costumes. Morgan doesn't like Nancy—the take-charge, assertive woman—preferring Giselle's princess wardrobe and focus on romance.
Early in the story, Robert tells Morgan that Nancy is "a lot like the women
in your book" and that, when they marry, Nancy will move in the apartment
and become Morgan's new mother. "You mean *step*mother," Morgan replies,
her correction reminding viewers that stepmothers are bad news in Disney
fairy tales (see Axelrod 2003; Haas 1995; Tatar 1985).[24]

Giselle stays in New York and marries Robert. In one of the final
scenes, a group of girls gathers excitedly in Giselle's new business, Andalasia
Fashions (which seems to have replaced Nancy's design studio). Presaging
what we witnessed at "Disney's *Enchanted* Experience," with which we
opened this chapter, the girls are dressed in pink and pastel princess and
fairy costumes, excitedly exploring Giselle's latest designs and thereby ensuring the perpetuation of princess culture by the next generation of consumers. Disney's portrayal of Morgan—her love of all things princess, along
with her rejection of Nancy—represents her antifeminist, backlash response
to societal changes and the progress women have made in changing sexist gender roles. Through Morgan, *Enchanted* sends a clear message that
feminism is not what girls really want, and it isn't going to make them
happy. Voiced by a young female, this commentary signals the audience
that "imposing" feminism on girls is harmful because it goes against their
allegedly natural desires.

Giroux observes and critiques the pedagogical function that Disney
movies serve especially for children, noting that "the significance of animated films operates on many registers, but one of the most persuasive is
the role they play as the new 'teaching machines,' as producers of culture.
I soon found out that that for my children, and I suspect for many others,

24   Christy Williams notes in her chapter in this collection that in *Ever After* (not a Disney
      film), the stepmother similarly "acts as a female agent of patriarchy, ensuring that
      male ideals of gender behavior and hierarchy are not solely perpetuated through male
      figures."

these films appear to inspire at least as much cultural authority as the public schools, religious institutions, and the family" (1997, 53). Princesses are big moneymakers for Disney, but their promotion does much more than generate a profit. It also inculcates archaic, patriarchal ideologies in each successive wave of children and reinforces oppressive value systems in older generations. Consumers are encouraged to internalize the messages about social relations, love, and power that are embedded in Disney fairy tale films. Writing about the potentially disturbing impact of princess culture, Meline Toumani described how a friend's daughters tried to convince their mother to let them wear their princess costumes over their pajamas so they wouldn't need to take them off when they went to bed. She comments that "the weirdest thing about the Princess craze is that it doesn't simply involve owning the same item that all the other kids have: it involves *becoming the character yourself,* a level of identification and involvement that deserves scrutiny for sure" (2007; emphasis added).

In response to social pressure, Disney has made a minimal effort in the recent past to incorporate moderately feminist elements into its fairy tale films, but these can be more accurately described as "faux feminism."[25] Usually this impulse involves trivializing feminist ideology or compressing the actions of female characters into the conventions of popular romance while maintaining that they are her choice, not actions instilled by patriarchal teaching and values. In her study of *Beauty and the Beast,* Allison Craven traces the way that Disney's version twists the older tale from a focus on Beauty's learning and understanding to falling in love. Citing the "domesticating effects of Disney's feminism on its heroines," she demonstrates the way that Disney films sometimes inject elements of self-determination or empowerment into the portrayal of female protagonists, only to undermine them with narrative conclusions that inevitably equate the heroine's fulfillment with heterosexual romance and marriage (2002, 126). She observes that—even when female protagonists are feisty or clever—their moments of agency reflect a "carefully scripted concept of pop femininity, constructed to be acceptable and entertaining to both children and adults" (Ibid., 130).

---

25 In *Feminism Is for Everybody,* for example, bell hooks critiques faux feminism or what she calls "lifestyle feminism": the idea that any perspective—no matter how damaging to women—can be part of a feminism that is individually, and individualistically, defined. She concludes, for example, that "one cannot be anti-choice and be feminist" (2000, 6).

Enchanted follows this pattern of faux feminism, in which fragments of feminist ideas are trivialized or subsumed within a dominant discourse of traditional gender roles (O'Brien 1996, 180). For example, Giselle demonstrates her resourcefulness by making a dress out of curtains in Robert's apartment.[26] However, her actions also reinforce her allegiance to domesticity and self-beautification: for example, using her creativity to make clothing, rather than find a way out of her dilemma. Giselle's gradual movement toward self-realization (by beginning to think for herself, recognizing she loves Robert rather than Prince Edward, assuming the role of warrior in her pursuit of the dragon, and starting her own business) is undermined by the narrative that ultimately defines her in relationship to a man. Although she lectures others about the depths and dimensions of love, her own focus is superficial. When Prince Edward finally finds her, Giselle's question is, "How do I look?" Robert's response, "Beautiful!" reaffirms that her appearance is what's important. Like the antifeminist postfeminism discussed by Kim Snowden in her chapter in this volume, *Enchanted* contends that women can have it all, so long as they do it within the roles of wife and mother in a nuclear family. Alternatively, we imagine Giselle coming to consciousness and starting a life of her own without being defined as a wife and mother. She could develop a critical sensibility about Robert, his cynicism, and his fear of commitment. She could encourage Morgan to read that book about women who have changed the world.

Marina Warner argues that the Disney version of fairy tales represents, above all, "Hollywood's cunning domestication of feminism itself" (1994, 313). In the end, *Enchanted* reinforces conformity to a nostalgic view of social and gender relations.[27] Characters who conform to heteronormative, racist, classist, and sexist ideals find themselves safe and happy. Personal growth remains minimal and superficial with social or political change

---

26   Here the filmmakers reference Julie Andrews, who played the main character in *The Sound of Music* (directed by Robert Wise, 1965) and is the narrator in *Enchanted*. Andrews's character also makes clothing out of curtains in *The Sound of Music*. In another homage, Giselle's song in Central Park, "That's How You Know," imitates Andrews as she runs over the top of a hill, singing "The Sound of Music."

27   Much like our interpretation of *Enchanted*, Williams in her chapter suggests that "the fragments of the 'Cinderella' tale that are manipulated most consistently in *Ever After*— the phrase 'once upon a time,' the dress, the rescue, and the godmother—placate a late-twentieth- and early-twenty-first-century audience's expectations of popular feminism but fail to move the 'Cinderella' story beyond the structural misogyny knit into the tale's plot."

precluded. Brenda Ayres aptly describes the continuing Disney agenda: "It is that Midwestern image—white, middle class, all-American, apple pie, Bible on the coffee table, anti-intellectual, heterosexual nuclear family— that has come to form the Disney ideal. Disney products colonize generations of children and parents to embrace this ideal and to regard divergence as inferior or evil. The Disneyfication of our children, then, is empire building, complete with an imperialistic colonizing force that effects either conformity to the ideal or denigration of the Other" (2003a, 16–17).

Of course, not all viewers happily accept the cultural narratives that Disney presents. Some voice their objections. To an online debate about gender roles in Disney fairy tale films, one blogger wrote, "And why does Disney feel such a need lately to show gutsy women who nonetheless are always needing to be rescued? Seems like they're trying to have things both ways—a strong heroine who really doesn't undermine the status quo. Grr. Argh" (e-mail posted by Erica Carlson, May 28, 2004, under Disney Movies vs Fairy Tales, SurLaLune fairytales.com). But perhaps the most urgent question is why contemporary audiences, particularly women, continue to support and promote the consumption of Disney fairy tale films.[28] Many who attended the Hollywood premiere of *Enchanted* were young mothers, who brought their children to view the movie. Afterward parents smiled and sometimes prodded their daughters—many of them wearing princess costumes—to stand alongside the Disney princesses. Women—who may know on an experiential level that Prince Charming and Disney's notion of happily-ever-after are fictions that do not elucidate or reflect their life experiences—clearly buy princess merchandise for their daughters and may even encourage them to pretend they will become princesses one day. To what degree do consumerism and cultural capitalism affect viewers' reception of Disney fairy tale films, and how does the "enchantment" of Disney ideology effectively "seduce its audience into suspending critical judgment on the messages produced by such films" (Giroux 1997, 58)?

Princesses and Disney's sexist ideology sell, and the Disney worldview is integral to the marketing of its products. Pamela Colby O'Brien observes, "As long as audiences approve of Disney's films and characters, the company has little incentive to reevaluate Walt's formula" (1996, 181). Disney's effective marketing to children means that mothers and families—even if they themselves disavow the films' and products' consumerist, heteronormative,

---

28   For a fuller discussion of this question, see Hines and Ayres (2003).

racist, and sexist messages—may feel that they cannot prevent their children becoming cultural consumers of Disney films.[29] Since economic profit remains central to Disney, its someday-my-prince-will-come formula is unlikely to change until more audience members object and are willing to signal their disapproval by altering their patterns of cultural consumption and choosing not to support the continuing production of patriarchal fairy tale films.

---

29   Thanks to Jack Zipes for this insight.

8

Fairy Tale Film in the Classroom:
Feminist Cultural Pedagogy, Angela Carter, and Neil Jordan's
The Company of Wolves

Kim Snowden

ACCORDING TO JACK ZIPES, READERS INTUITIVELY KNOW that a narrative is a fairy tale, and the same can be said of fairy tale film (1997, 61).[1] But even though the genre is recognizable regardless of form or medium, audience approaches can be unpredictable. In this chapter, I want to explore a particular audience's reactions and understanding when a specific familiar text is adapted to film. I currently teach a course on the representation of female archetypes in fairy tales. My students and I work with a number of traditional motifs in film and literature, focusing on versions and references in popular culture. My interest in cultural pedagogy from a feminist perspective leads me to ask, what do my students learn from fairy tales and fairy tale films, and how do these texts inform their understanding of socialization relating to sexuality, gender, race, and class differences? In particular, what do fairy tales teach girls and women about femininity, and how do these stories reinforce or subvert broader cultural concepts about gender and sexuality? Marina Warner calls this implicit pedagogy the "suspect whiff of femininity" in fairy tales (1994, xiv). How do contemporary revisions,

---

1   I assume that readers have a working knowledge of the origins, histories, and definitions
     of fairy tales. For recent overviews of fairy tales and the challenge of defining them,
     see Kevin Smith (2007) and Zipes (2007). Like Marina Warner, I focus on tales that
     center on familial relationships, especially those that deal with marriage, romance, and
     the notion of a "happy ending" (1994). With her I am interested in their construction
     of gender.

including literary and film versions, challenge or reinforce this "suspect whiff" and the feminine ideals it engenders?

This chapter explores these ideas in the light of contemporary feminism and the increasing popularity of postfeminist ideology. In my classroom, I employ the term *cultural pedagogy* to refer to the ways that my students learn about gender, race, class, and other social characteristics through their representations in literature, film, visual art, and popular culture media such as television, advertizing, magazines, and the Internet. Feminist theory, in developing feminist cultural pedagogy, approaches these images with a critical eye. If the gendered values of fairy tales inform and are informed by Euro-North American cultural pedagogy, how do my students respond to them? How do contemporary versions of fairy tales in film complicate these readings, and what challenges do they raise in the classroom?

In answering these questions, I focus primarily on Angela Carter's wolf stories in *The Bloody Chamber and Other Stories* and the 1984 film adaptation, *The Company of Wolves*, cowritten by Carter and Neil Jordan. I contend that reading Carter's work as antifeminist and reinforcing the patriarchal constraints of the genre is a misunderstanding of her complex intent.[2] Indeed, using the stories and film in a classroom context allows the possibility for a deeper understanding of Carter's feminism and challenges the postfeminist ideology that many students use as a referential framework.[3] Similarly I see Jordan's film as an example of the complexities of Carter's feminist politics.[4]

---

2   See Joseph Bristow and Trev Lynn Broughton (1997) and Lucie Armitt (1977) for an analysis of Carter's reflections on feminism and an overview of critical debates about reading her work as feminist. Both cite Duncker (1984) as a critic who considers fairy tales to be inherently patriarchal and sees Carter's adaptations as reinforcing this ideology. Cristina Bacchilega challenges Duncker's reading and suggests that Carter avoids a simple rejection of oppressive ideologies that may exist in fairy tales and, instead, acknowledges and confronts patriarchal attitudes by exploring fairy tales' "'several existences' as a genre in history, as well as its stylized configurations of 'woman'" (1997, 52).

3   The term *postfeminism* often refers to a body of analyses and theories that challenge and critique much of the work of feminism's so-called second wave. It is often confused with third-wave feminist politics. I use the term in the sense that emerged in the 1980s and 1990s with the backlash that considers feminism outdated, irrelevant, and unnecessary. See Natasha Pinterics (2001) for a discussion of the problem with the "waves" distinction and a clarification of postfeminism's relationship to recent feminist thinking.

4   I differ with critics such as Sara Martin (2001) and Carole Zucker (2000).

Fairy Tales in the Classroom and the Possibilities of Feminist Pedagogy

I teach fairy tales, Carter, and Jordan in a course entitled "Women in Literature." A service course at the university—rather than one directly linked to a disciplinary major—it is described as an introductory survey of "literature by and about women." It fulfills the basic literature requirement for any undergraduate degree. Although listed as a women's studies course, it is not required for a major or minor in the department. However, most majors and minors do take it. But as it is one of the few year-long courses and is taught annually, the majority of students are there to fulfill a credit requirement and have no background in either literature or women's studies. Many express their wariness of women's studies and, more so, the idea of feminism. Understandably they fear their peers will mock them for taking a course that can be dismissed as ideology, not academics, but they also resist associating with a philosophy they misunderstand as a polemic.

Of course, some students in every class do not fall into this category and are taking the course *because* it is women's studies. Often proud feminists, these individuals seek to learn about the discipline itself. However, in the six years that I have been teaching this course, those who identify themselves as feminists are in the minority. Indeed, the majority are more comfortable with varying forms of postfeminism. This group includes the students to whom I refer throughout this chapter.[5]

A "postfeminist theater"[6] of covert feminism is part of my teaching because many students accept the postfeminist rhetoric that feminism has met its goals and there is nothing left to fight for. Alternatively, some subscribe to the postfeminist logic that "one might now affirm that one was indeed a feminist, but feel no need to lay claim to this as a significant political identity" (Whelehan 2005, 159). I risk alienating or losing them entirely if I come across, at least initially, as an overt feminist. I need to be aware—as Susan Faludi (1991), Rita Felski (2003), Imelda Whelehan

---

5   I am not creating a rigid dichotomy between students who identify themselves as feminists and those who don't. Many fall in between, and others do not define themselves in relation to feminism at all.

6   This term comes from Canadian journalist Jennifer Wells (2008). She uses it to refer to powerful public females who, to remain popular, must avoid promoting their feminist agendas overtly. Unlike postfeminism per se, which uses feminist rhetoric to advance a backlash approach, postfeminist theater incorporates postfeminism as a means to advance a feminist agenda.

(2005), and others have discussed—that postfeminism plays a central role in the backlash against feminism. In this context, feminism as an overall philosophy uses the feminist politics of the second wave as its only possible referent.[7] As Faludi points out, much of this ideology is based on the idea that "the very steps that have elevated women's position have actually led to their downfall" (quoted in Loudermilk 2004, 7). Mass media claims that feminism is dead while simultaneously using it as its "favorite punching bag" (Valenti 2007, 11). Thus, in these students' eyes, to be a feminist is to be outdated, shrill, and "anti-everything" (Ibid., 6).

Yet postfeminism carries out its backlash in feminism's name, and postfeminists "use feminist rhetoric to advance their agenda" (Loudermilk 2004, 7).[8] Similarly many mainstream films using fairy tale motifs and stories and marketed toward a teenaged and early-twenties female audience appear to draw on feminist ideals. For example, *She's All That* (directed by Robert Iscove, 1999), *Ten Things I Hate about You* (directed by Gil Junger, 1999), *A Cinderella Story* (directed by Mark Rosman, 2004), and *Ever After* (directed by Andy Tennant, 1998) play on the theme of a Cinderella-style rags-to-riches story and represent young women at pivotal points in their lives, faced with difficult and challenging choices.[9] Yet these characters' ambitions are invariably derailed when romantic dilemmas supersede them. While

---

7   Second-wave feminism—often characterized by the catch phrase "the personal is political"—refers to action and awareness centered on women's rights from the 1960s to 1980s. In most of Europe and North America, it evolved alongside student and antiwar protests and the civil rights movement. Largely an activist and consciousness-raising movement, but supported by the development of feminist theory and women's studies departments in universities, it focused on women's sexual freedom, reproductive rights, legalizing birth control and abortion, and equal pay. In addition, it raised awareness about domestic violence, sexual harassment, and violence against women (Code 2000, 209). Recent feminist writing has criticized the second wave for being classist, heterosexist, and racist. Many feminist groups have worked to create more diversity within the larger movement, yet second-wave feminism remains the best known and most often referenced feminist movement. For more on the feminist movement and the specifics of second-wave politics, see Lorraine Code (Ibid.).

8   For more on the backlash against feminism, see Faludi (1991). Kim Loudermilk explores this phenomenon in terms of feminist writing (2004). Similar arguments are found in Whelehan (2005) and Felski (2003).

9   Christy Williams's analysis of *Ever After* in this volume argues that the film—celebrated by critics as a feminist revision of Cinderella—actually presents a narrow version of feminism with few alterations of the original's patriarchal vision. Its postfeminist position doesn't address the realities of contemporary feminism or its place in the lives of its intended audience of girls and women. Rather than challenging fear of feminism, *Ever After* placates it.

these films may have active, engaged, and smart heroines, they ultimately prioritize romantic, heterosexual love and standard norms of beauty as the most prized achievements their characters—and by implication their audiences—can hope for. These are the fairy tale visions that my students are most familiar and, seemingly, most comfortable with. They accept the films' representation of girls and young women as having an endless range of wonderful options from which they may freely choose. They may be able to identify the gender, class, race, and other limitations of these ideas, but they still seem to accept them as the norm.

It is within this context that I teach Angela Carter's work and *The Company of Wolves* in a section called "Little Red Riding Hood and Wolves." We explore the archetypes and representations of gender in various versions of "Little Red Riding Hood" (ATU 333), most commonly those of Charles Perrault ([1697] 1961) and Jacob and Wilhelm Grimm ([1812] 1981), compared to Carter's three wolf stories and the film. In six years of teaching these texts to undergraduates, I have yet to encounter a student who has seen *The Company of Wolves* before viewing it in my classroom. Usually all have seen the films I've already mentioned as well as most Disney fairy tale films. How, then, does Angela Carter fit into their cultural pedagogy?

Fairy Tales as Femininity: The Possibilities of Fairy Tales as Feminist Pedagogy

At the beginning of every semester, I ask my students to fill out a questionnaire about why they chose to take my class. Inevitably at least half say that they are excited about the chance to read and study fairy tales. I teach literary fairy tales and written versions of traditional oral stories in the context of their form and function as written texts but also as part of cultural pedagogy. We explore contemporary and feminist versions and examine the use of archetypes and the representations of women, female desire, and agency.

Fairy tales are part of most of my students' reading background but also their viewing history. Many know these texts through the collections of the Brothers Grimm or the literary fairy tales of Hans Christian Andersen. Some are also familiar with other collections and writers. But most know fairy tale through film, especially the Disney versions. For this generation of students, Disney is synonymous with fairy tales. Unfortunately, this equation not only limits their understanding of the genre's rich and diverse history but also establishes a specific type: a formula that they come to expect and desire. As Jack Zipes points out, "The reception of folk and fairy tales in the Western world (and to a great extent throughout the world) has been heavily influenced by the Walt Disney industry and other similar corporations so that most people have preconceived notions of what a fairy tale is and should be" (1979, 105). The Disney model also instills a conventional and stereotyped idea of the way gender is constructed in these texts. Even students who can identify and critique social constructions of gender in other genres and media resist judging fairy tales: they are untouchable.

The Disney Studios began mass-market commodification of fairy tales during the 1930s. The company, always at the forefront of animation, prioritized new technological advances over "the narrative depths of the fairy tale" (Zipes 1997, 94). Disney standardized the formula for fairy tale films by entrenching a recognizable and pervasive brand (Ibid., 92). Features that appear in every film include music and songs that reveal the characters' inner thoughts; the sequential plot that relies on a woman/girl being rescued by a worthy man; the inevitable resolution based on heterosexual marriage or betrothal; and the secondary characters, usually funny animals, who inform and elaborate this primary narrative and guarantee its outcome (Ibid., 95).[10]

Many students think that this formula has evolved over time. They see the gender depictions in earlier works as laughably dated, but they contend that more recent Disney films can be read as feminist. Yet, as Zipes argues, many new developments actually result from advances in animation rather than a change in the formula. The films may appear to be more in step with current mores and ideology, but what lies beneath is still the "well-ordered, clean world in which evil is always recognizable and good takes the form of a male hero who is as dependable as the phallic principles that originally stamped the medium of animation at the beginning of the twentieth century" (Zipes 1997, 92). Now, as then—as Linda Pershing and Lisa Gablehouse indicate in their discussion of *Enchanted* (directed by Kevin Lima, 2007) in this volume (see also Cristina Bacchilega and John Rieder's article in this anthology)—Disney films sell the ideology they have always espoused. Despite the inclusion of strong women, female warriors, liberal feminists, and powerful, magical girls, Disney and most mainstream contemporary fairy tale films ultimately send the same postfeminist message: women can

---

10   Zipes explores this formula up to *The Lion King* (directed by Roger Allers and Rob Minkoff, 1994), but it equally applies to the films that followed.

be all of these things as long as they ultimately conform to social norms of heterosexual marriage.[11]

Audiences are familiar with the structures and expectations of fairy tales; those things are what makes them so readily recognizable. "The existing canon indicates a central fact about the study of fairy tales: we cannot help but know what a fairy tale is before we know what a fairy tale is" (Martin 2006, 15). Ann Martin's idea of "intuitive cultural knowledge" (Ibid.) is evident when my students discuss different versions of fairy tales they recall from their childhoods, which encompass diverse cultural and literary backgrounds. As Marina Warner points out, much of this intuition is linked to very limited knowledge of gender roles, domesticity, female sexuality, female heroism, and femininity (1994, xiv). Further, these narrow structures are reproduced and rewritten into Disney films and contemporary popular culture and media. So what does it mean when students intuitively understand a cultural text that is created within such narrow and oppressive gender frameworks?

Warner suggests that the complexities of fairy tales and the richness of their histories have been erased by companies like Disney and its affiliates, who have "naturalized" specific versions of fairy tales through images and texts "with certain prejudices and values deeply instilled" (1994, 416). She says that

> the misogyny present in many fairy stories—the wicked stepmothers, bad fairies, ogresses, spoiled princesses, ugly sisters and so forth—has lost its connections to the particular web of tensions in which women were enmeshed and come to look dangerously like the way things are. The historical context of the stories has been sheared away, and figures like the wicked stepmother have grown into archetypes of the human psyche, hallowed inevitable symbols, while figures like the Beast bridegroom have been granted ever more positive status. . . . The danger of women has become more and more part of the story, and correspondingly, the danger of men has receded. (Ibid., 417)

This naturalization of a cultural approach is precisely why I teach fairy tales and focus specifically on ones with plots that center on marriage and

---

11   Exceptions to the pattern of postfeminism defining fairy tale film discussed in this volume include the independent production of *The Juniper Tree* by feminist director Nietzchka Keene (1990; see Pauline Greenhill and Anne Brydon's chapter); Guillermo del Toro's *Pan's Labyrinth* (2006; see Cristina Bacchilega and John Rieder's article and Tracie Lukasiewicz's chapter), *Eyes Wide Shut* (directed by Stanley Kubrick, 1999; see Sidney Eve Matrix's analysis), and the works of Tim Burton (see Brian Ray's article).

family. Indeed, these are the narratives usually reproduced in the most popular contemporary fairy tale films. Fairy tales offer my students a way to look at the realities and complexities of gendered experience through texts that appeal to their sense of nostalgia for wonder and enchantment: students recognize them as part of their cultural pedagogy. But the contemporary versions that are also part of their learning are steeped in sexism that teaches them, as Warner says, that this cultural patterning is "the way things are" (Ibid., 417).

This preconception often creates a dilemma in the classroom. Many students voice their frustration at not knowing what they are supposed to feel about certain stories. For example, they often cite Belle in Disney's *Beauty and the Beast* (directed by Gary Trousdale and Kirk Wise, 1991) as a character who is special because she appears to be Disney's first and strongest feminist character. However, they can also read the film in the light of critics such as Zipes and Warner, who identify Belle as constructed within limited feminist frameworks that may reinforce sexist constructions of gender. So, they ask, should this critique prevent them from enjoying the film or liking Belle's character? Is Belle feminist or not? Is Disney antifeminist? Are they antifeminist if they enjoy the film? Much of the reason for these concerns relies on feminism being understood as dichotomous and one dimensional. If, as I contend, there is more than one way to define feminism—both for the students and the characters they study—these questions become less divisive and the answers more complex and compelling.

The students' questions illustrate one of the dangers of postfeminism: feminism's complexities, diversities, and realities get lost in ideology. If students must distance themselves from a feminism that is now perceived as irrelevant, many fear that reading fairy tales within feminist frameworks must inevitably result in the conclusion that all fairy tales are bad and sexist and should therefore be avoided. Instead, I try to lead my classes toward the realization that there are multiple ways to understand feminism and reading fairy tales from feminist perspectives does not mean that they cannot enjoy them. Indeed, such readings can actually enhance students' appreciation of the films.

However, I also want to draw students' attention to the ways that many contemporary fairy tales and fairy tale films reinforce narrow frameworks and socially constructed ideas about femininity, sexuality, and beauty, as well as suggest that heterosexual marriage should be young women's sole desired goal. As Warner says, these representations undermine both the inherent complexities and any possible feminist readings of traditional fairy tales (1994, 416). Instead, such concepts reinforce oppressive ideals of gender.

So how can students in a feminist classroom read Carter? Can her work become part of the same cultural pedagogy that most contemporary fairy tale depictions in film and television currently occupy, or does her work offer possibilities for feminist interpretation? My observations suggest that Carter occupies a place that is almost too feminist for students. They are more comfortable with seeing her work reinforce sexist stereotypes than with contemplating the possibility that she challenges both narrow feminist and antifeminist constructions of femininity and female sexual desire.[12] On the other hand, they are quick to embrace other class material—such as the film *Ginger Snaps* (directed by John Fawcett, 2000) and the television series *Buffy the Vampire Slayer* (created by Joss Whedon, 1997–2003)—as feminist examples of the way archetypes and images can be rewritten and retold in contemporary contexts. But even here, their analysis too often falls victim to postfeminist ideology.

I suggest that students are drawn to these images precisely because they erase any discomfort with feminism by reasserting the characters' relationship to the feminine in recognizable ways. Buffy uses her physicality for purposes other than simply to attract cute boys. However, she does so within conventional accepted frameworks of femininity. Buffy never fails to remind the audience that though she is the slayer, violently and mercilessly dispatching vampires and demons, she is also desirable to boys and constantly makes references to things traditionally associated with the feminine, such as shopping, clothing, and shoes; these are as much a part of her daily routine as saving the world. She stands up to male, adult authority figures' and vampires' aggression without fear but also without losing one iota of her conventional attractiveness—to boys and her audience.

Ginger, on the other hand, personally critiques attempts to restrict and define her sexuality, but she is apparently punished for it. She is initially defined against traditional conventions of beauty and, therefore, is an outcast in her high school. During her transformation, she begins to embrace a feminine sexuality that is appealing to boys and problematically

---

12   As discussed by Kimberly J. Lau, Carter's work exemplifies "an alternative erotics located in the very infidelities to the usual, enchained erotic" (2008, 77). She argues that "women writers seem to have found in fairy tales a means of rearticulating women's sexual agency by drawing attention to their/our positioning within a culture that fetishizes young girls as objects of sexual desire" (Ibid., 79).

associated with the animal/monster she becomes. The horrendous alteration of her body and mind eliminates any possibility of individual action or personal choice. Her werewolf nature entirely consumes her. In contrast, Carter's constructions of femininity and sexuality are both recognizable and unrecognizable to my students because she refuses to conform to one static notion or dichotomy of either femininity or feminism. Thus, her work is crucial to my class's analysis of gender and archetypes in fairy tales.

Ann Martin invokes "popular metaphors: 'a wicked stepmother'; 'a Cinderella story'; 'a fairy tale ending'" (2006, 15). The latter centrally relates to many of the texts that we address in class that end in marriage or betrothal. They assert that marriage is every young girl's happily-ever-after. That this univocal conclusion has become the touchstone of most contemporary fairy tale films is the reason I choose to teach *other* fairy tales that also have young women's comings-of-age, marriage, and family as their central plots but resolve them in different ways. For example, stories in Carter's *The Bloody Chamber and Other Stories* employ similar plots, but they challenge the equation that happily-ever-after equals heterosexual marriage.

In an essay about the influence fairy tales had on her writing, Midori Snyder discusses heroines who were active, courageous, and smart:

> They were certainly a far cry from the "waiting-to-be-awakened" girls
> or the girls expected to be fitted with a shoe, a prince, and a future
> all at the same time. Yet even in their plucky natures and heroic
> tales, there was still something that troubled me. Perhaps it was the
> assumption of happily-ever-after, or at least the seeming surrender
> of all that reckless adventure. Their rites of passage completed, the
> journey to find a husband over, there was an expectation that these
> young women would settle once again into neatly defined roles and an
> untroubled routine. (2002, 325)

Carter's work similarly allows students to deconstruct the way the apparently neatly defined roles work in traditional tales but also opens up a discussion about the complexities of feminism and postfeminism and breaks down dichotomies and stereotypes concerning female sexuality, agency, and women's happily-ever-afters.

Angela Carter in the Classroom

Carter's stories and Jordan's film serve multiple and diverse ends in the classroom. First, I want my students to be aware of Carter's dialogue with traditional versions of "Little Red Riding Hood." This interaction occurs in the film—collaboratively written by Carter and Jordan—through the many references to Carter's story and Perrault's version of the fairy tale.[13] The film and story also both refer to oral storytelling traditions, particularly passing down stories through generations of women. In the film, the young girl Rosaleen (Sarah Patterson) is portrayed as a heroine. Curious, self-aware, fearless, she refuses to deny her emerging sexuality or allow herself to become part of a traditional narrative of punishment or victimization, thereby encouraging the viewer to do the same. Though the film and story endings differ, the former still references Carter's larger body of work and her feminist politics.

Second, both Carter and Jordan disrupt the traditional rites of passage for young women often found in family- and marriage-centered fairy tales. They do so through Rosaleen's relationships with her male peers and the huntsman/werewolf (Micha Bergese) and also her relationship with her mother (Tusse Silberg). Rosaleen unconventionally rejects traditional courtship rituals and, instead, acts on her own desires with the hunter/werewolf. And, at the same time, she challenges the assumption that her rite of passage requires severing the bond between mother and daughter. The result is a narrative that allows Rosaleen to act on her own choices with her mother's blessing.

Third, through the use of a frame story that has a contemporary version of Rosaleen dreaming of herself as Little Red Riding Hood and her transformation into a wolf, Jordan challenges the traditional negative association of women's sexuality with beastliness and, in doing so, resists the possibility of the more traditional happy ending that would have Rosaleen rescued and set on the proper path to heterosexual marriage.

Postfeminism affects the way some of my students view *The Company of Wolves.* Because they are more at ease with contemporary depictions of fairy tale motifs in film and television than with Carter, their reactions vary. They may see it as a horror film, a comedy, and/or an adaptation that simply doesn't make sense. Indeed, there are many seemingly nonsensical aspects to Jordan's film such as giant dollhouses, oversized toys, cars out of place

---

13 Perrault's version of "Little Red Riding Hood" is just one of many intertextual references in Jordan's film. I mention it here because it is the version on which Carter's "The Company of Wolves" is based.

and time, and animals where they don't belong.[14] Carter commented that—unlike the story—the film remains curiously open ended (Martin 2001, 19). While the adaptation was a collaborative process, it was also an interpretive one. The film can be seen as a dialogue with Carter's three Red Riding Hood/wolf stories ("The Werewolf," "The Company of Wolves," and "Wolf-Alice") but also a reference to Carter's own dialogue with Perrault.

Sara Martin considers these overlapping discourses as one aspect of the film's failure. She argues that *The Company of Wolves* has no unified centre and no fundamental meaning because Jordan attempts to locate his work not only in Carter's story but also in other werewolf and horror films of the 1980s: "The problem . . . is that Jordan attempts to hold different conversations at the same time that do not quite deal with the same subject: his absorbing dialogue with Carter—a consequence of her own dialogue with Perrault—leaves little room for the innovating, daring mixture of the tale's wolf with the horror film's werewolf. In the end, the fairy tale dominates the horror film, a victory that undermines the role of the immature heroine" (2001, 30).

Martin contends that Jordan fails to allow Rosaleen to embrace completely the role of fairy tale or horror-film heroine or any subversive combination. The uncertainty of Rosaleen's location is precisely what makes the film problematic for students to accept in a feminist context because it does not clearly align itself with a feminism that they recognize. If my students and I read *The Company of Wolves* as a film that incorporates many different dialogues among genres and ideologies (traditional fairy tales, fairy tale films, adaptations, horror films, feminism, Carter, Perrault), we are forced to face our discomfort with the fact that there may not be one simple way to understand Rosaleen or her place in the world of feminist fairy tales, or one simple way to understand Carter's feminism and representation of the feminine. As the characters in *The Company of Wolves* repeat, "Seeing is believing," but in the classroom, students are often unable to believe what they see because—refusing to remain static—it challenges their preconceptions of both fairy tales and feminism.

---

14   Of course, such features are very much part of both traditional and literary fairy tales as well as fairy tale film. Consider, for example, the helicopter that brings the Lilac Fairy and the king to Donkeyskin's wedding in *Peau d'âne* (directed by Jacques Demy, 1970), or the disembodied hands that serve food to Belle in *La Belle et la bête* (directed by Jean Cocteau, 1946).

Carter's dialogue with the history of traditional fairy tales informs an understanding of its feminist underpinnings. She engages with the way these narratives explore the role of women in patriarchal contexts but also with examples that specifically detail relationships between adults. Carter says that she is interested in fairy tales that express the "latent content of stories" that are often about cannibalism, incest, bestiality, sexual desire, and female sexuality (Day 1998, 133). Aidan Day describes Carter's fairy tales as informed by psychoanalysis but "better described as materialist, rationalist 'fables of the politics of experience.' Specifically, of course, it is the gender politics and the intimately related class politics of experience that they are preoccupied with" (Ibid., 134).

However, Carter's handling of gender—along with her fascination with "female sexuality through images of passivity, violence, bestiality and sadomasochism"—often raises questions (Armitt 1997, 88). As Lucie Armitt points out, Carter has been criticized by feminist literary critics such as Patricia Duncker (1984) for her treatment of the feminine, domesticity, and other symbols that are considered part of the patriarchal content of fairy tales. The result is that "patriarchy and its constraints can be made to appear inescapable" (1997, 88). However, Armitt also rightly insists that Carter's work should not be dismissed as antifeminist. Instead, she suggests that Carter's work deals with the complexities of female desire and sexuality within patriarchal contexts (Ibid.).[15]

Hermione Lee agrees that Carter should be identified with "a feminism which employs anti-patriarchal satire, Gothic fantasy, and the subversive rewriting of familiar myths and stories, to embody alternative, utopian recommendations for human behavior," but she should never be considered "politically correct" (1994, 310, 311). Carter's dialogue with feminist discourse draws attention to the fact that feminism cannot be seen as a polemic or from a unitary perspective (Day 1998, 149-50). Her work, then, is a perfect source for *creating* feminist cultural pedagogy: teaching students feminism's heterogeneous forms. Rather than detracting from them, Jordan's film reflects these complexities. What others read as his inability to align the film successfully with one genre, my students and I interpret as an example of the enigmatic nature of Carter's work. The questions raised

---

15   Armitt deals extensively with the elements of Carter's fiction that many critics have called misogynist, such as "the enclosing effects of domesticity" and the use of the gothic in her work (1997, 88).

in my classroom about the film ultimately lead to eye-opening discussions about fairy tale film and fairy tales as cultural pedagogy.

Carter contributes to feminist cultural pedagogy through her dialogue with traditional fairy tales. Her short story, "The Company of Wolves," references Perrault's version of "Little Red Riding Hood," and her narrative reflects both the changes that he made from the original oral tale and her criticisms of them. For example, as Zipes points out, the French oral tale on which Perrault based his 1697 version presents the young girl as a capable, brave, and smart person who escapes from the wolf and "learns to cope with the world around her" (1986, 229). The original tale ends with the young girl returning home, an act that also secures her safety from the wolf because he cannot enter her house (Ibid.).[16] Zipes indicates that Perrault (and subsequently the Grimm brothers) transformed the tale into "a narrative about rape in which the heroine is obliged to bear the responsibility for sexual violation" (Ibid., 227). These narratives strip the character of Little Red Riding Hood of any agency in her sexual desires or ability to make choices free from blame or victimization. Carter's heroine challenges Perrault's construction of Little Red Riding Hood's sexuality as deviant and rape as the inevitable and deserved outcome, one that is problematically connected to her coming-of-age.

Zipes suggests that Perrault's addition of the little girl's red cape/hat not only symbolizes her coming of age with menstruation but also taints her and marks her as sinful "since red, like the scarlet letter A, recalls the devil and heresy" (1986, 230). He and other critics have paralleled the devouring of Red Riding Hood to a sexual assault. Compared to the one in the original oral story, Perrault's heroine is naïve and spoiled and thus deserves her fate. She is made to be responsible for—and even to desire—her own rape (Ibid.).[17] Carter rejects this misogynist and essential connection of blood/red/sex/violence that is supposed to shame Little Red Riding Hood. The writer reclaims her from her status as a "female object of male desire" (Zipes 1986, 229). Carter uses the red shawl to address the reality of the young girl's sexual awakening through her awareness of her body and insistence on talking about blood and menstruation as a natural process. In the story, the young girl refers to her scarlet shawl as "the color of her menses" (Carter

---

16   The original French tale can be found in Zipes (1986, 228–29).

17   For a more in-depth analysis of the literary development of sexual violence in "Little Red Riding Hood," see Zipes (1983, 1986). For an exploration of the use of the same narrative to explore pedophilia in films, see Greenhill and Kohm (2009).

1979, 117), and in the film, Rosaleen is quick to mention that her shawl is red—like blood.

Jordan also disrupts traditional rites of passage for fairy tale heroines, especially those in tales that connect coming of age to the pursuit of marriage. Rosaleen's parents tease her about the local village boy who wants to court her. They clearly assume that she will marry one of the few village boys her age. At the same time, Granny (Angela Lansbury) prepares Rosaleen for womanhood by regaling her with stories and folktales about women and werewolves, each concluding with the warning that all men are beasts and women are responsible for inciting their beastliness/lust and must bear the consequences. These stories also reinforce the expectation that Rosaleen will soon marry and, at the same time, serve as a reminder of the narrow, gendered roles and constructions of sexuality to which Granny subscribes.

However, Rosaleen rejects these traditional roles and stories. The narrative that she hears from Granny but retells to her mother and the werewolf invokes women who stray from the path and are comfortable in the forest, who are kin to the wolves, recognizing themselves in these animals' otherness. By questioning the passivity of the women in Granny's stories—at one point, referring to her sister who was killed by wolves, she asks, "Why couldn't she save herself?"—Rosaleen weaves her own versions of fairy tales and assumes the role of the female storyteller. Cristina Bacchilega says that the film reinterprets "blood-line as narrative tradition" and Rosaleen strengthens the "primarily female genealogy" through becoming a storyteller (1997, 67). She does so without losing the pleasure of telling a story but shifts her narratives away from Granny's moralizing tone.

Of course, Rosaleen does not reject the rituals of courtship completely. In fact, her curiosity leads her to test them with a walk in the woods with a village boy, even experimenting with a kiss. However, she easily tires of him and decides that she is meant for something or someone better. In making this choice and assuming that she can and will move beyond the narrow expectations of the village, Rosaleen again shifts the traditional narrative. What is important for my teaching is that Rosaleen does not reject the idea of marriage; instead, she recognizes other options. Traditional rites of passage do not define her coming of age; she defines it.

This narrative shift is also evident in Rosaleen's relationship with her mother. In Carter's "The Bloody Chamber," the narrator says that when she herself married she "ceased to be her [mother's] child in becoming his wife" (1979, 7). This comment suggests that a daughter can never go back;

the transition from childhood to adulthood relies on rejecting the parents, especially the mother, signaling women as objects of exchange between men and part of the transmission of property in a patriarchal economy.[18] In *The Company of Wolves*, in contrast, Rosaleen finds a baby doll in a bird's nest that she gives to her mother, thus making children or their avatars subject to women's exchange. This moment occurs after Rosaleen has rejected the village boy but before she embarks on her journey through the forest to Granny's house. Viewers recognize this travel as part of the traditional "Little Red Riding Hood" narrative and associate it with her transition from child to young woman.

When Rosaleen gives the doll to her mother, she relinquishes childhood but also leaves part of herself with her mother. Her act allows the possibility of her return and also continues and strengthens not only the bond between women but also the links in the female familial line. Enacting a connection with the mother is also related to the original French tale that concludes with the young girl's escape and return home. In this version, the wolf chases her but is forced to admit defeat once she is safely inside her home and thus returned to her mother's care. In many subsequent versions, however, Little Red Riding Hood is either killed or rescued. It is neither her agency nor her return home that keeps her safe. Instead, the patriarchal male hunter saves her, and sometimes also her grandmother, reinforcing his power and their weakness.[19] In *The Company of Wolves*, Rosaleen is also saved by her mother, who is able to recognize that her daughter has transformed into a wolf.

"She Knew She Was Nobody's Meat": Rosaleen's Sexuality

The young girl's "seduction" of the wolf/werewolf in the story and Rosaleen's subsequent metamorphosis into a wolf at the end of Jordan's film present troubling dilemmas to students. The relationship of female sexuality to the beastly and, further, the possibility of sex with the beast become problematic for students because they immediately associate these ideas with patriarchal constructions of female sexuality and believe Carter is perpetuating damaging images. Certainly female sexuality has long been connected with danger

18   Gayle Rubin (1975) and Luce Irigaray (1985) have most famously discussed the exchange of women.

19   Carter explores the relationship between mothers and daughters and uses the return to the mother in many of her fairy tales, most notably "The Bloody Chamber," where the mother rescues her daughter from Bluebeard (1979, 40).

and represented as uncontrollable and wild, something animalistic. But this association is precisely Carter's point. Aidan Day suggests that Carter uses animals in her stories to represent a libido and desire that are common to both men and women and fall outside traditional constructions of both male and female sexuality: "She uses the image of animals to signify a libido that has been culturally repressed in some women and which needs recognizing and articulating in order that they may define autonomous subject positions for themselves. A recognition of the materiality of the flesh is not the same as attributing particular essences to the flesh" (Day 1998, 147), as Carter's comment that "she was nobody's meat" underlines (1979, 18).

In the film, this signification is particularly evident in the way that seeing functions. *The Company of Wolves* effectively subverts the male perspective. According to Laura Mulvey, in classic Hollywood films, "pleasure in looking has been split between active/male and passive female" where women are "simultaneously looked at and displayed," connoting a "to-be-looked-at-ness" but inability to return the look (1975, 11). Mulvey's perspective has been criticized for assuming a male viewer and precluding the possibilities of female spectatorship and pleasure in viewing, but her ideas have inspired not only feminist film critics but also filmmakers.[20] In *The Company of Wolves,* Rosaleen refuses to be objectified by the werewolf or sacrifice her own desires.

First, when she encounters the hunter in the forest, she plays along with his seduction, enjoying the game, exploring her feelings with a mixture of naïvety and boldness that keeps the viewer guessing about her knowledge and experience. That Rosaleen is driven by her desires at the possible expense of her safety is disconcerting. But at the same time, she appears to be aware of her role in this "rustic seduction" (Carter 1979, 115) and gets pleasure from it. When she arrives at Granny's house and is confronted by the werewolf, she seems, again, aware of the danger. Yet she sees it as a challenge, dismissing her fear as useless. She takes control, asks him questions, and takes off her own clothes. Rosaleen is aware of her surroundings and means of escape but is also obviously drawn to the werewolf by desire and curiosity. She understands the power of her sexuality, not as an object of male desire but something pleasurable to her. Rosaleen does not use her sexuality to tame the beast or lull him into a false sense of security and escape. Instead,

---

20   Other essays in this volume address feminist film theory and seeing in more detail. See, for example, Pauline Greenhill and Anne Brydon's chapter on *The Juniper Tree* and Sidney Eve Matrix's discussion of ways of seeing in *Eyes Wide Shut.*

she discovers the pleasure in controlling her own desires and, in doing so, frees herself from male dominance (see Lau 2008, 81–88).

Catherine Lappas says that the film provides "an interesting moment for female spectatorship—a pleasurable moment in which woman acts as a distinct subject with agency and identity" (1996, 116). In the classroom, students can initially interpret Rosaleen's seduction of the werewolf as a problematic use of female sexuality to tame the beast. But they then explore this scene as a possible subversion of the woman-as-object/man-as-viewer dichotomy. Rosaleen's pleasure and her somewhat naïve and experimental approach to sexual agency and autonomy allow an interpretation of desire that falls outside the male perspective. Rosaleen controls her own body and safety. The film, then, subverts the victimization and voyeurism that Zipes says are inherent in the original tales of "Little Red Riding Hood" by allowing Rosaleen to engage actively with her desire as part of her self-identification and coming-of-age.

The ending to the film that changes Rosaleen into a wolf also troubles many in my classroom. Similarly, some critics read the conclusion as Jordan punishing Rosaleen for her active desire by transforming her into a beast. But viewers must recognize that the film is framed by a contemporary Rosaleen dreaming. The dream and real worlds collapse onto one another at the end as the dream-world wolves break through the boundary and attack Rosaleen. Sara Martin believes that Jordan's ending—supposedly written on his own and not endorsed by Carter—undermines Carter's message of female liberation. She suggests that both the metamorphosis into a wolf and the possible killing of the dreaming girl can be read as "Rosaleen's fall into monstrosity" and her subsequent punishment for her active part in her fall (Martin 2001, 20).[21] But my classes often conclude that this collapsing of frames offers the potential for a reading that reclaims female subjectivity and agency by embracing the Other within the self.[22] Specifically the abject Other survives, and Rosaleen must literally confront it.

---

21   Bacchilega agrees that the ending of the film "undoes" much of the feminist potential by punishing Rosaleen (1997, 69).

22   In feminist terminology, the association of women with the Other refers to their oppression in patriarchal societies. "Women, under oppression, are forced to deny their freedom and accommodate themselves to a life of immanence as the Other, while men claim subjectivity for themselves alone. Man is the positive, the norm, the universal; while woman is the negative, a deviation, a distortion" (Code 2000, 374).

Gina Wisker suggests that the emphasis on the self/other demonstrates Carter's fascination with horror writing and the gothic. Carter's work, as part of the history of the gothic in literature, explores the repressed and rejected Other in terms of gender (1997, 117). Wisker reads Carter's writing in relationship to abjection and dealing with opposites, such as repulsion and desire, but never privileging one over the other. Carter "shows us that . . . we ourselves produce what we most fear" (Ibid., 126).[23]

In *The Company of Wolves,* Rosaleen is the Other to her dreaming self. The dream Rosaleen fears girls like her sister, ones like her dreaming self— the passive, sleeping beauties. At the film's conclusion, Rosaleen empathizes with the werewolf, allowing him to accept the Other as part of himself. In the process, she transforms into a wolf, thereby fully embracing the Other within. The passive, sleeping heroine (significantly her bedroom is located in a decaying mansion) perhaps awakens and is possibly devoured and incorporated by her powerful, sexual, desiring Other, allowing a new under-standing of femininity, sexuality, and power. And this is Julia Kristeva's point, as described by Wisker: "By recognizing the Other and the abject as part of ourselves, we can . . . overcome the need to find victims, scapegoats, enemies" (Ibid., 126).

Saving Ourselves

In an episode of the television series *Buffy the Vampire Slayer* called "Fear, Itself," Buffy and her friends prepare to go to a Halloween party at a fraternity house on campus.[24] She is dressed as Little Red Riding Hood, but when asked what she has in her basket, she replies, "Weapons." The characters refer to a previous episode where a magic spell gone awry turned all of them into their costumes. In that installment, Buffy, dressed in a ball gown/princess outfit, instantly became helpless and afraid, unable to defend herself, and dependent on men for rescue. In "Fear, Itself," Buffy chooses to be Red because she doesn't want to be helpless again, and she correctly defines that character as a strong, independent, self-reliant woman. Even more significant is the fact that in the same episode, Buffy's mother adjusts the costume to fit her, remembering how she wore it as a little girl.

---

23   Abjection, in Kristevan terms, refers to what the body must reject to create a recognizable autonomous subject. The abject is "ejected beyond the scope of the possible, the tolerable, the thinkable" (Kristeva 1982, 2).

24   The episode originally aired in 1999: season four, episode four.

In altering the outfit for grown-up Buffy, she also changes the narrative to allow Little Red Riding Hood to evolve as a female symbol and character. While the character stands for Buffy's childhood nostalgia and the meaning of fairy tales to little girls, she is also a powerful reminder that Buffy's understanding of Little Red Riding Hood strays far from the submissive and naïve victim of Perrault's story.

This episode links Rosaleen to the adult Buffy. Buffy is a safe feminist choice for my students because her association with the feminine allows them to access her power without undermining their relationship to the heterofemininity they fear they must sacrifice to accept feminism. Irene Karras calls Buffy a "girlie feminist": she uses her femininity as a source of power, rather than embodying the typical traits of a masculine hero (2002, para. 14). Karras argues that Buffy is a successful feminist character because she embraces both the feminine and her female sexuality but does so outside of patriarchal understandings of these qualities. Like Rosaleen, Buffy's rite of passage to become a slayer happens at the onset of menstruation—her burgeoning sexuality is equated with her power. As she grows up and becomes more aware of herself as a sexual, desiring woman, she also begins to own her power, and we understand her as a traditional object of the male gaze who not only looks back but is not punished—indeed, she is rewarded—for doing so. Buffy's gaze—her percipient eye for the vampire and demon—is what makes her the successful slayer she is.

My hope, then, is to create a dialogue in the classroom between Buffy—and other characters like her—and Rosaleen so that students can understand them all as part of a feminist cultural pedagogy. Karras says that Buffy represents third wave feminists' struggle "to define their femaleness in a world where the naming is often done by the media and pop culture, where the choice for young women is to be either a babe or a bitch . . . and third wave activism builds on the second wave by focusing on the relationship of texts to one another and to the world" (2002, para. 7). Postfeminist ideology wants my students to believe that they must choose between being a babe or a feminist bitch. Many young women embrace postfeminist ideology precisely because they see feminism as devaluing the feminine (and, to some degree, the masculine). Unlike Carol Clover's "final girl"—the lone survivor at the end of the horror film whose heroic power is undermined by her status as victim of the male perspective and her association with masculine traits (as indicated by her androgynous name and figure), Rosaleen and Buffy survive without sacrificing their femininity.[25] This is where their potential for subversion lies. My students have the ability to "unlearn" and "relearn"— to ask, as Rosaleen herself does, "Why couldn't she save herself?"

---

25 Irene Karras, Sara Martin, and Catherine Lappas all discuss Carol Clover's concept of the "final girl" (1992), an androgynous and androgynously named figure in slasher films who "endures a relentless persecution that claims the lives of all those around her and that finally leads to her horrific confrontation with death, embodied by the monster, which she survives whether she is rescued by others or rescues herself" (Martin 2001, 18–19). Clover sees the final girl's victory as undermined by her association with masculinity: "her inevitable sexual reluctance, her apartness from other girls, sometimes her name . . . her unfemininity is signaled clearly by her exercise of the 'active, investigating gaze' normally reserved for males and hideously punished in females" (Clover 1992, 83). Martin counters that Clover's insistence on the final girl's victimization as key to male scopophilic pleasure does not allow for female spectatorship and undermines her role as a survivor and heroine.

9

A Secret Midnight Ball and a
Magic Cloak of Invisibility
The Cinematic Folklore of Stanley Kubrick's *Eyes Wide Shut*

Sidney Eve Matrix

> *He placed himself out of the way in a corner, admiring the grace and beauty of the princesses. Their loveliness was of every kind. With what eagerness they danced!*

"The Twelve Dancing Princesses,"
Jacob and Wilhelm Grimm [1812] 1890[1]

THIS CHAPTER DEMONSTRATES THE INTERTEXUAL RELATIONSHIP between Stanley Kubrick's final film, *Eyes Wide Shut* (1999), and the international fairy tale known as "The Twelve Dancing Princesses" (ATU 306)—also variously called "The Worn-Out Dancing Shoes" and "The Secret Ball."[2] I argue that approaching *Eyes Wide Shut* through the analytic lens of its borrowings from ATU 306 illuminates the film's central themes of desire, duplicity, and power as classic tropes with a decidedly modern twist. As the case of *Eyes Wide Shut* attests, the age-old story of the disobedient, undomesticated female has considerable cultural elasticity, remaining relevant today as a

---

1   I use the SurLaLune Web site as a source because of its ready availability as well as its aggregation of different versions across media forms from literature and film, including popular interpretations and variations.

2   In this chapter, I refer to a Portuguese version of ATU 306, "The Shoes That Were Danced to Pieces." It is among dozens of variants included on the Web site SurLaLune Fairy Tales, maintained by Heidi Anne Heiner (http://www.surlalunefairytales.com). Cristina Bacchilega and John Rieder similarly consider gender ideology in fairy tale films in their article in this volume. See also Jennifer Orme's (forthcoming) consideration of Jeanette Winterson's riff on ATU 306 in her novel *Sexing the Cherry*.

cautionary tale about the perceived threat of female agency and sexuality to the maintenance of patriarchal cultural arrangements and, correspondingly, men's convoluted and misguided attempts to control and dominate women and girls (Bacchilega 1997). A closer look at the details of both *Eyes Wide Shut* and "The Twelve Dancing Princesses" reveals each to be a story about the enigma of female desire, the difficulties of domesticity, and the challenge of marital fidelity for both genders.

Eyes Wide Shut

> Bill: *Women don't, they basically just don't think like that.*
> Alice: *If you men only knew.*
>
> conversation between the Harfords—husband and wife—in *Eyes Wide Shut*

Stanley Kubrick and Frederic Raphael adapted the screenplay of *Eyes Wide Shut* from a novella by Arthur Schnitzler titled *Dream Story (Traumnovelle)*. Numerous commentators (including Acevedo-Munoz 2002, Hensher 1999, and Alison 2003) have described the relationship between the 1999 film and its 1926 literary source as a largely faithful, if modernized, adaptation. The narrative of *Eyes Wide Shut* reproduces Schnitzler's story line—although Kubrick added scenes and characters and shifted the setting from 1920s Vienna to 1990s New York. As any artist knows, an adaptation is generally received and reviewed by those aware of its source in light of whether it does justice to, or improves upon, the original. In the case of *Eyes Wide Shut,* most critics in the popular press initially panned the film, criticizing its casting, production design, screenplay, and most (if not all) of the innovations that deviated from *Dream Story.* Subsequently a second wave of reviewers—largely academic—provided in-depth analyses of the strengths and weaknesses of *Eyes Wide Shut* and its engagement with Schnitzler's work, considered the film as part of Kubrick's oeuvre, and assessed it in light of the auteur's death immediately after its completion.

I will reference and integrate some of the insights from both the academic and journalistic assessments as I extend this critical engagement with Kubrick's film in a different direction by considering its intertextual relationship to a different, mainly European story—namely ATU 306. My intention is not to suggest that *Eyes Wide Shut* is a faithful recreation of this tale, nor to claim that the film is straightforward fairy tale cinema, but rather to indicate that through the use of a series of parallel motifs, the film accomplishes a compelling modern resuscitation of the tale—however accidentally. In so doing, *Eyes Wide Shut* gains the status of cinematic folklore.[3] By identifying a suite of folkloric motifs linking ATU 306 and *Eyes Wide Shut*, this chapter illustrates the transmediality that is characteristic of cinematic folklore—the tropic borrowings, recombinations, and reaccentuations of traditional material inherent in fairy tale film adaptations (Stam 2004, 25). This analytic approach adds a layer of significance to Kubrick's work, which may contribute to an appreciation of its generic and cultural impact and lasting resonance while, at the same time, developing a more nuanced understanding of the qualities that comprise the genres of cinematic folklore and fairy tale film.

Before going further, I should summarize the general plot of *Eyes Wide Shut,* a film about desire and fantasy but more specifically about the often-unsuccessful, unsatisfying containment of male and female sexuality within the institution of marriage. The hero, Dr. William "Bill" Harford (Tom Cruise), is a lousy husband who has become immune to his wife's beauty and grown complacent about their sexual exclusivity. Blind to Alice's (Nicole Kidman) attractiveness, Bill takes her commitment to monogamy for granted, admitting that he has never felt jealous or worried about losing his wife because they are married and in love and have a child. To convince Bill that women—even wives who love their husbands and children—indeed have complex sexual desires and needs that may put stress on a monogamous marriage, Alice confesses her illicit fantasies about sex with a stranger. Her goal is to enlighten her husband and get his attention when she reveals that in fact just last summer, she flirted with the idea of leaving him to run off with a sexy sailor she glimpsed at a seaside resort while they were on vacation. This storytelling is intended to penetrate her husband's ballooning

---

3   *Eyes Wide Shut* can also be considered cinematic folklore insofar as it participated in the kind of cultural storytelling typical of paparazzi-fueled tabloids. Reviewers widely suggested that in casting the real-life couple Nicole Kidman and Tom Cruise, Kubrick was banking on some of the massive cultural fascination with A-list actors' lives. In this sense, the furor over sexually explicit and nude scenes in *Eyes Wide Shut* is connected to the audience's voyeuristic desires for a glimpse at the chemistry between these celebrities as the camera penetrates the sanctity of the (albeit fictional) marital bedroom—a desire the trailers for the film invited and exploited. Because it stoked the fires of the celebrity machine, *Eyes Wide Shut* is a popular culture production that functions as contemporary cinematic folklore in its own right. For more on the public's voyeuristic fascination with Kidman and Cruise, see Pocock (2000). For more on the relationship between popular culture and folklore, see Narváez and Laba (1986).

arrogance and neglectful attitude, and it finds, but overshoots, its mark; Alice's shocking revelation sends Bill into a tailspin crisis of masculinity that lasts three days.

Leaving Alice behind at home—enclosed in the world of domesticity and child care (she is pictured in the kitchen and mothering her daughter in numerous scenes), off goes Bill into the New York night on a journey that is both literal and psychological. For the next two hours, the film follows Bill as he seeks to come to grips with this seemingly new information about the nature of female sexuality and understand and accept what it means for his marriage and his manhood. His pride wounded, Bill contemplates revenge against Alice for her imaginary affair with the naval officer and opts to experiment with sexual infidelities of his own.

Prowling through the dark city streets, Bill fends off the inappropri-ate amorous advances of two women (first, his client and then, an under-age girl); he then dallies with a prostitute and finally bluffs his way into a late-night orgy—from which he barely escapes unharmed. After indulging in some seriously dangerous voyeurism, flirting, fantasizing, and foreplay (though not coitus), coupled with several awkward and agonizing erotic entanglements and guilt-ridden soul searching, a confused and exhausted Bill returns home. The next day he learns that two of the women he sought for intimate (albeit unconsummated) encounters are literally *femmes fatale*: one has overdosed on drugs and died, and the other has contracted HIV.[4] The links among sex, women, and death could not be clearer, and Bill is traumatized, seeking refuge in his imperfect, but comparatively safe, mar-riage. After confessing his digressions to Alice, their relationship is shaken and transformed but ultimately set on a course of repair. The film con-cludes with scenes of the couple and their uncomfortable, unsettled, and unconvincingly happy ending—Bill and Alice bound together in suffocat-ing security.

---

4   Incidentally, as Andrews (2006, 64) observes, the sex/violence theme was connected to a kind of "sex-fear" in the 1990s golden era of erotic thrillers, a fear of feminism and AIDS. Predictably, then, when Kubrick's film directly employed these two terrifying specters, the critical response from audiences was mixed between those who believed the film was a pro-feminist critique (see for example Whitinger and Ingram 2003; Acevedo-Munoz 2002; Alison 2003) and those who thought it was simply misogynistic and exploitative (see for example Decter 1999; Denby 2000; Saur 2001).

Each Night, Locked in by Triple Bolts, Each Morning, Danced-Out Shoes

When they were asked what they had been doing all night, they always answered that they had been asleep; and, indeed, no noise was ever heard in the room, yet the shoes could not wear themselves out alone!

"The Twelve Dancing Princesses"

Numerous collectors published ATU 306 in a number of variants, so for my purposes, I have assembled an overview of the narrative twists and turns from versions in the Russian, French, and German traditions—as they are reproduced on the SurLaLune Web site.[5] The story goes this way: Once upon a time, a king has several daughters whose dancing slippers appear mysteriously worn out each morning, though—to the best of the father's knowledge—they do not venture outside their bedchambers at night. The confused royal parent offers a reward to whoever can solve the mystery of the danced-out shoes. The hero (Michael, the stargazer, a cowboy) volunteers his service to the king. Unbeknownst to the princesses, Michael follows one night as they sneak down a secret staircase to an underground world. Hidden in a magic cloak of invisibility, the hero watches the princesses arrive at an enchanted castle, where they dance with a collection of male partners until dawn. Before departing, Michael pockets a token from the underground world as proof that he has successfully unraveled the mystery of the princesses' danced-out shoes. He keeps the secret for three days, following the princesses to indulge his voyeurism each night. The youngest princess grows increasingly suspicious and filled with the uncanny sense that someone is stalking, watching, waiting—but her sisters dismiss these anxieties. Eventually Michael presents the pilfered token to the king and his disobedient daughters as irrefutable proof of the midnight adventures and indiscretions and is rewarded with marriage to the princess of his choice—usually the youngest.

5　　As N. J. Girardot has commented, critical interpretation of a fairy tale "requires careful consideration of the different variants of a single tale type," and doing so "presents us with many interesting transformations and substitutions" while also identifying "the basic frame of formulaic form, main events, and episodic sequence" of a tale (1977, 279). Here Girardot is borrowing from Alan Dundes (1965). The SurLaLune Web site offers the Grimm text plus seventeen "similar tales across cultures," which I draw upon, and seventeen "modern interpretations" (http://www.surlalunefairytales.com/twelvedancing/index.html).

Fairy Tales for Adults

And I knew you could see me in the arms of all these men.

Alice Harford, *Eyes Wide Shut*

Eyes Wide Shut is an erotic thriller that may at first seem very distant from the folk stories collected by the Grimm brothers, published in *Childhood and Household Tales,* and selected by Andrew Lang for inclusion in *The Red Fairy Book.* However, not all fairy tales are designed for children. Some are directed at adults, and many have psychological themes, a common one focusing on dilemmas stemming from sexual anxiety and transgressions (Jones 2002, 20). As Steven Swann Jones observes, in tales for adults, the protagonists are usually married and facing moral, emotional, and psychological difficulties associated with their life together—such as anxieties about fidelity, child raising, domestic finances, or communication (Ibid., 25). In fact, according to Jack Zipes, many of the best-known fairy tales are stories that describe how agonizingly complicated or seemingly impossible it is to change or curb natural instincts, including sexual desires (2006b, 131).

Moreover, even the graphic nudity and sexual scenes that threatened to earn Kubrick's film a much-dreaded NC-17 rating are not necessarily out of place in the fairy tale tradition.[6] As many folklorists have noted, anyone encountering the classic versions of tales collected by Perrault or the Grimms will be shocked at the rawness there—sex and violence are key elements of many of them. In well-known stories—ranging from the "Cinderella"/"Donkeyskin" cycle (ATU 510) and "Little Red Riding Hood"/"The Story of Grandmother" (ATU 333) to slightly less famous tales like "Bluebeard" (ATU 312) and "The Juniper Tree" (ATU 720)— scenes of incest, cannibalism, murder (infanticide, parricide, matricide, and intimate femicide), rape, torture, bestiality, and a grab bag of other cultural taboos are commonplace (Tatar 1987).[7] Considering these thematic links among sex, danger, and violence, it does not seem far-fetched to suggest

---

6   According to the Motion Picture Association of America rating system, a film categorized as NC-17 contains what was previously called X-rated material (graphic violence and pornography). This prohibitive rating limits the media advertising and theatrical distribution of adult-only films.

7   Pauline Greenhill and Anne Brydon discuss a fairy tale film version of "The Juniper Tree" in this volume. As well, Cinderella and the glass slipper are the focus of Ming-Hsun Lin's look at princess figures in the Harry Potter series.

a generic verisimilitude between a nineteenth-century fairy tale version of
"The Twelve Dancing Princesses" and a twenty-first-century Hollywood
film such as *Eyes Wide Shut*. The connections go much further, though,
when exploring the similarities between these two narratives.

Fidelity Tests

*Women, don't give in to your sexual curiosity; men, don't permit yourself to be carried away
at being sexually betrayed.*

Bruno Bettelheim, 1976 (302)

*Don't you think one of the charms of marriage is that it makes deception a necessity for
both parties?*

Sandor Szavost, *Eyes Wide Shut*

As I have already noted, there are numerous versions of the globe-trotting
ATU 306 fairy tale, and many details vary among them. In all versions, the
hero must learn the secrets of the danced-out shoes if he wants to pass the
central and most obvious suitor test and win the princess prize and a royal
wedding. But this motif of a fidelity test plays out differently across versions,
with significant variations concerning gender, sexuality, and power. For
example, in a French variant (published by Andrew Lang in 1890, according to the SurLaLune Web site), long before the wedding, the loyalty and
love of *both* the hero and his soon-to-be-wife—the youngest princess—are
tested. Michael proves his devotion to the youngest princess by keeping her
secret adventures under wraps for three nights. By delaying his report to the
king, however, the hero puts himself at great personal risk because the other
princesses realize he knows too much and decide to set a trap and imprison
him underground. Luckily, at the last moment, the youngest princess realizes she, too, has fallen in love, and thus intervenes and saves his life—passing a suitor test of her own. This is one of several tales for mature audiences
where men and/or women must prove themselves to each other—"East of
the Sun and West of the Moon" (ATU 425A) and "Bluebeard" are other
obvious examples.

In a Portuguese variant—"The Shoes That Were Danced to Pieces"—
the suitor-test motif plays out differently again. Here the princesses fail
to demonstrate their worth and marriageability. This is evident when the

hero—who has accurately solved the mystery of the danced-out shoes and deserves his promised remuneration—instead opts out of the king's offer altogether, refusing to accept the tainted hand of any deviant princess who has danced with devils at a secret underground ball. The idea that females who have expressed their desire for freedom, romance, privacy, and adventure are dangerous and damaged goods is present in many cautionary tales about disobedient women and girls, for example "The Red Shoes" (Hans Christian Andersen) or "Little Red Cap" (ATU 333)—incidentally both these fairy tales have inspired erotic thrillers for the silver screen.[8]

It is clear that both men and women are tested for their fidelity and fitness for marriage in ATU 306. Likewise, it is equally possible for men and women to pass or fail such trials, which are at base tests of commitment, maturity, and trustworthiness. But it is best not to push the theme of sexual equity in fairy tales too far since it is also the case that the naturalness of patriarchal marriage and family structure and its sexual double standard remains unquestioned across versions of ATU 306. For example, in this story, the male hero is rewarded by inheriting the kingdom and the princess for a wife because he is adventurous and cunning. On the flip side—whether the variant is in French, Russian, Portuguese, German, or another language—the princess is punished for stepping out to indulge her feminine *jouissance*. This transgression results in her incarceration in a patriarchal marriage—though in some variants, she, too, falls in love with the hero before betrothal. Either way, however, the youngest princess may or may not desire/admire the hero—before or long after the wedding—but that is of no importance to the king. In the patriarchal home ruled by the law of the father, her fate—like that of her sisters—will be decided in negotiations between men (similar to what Gayle Rubin [1975] describes as "the traffic in women").

---

8   There are many examples of erotic-thriller fairy tale films. For example, "Little Red Riding Hood" is the back story of the pedophile crime films *Freeway* (directed by Matthew Bright, 1996), starring Reese Witherspoon and Kiefer Sutherland, and *Hard Candy* (directed by David Slade, 2005) (see Greenhill and Kohm, 2009). *The Red Shoes (Bunhongsin)* (directed by Yong-gyun Kim, 2005) also comes to mind as a South Korean folklore, horror, and erotic-thriller crossover film—one that credits Hans Christian Andersen as a writer. In a similar vein, the Japanese cyberpunk film *964 Pinocchio* (directed by Shozin Fukui, 1991) is a cult favorite erotic horror film about the terrible adventures of a lobotomized sex-puppet. Perhaps in its time, Fritz Lang's *Secret Beyond the Door* (1948) was considered an erotic psychological thriller based on the "Bluebeard" tale. For more information on this tale—its versions and interpretations—see Maria Tatar (2004).

The suitor test and the glimpse into men and women's experiences of patriarchy are key themes from ATU 306 that carry over to *Eyes Wide Shut.* The commitment of both Bill and Alice is tested by their sexual curiosities, tempting them to venture outside the bounds of marriage to satisfy their desires. At the heart of *Eyes Wide Shut* is a romantic contest where appropriate forms of sexual conduct are defined and against which male and female behaviors are measured, endorsed, rewarded, or punished as deemed appropriate (Warner 1994, 135). The audience learns early on that Alice has only imagined her infidelities—and her fantasies are just that—part of a dream story she recounts to Bill in vividly embellished detail. On the other hand, although Bill's attempted adultery is never actually consummated, the viewer watches as he kisses, gropes, grinds upon, and ogles scores of mostly naked and scantily clad women over the course of three days—behavior that, when revealed to Alice, understandably devastates her. Of course that is the intention, in part, of Bill's erotic adventure in vindictiveness—he seeks to punish Alice for her adulterous fantasies by acting out some of his own.

It becomes clear as the film follows Bill through the streets of the city that his self-assurance and marital fidelity are being tested. He is consumed with visions of Alice's dream story—they threaten to overwhelm him. It is his devastating jealousy that motivates Bill to seek out other women with the misguided idea that he can use them to free his mind from the haunting images and fear of losing his wife to another man. Had he listened more carefully to Alice's dream story, he would have learned that it concerned far more important insights into her identity than her fleeting desire, *once upon a time,* to flee with a romantic stranger. Alice recounts her realization that—after confronting and dispelling momentary fantasies of infidelity— she is even more deeply satisfied and committed to her marriage. "At that moment, you were even more dear to me," she confesses. The fact that Alice's story is a tale of successfully completing her own suitor test falls on Bill's deaf ears. Seemingly shocked to learn that women have residual sexual curiosity that is not extinguished by marital vows, a visibly shaken Bill stumbles through the night.

They Went Down, Down, Down: Midnight Revelry at an Enchanted Mansion

I need a tux, a cloak with a hood, and a mask.

Bill Harford, *Eyes Wide Shut*

Teach me how to become invisible.

Michael, "The Twelve Dancing Princesses"

"The Twelve Dancing Princesses" tells the way one man does the king's bidding through a dangerous underground voyage to a secret ball at an enchanted castle, where the princesses dance with passionate abandon in the arms of handsome masked strangers. In *Eyes Wide Shut*, an unlikely hero similarly searches for a group of legendarily beautiful women—not princesses, but (as it turns out) prostitutes. Wandering through the city, Bill runs into an old friend (Nick Nightingale, played by Todd Field) who tells him about a secret masquerade sex party later that night, and Bill becomes determined to attend it. In the film—as in the fairy tale—duplicity, discretion, and disguise are paramount, so Bill rents a cloak and mask from a costume shop.[9] The invitation-only party takes place at a magnificent mansion, where the *mise en scène* is gothic ritual as a collection of women—naked except for masks, thongs, and stilettos—wander through enormous, cavernous, candlelit rooms, engaging in exhibitionist sex acts as they are exchanged and shared among masked male guests. Bill stands on the side-

---

9 The motifs of disguise and an elegant ball also appear in a considerably more famous fairy tale, one where the protagonist passes as an insider to attend a dance at a majestic castle—namely "Cinderella" (ATU 510A). In it the lowly and persecuted heroine risks all to experience the magic of a royal fete and a waltz with the prince of her dreams. Like Michael the gardener, Cinderella's charm and beauty win her the favor of a royal suitor, and an unlikely marriage ensues between a common servant and a member of the elite—such that some variants of the story are classified as ATU 510B: "unnatural love" tales. In some variants of ATU 510, the heroine also descends from royal bloodlines but is thrown into temporary servitude because of unusually cruel, wicked, or deviant (step)parents, as in "Donkeyskin" or "All-Kinds-of-Fur," whose eponymous heroine is subject to the incestuous wishes of her father. In these tales, marriage returns the heroine to her original social class and elevates her status (from child to married woman and/or, in some cases, from exiled princess to queen). Conversely, it is clear that marriage is a ride up the class elevator for the lowly cowboy in the story "The Danced-Out Shoes."

lines, invisible in his cloak,[10] as he watches the scene, presumably with eyes very much wide open.

The potent mix of pleasure and danger that draws Bill to the intriguing underground event intensifies when he witnesses the display of absolute male dominance and female submission. Like Michael, Bill is "quite bewildered at the magnificence of the sight" (Lang 1890). Inadvertently both Michael and Bill become completely entangled in the mysterious midnight revelry they witness from the safety of their respective invisible perches. In the process of investigating the strange and wonderful happenings underground at the secret ball, each hero is progressively entranced by the sight of the extraordinary and exotic women performing with such exuberance and abandon. In dancing slippers or stilettos, as it were, the women form a powerful spectacle for the male voyeurs to consume hungrily. And yet, the more they look, the more famished each man becomes. In both film and fairy tale, the male investigators risk detection to return to the scene of the late-night carousing for a second look, and in the case of "The Twelve Dancing Princesses," Michael returns not once, but twice, to indulge in voyeurism and wonder at the sight of the lovely princesses three nights in a row. Surely these fabulous females ooze what feminist film theorist Laura Mulvey (1975) described as to-be-looked-at-ness. Of course, by extension, both the princesses and the prostitutes serve as the *femmes fatale*, a phallic female whom men desire, fear, and cannot resist, even when that longing places them in precarious positions and dangerous territories.

The burning desire to consume, possess, or otherwise intimately bond with these fantastic (and potentially fatal) women motivates both Michael and Bill to take enormous personal risks—indeed, they flirt with death to gain closer access. As Mary Anne Doane (1991) could have told these unlucky fellows (had they asked), their efforts are doomed to failure: the *femme fatale* is, at base, ultimately and exquisitely unknowable. Part of what makes the lovely, vivacious, undomesticated, and sexually expressive women in *Eyes Wide Shut* and "The Twelve Dancing Princesses" so irresistibly

---

10　Although Bill is suitably concealed at the orgy—as was Michael at the ball—both men misstep and inadvertently alert others to their trespassing. In "The Twelve Dancing Princesses," Michael carelessly treads on the princess's dress while in *Eyes Wide Shut*, Bill neglects to cover his tracks, leaving a trail of clues that signal he is not an elite club member (the taxi waiting at the gate, the receipt in his pocket from the rental shop) but, rather, an intruder. In each case, these mistakes are significant because they may very well cost the hero his life—if it is not for the woman who intervenes and saves him.

intriguing is that they remain enigmatic to the male voyeur. The spectacle of their magnificent womanliness is a masquerade, Doane explains, borrowing from Joan Riviere (1929)—a performance enacting the only source of power allowed to women under patriarchy: sex appeal.

The power of seduction wielded by beautiful women is not sufficient, however, to prevent them from being abused and controlled by the same men who exhibit intense fascination. At the orgy, the prostitutes' performance of masked hypersexuality makes the women anonymous and interchangeable objects for male pleasure—a ritualistic exaggeration of women's everyday lot under patriarchy.[11] This is a truism that Alice Harford knows and resists with futility when she confronts her husband about the normalization of women's sexual objectification at the hands of men. It is her rage at this status quo that drives her husband away and sets in motion the chain of events that culminates in his presence at the mansion. A self-fulfilling prophesy if there ever was one, Alice's outburst of frustration with everyday sexism and misogyny inspires her husband's encounters with a series of prostitutes later that same night. Yet even after indulging himself, Bill moves no closer to understanding the nature of female desire, women's lot under patriarchy, or the true social function of marriage—all things that Alice, the prostitutes, and the disobedient dancing princesses undoubtedly know deeply and intimately with every breath they take.

From Voyeurism to Violence

I don't think you realize the danger you're in now.
You can't fool them for much longer.

Masked Woman, *Eyes Wide Shut*

The enchanted castle has no more secrets for you.

Youngest Princess, "The Twelve Dancing Princesses"

In both the fairy tale and film, the fantastic/fantasy women out of bounds pose at least a mild threat to the patriarchal cultural order of things in general and the male ego in particular. The women must be placed under absolute male control—their headstrong desire subdued, their passionate

---

11   This insight belongs to Charles Helmetag's critical review of Kubrick's film, where the prostitutes are described as anonymous and interchangeable (2003, 280).

energy harnessed and safely contained by husbands, fathers, and other powerful men.[12] In the case of "The Twelve Dancing Princesses," it is (in the
first instance) a father who tries to assert his paternal dominance by tam-
ing his daughters' forbidden adventures. In the second instance, the hero/
husband systemically tracks and tames his lovely princess prize. In *Eyes Wide
Shut*, it is (in the first instance) a husband who tries to boost his male ego
through sexual conquests with anonymous women. In the second instance,
the brotherhood of men organize and attend members-only group sex parties and are responsible for the deaths of one or more of the unfortunate
prostitutes who unsuccessfully attempt to break the rules and pay with their
lives. In both the fairy tale and the film, male ownership of women is a
prominent theme.

Likewise, in both narratives, men act instinctively, defensively, even violently in response to the threat of female sexual agency. And for their part,
the women express no remorse for their wild behavior. It should come as no
surprise, then, that in the erotic thriller, several promiscuous women lose
their lives while the randy (and married) men escape relatively unscathed
from their sexual escapades. Of course, in fairy tales—as in life—the stakes
are very different for men and women where sexual transgression is concerned. As many feminist folklorists have observed, in fairy tales, no pen-
alty is too harsh for women who dare to overstep their bounds. Having
said that, it is important to note that this film and its fairy tale predecessor
both include instances where males and females are perpetrators as well as
victims of violence. From the enchanted princes trapped underground and
the attempted murder of Michael at the secret ball in "The Twelve Dancing
Princesses," to the bruises on Nick Nightingale and stalking, gay baiting/
bashing, and death threats against Bill in Kubrick's film—it is clear that
weaker men, too, are at risk in a patriarchal social system.

---

12 Nancy Tuana (1993) explains the philosophical arguments for, and historical
    conditions of, keeping women under man's control to preserve patriarchal order in
    culture, science, and religion.

Characterization and Redemption

I am ready to redeem him.

Masked Woman, *Eyes Wide Shut*

Don't drink!

Youngest Princess, "The Twelve Dancing Princesses"

As mentioned earlier, in both the fairy tale and the film, once the hero is discovered and identified as a trespasser at the ball or party, he is in grave danger. In both instances, he is saved by a woman who, in the process, sacrifices herself or her freedom. For the youngest princess in ATU 306, her choice to intervene and rescue Michael is motivated by her love for him and leads directly to their marriage. In some versions of the tale, her act initiates a string of events that ends with all of her sisters married to disenchanted princes set free from the underground ball—a massively happy ending for all concerned. Things are considerably darker and more tragic in the film—when Bill learns that the woman who tried to warn and save him turns up dead at the morgue the next day. Despite these differences, however, it is highly significant that the theme is the same: men are saved by the selfless love of a good woman.

This take-home message is a thematic staple of fairy tales such as "Six Swans" (ATU 450), Hans Christian Andersen's "The Little Mermaid," "Beauty and the Beast" (ATU 425C) and other search for the lost husband (ATU 425) and animal bridegroom (ATU 425A) tales. *Eyes Wide Shut* gives the viewer what appears to be a double dose of this fairy tale theme: the selfless prostitute saves Bill from the wrath of the orgy participants, and later his selfless wife, Alice, recommits to their marriage, rescuing Bill from his torment of jealousy and guilt. One female rescuer dies alone, the other lives on, cocooned in upscale domesticity. Why the disparity between the fates allotted to different types of women? The answer to this question becomes clearer with more reflection on the fairy tale. Especially in the Russian version of "The Secret Ball" (another variant of ATU 306), where the princesses who danced with devils are rejected by the hero as unsuitably tainted (as they are in the Portuguese version discussed above), there is evidence of the seemingly timeless sexual double standard and remarkably resilient

Madonna/whore dichotomy characteristic of this tale type, more or less intact from the Grimms to Kubrick.[13]

To be fair, all of the characters in *Eyes Wide Shut* are types: doctors and piano players, wives and mothers, pushy powerful patriarchs (like Victor Ziegler/Sydney Pollack and Sandor Szavost/Sky Dumont) and thugs, models, and prostitutes. This convention echoes fairy tales, where all the characters are types and almost invariably fall into two general categories: good or bad. Fairy tale characters are rarely ambiguous, lack psychological depth, and are relatively undeveloped. This makes the moral lessons unmistakable: the bad are punished, the good are rewarded, the lovely princess lives happily ever after, and the evil stepmother dies a terrible death. Consuming fairy tales from childhood to adulthood enables audiences to recognize these predictable tropes. However, in this instance, what works for the heavy-handed moralistic tales of children's literature does not necessarily suit adult cinematic folklore.[14]

When *Eyes Wide Shut* used character types, or caricatures, and generic simplifications common to the fairy tale to develop a deeply disturbing psychological and erotic thriller, reviewers were hugely disappointed and criticized Kubrick for his wooden characters and their lack of intensity or chemistry (Mattessich 2000; Blake 1999). They also slammed the film for what they described as its simplistic characters lacking believable personas and the actors' wooden delivery of (what sounded like) awkwardly stilted and highly staged dialogue.[15] However, looked at through the lens of fairy tale cinema, perhaps these formulaic elements make more sense. By condensing the characters into simplistic types, Kubrick creates a highly charged thriller of moral confrontation involving the pleasures and perils of sex that sharply distinguishes villain from hero(ine) (Williams 2005, 32). The result is a clear take-home message, which David Andrews elegantly distilled as *it's dangerous not to satisfy your spouse* (2006, 65).

It is not only fairy tales that contain standard character types. In other Hollywood genres, there are iconic stock characters and classic narrative strands specific to horror, sci-fi, and comedy films. Correspondingly, then,

---

13 For a discussion of Freud's Madonna/whore dichotomy and its implications, see Joyce McDougall (2004).

14 Kim Snowden's discussion of her students' difficulties with film and prose versions of Angela Carter's fairy tale revisions in this volume poses similar interpretive issues.

15 Similar criticisms were leveled at Nietzchka Keene's *The Juniper Tree,* as discussed by Pauline Greenhill and Anne Brydon in this collection.

in her study of erotic thrillers, Linda Williams (2005) describes the predictable triangulation of a bored and neglected wife; a lousy, guilty, and paranoid husband; and a generally disposable, highly sexed, and loose woman or *femmes fatale*. This configuration not only delivers sexual intrigue and dramatic tension but also supplies a recognizable cast of character types viewers expect in erotic thrillers. Kubrick followed this generic convention exactly, which might have been the problem—since his reputation as an award-winning filmmaker had raised audience expectations for cinematic innovation in his work. Moreover, it is also true that the complexity of characterization in award-winning erotic thrillers of the 1980s and 1990s—such as Alex Forrest (Glenn Close) in *Fatal Attraction* (directed by Adrian Lyne, 1987) and Catherine Tramell (Sharon Stone) and Nick Curran (Michael Douglas) in *Basic Instinct* (directed by Paul Verhoeven, 1992)—had set the bar very high for Kubrick's long-awaited contribution to the genre.

Transformation and Initiation

From a broader point of view it is what Max Luthi calls a story that is concerned with the process of human maturation, a tale that depicts some essential threatening transitional episode in personal growth and socialization.

N. J. Girardot, 1977 (280)

As soon as you were gone, it was completely different. I felt wonderful.

Alice Harford, *Eyes Wide Shut*

As Marie-Louise von Franz has noted, even fairy tales with titles featuring women, or stories that appear to be centrally concerned with a female character, are often about men and the development of their emotional maturity (1972, 2). Von Franz observes that fairy tales are usually transcribed or authored by men (though told by women in the oral tradition), and as a result, the representations of women reflect male fantasies of womanliness—or what Jungians call *the anima*.[16] Perhaps the best example of this transformation of women into sexual stereotypes occurs in Kubrick's

---

16   Of course, collection and redaction are by no means as simply gendered as this generalization suggests. Both Nina Auerbach and U. C. Knoepflmacher (1992) and Elizabeth Wanning Harries (2001) have extensively discussed women writers' fairy tale creations.

ritualistic orgy scene, where one reviewer described the masked prostitutes as "not so much real women as abstract projections of someone else's sexual desire" (Rasmussen 2001, 347).

Von Franz continues, "A feminine figure in a fairy tale with the whole story circling around it does not necessarily prove that the tale has to do with a woman's psychology. Many long stories of the sufferings of a woman have been written by men and are the projection of their anima problem" (1972, 2). The story of "The Twelve Dancing Princesses" is a case in point. It tells of two men (a father and a suitor) who join forces to restrain and rule over some willful young women. Although ATU 306 is explicitly about a dozen princesses and their slippers, it is really, of course, about the perceived threat that powerful and self-actualized women pose to patriarchal masculinities. Fast-forward a few centuries, and the story is modernized in a film about a different set of men seeking control over another group of naughty and fascinating females (some of whom are hired for sex and others who marry for sex—or so the smarmy Hungarian Sandor Szavost explains to Alice on the dance floor). In each case, the women are mere props—eye candy—whose main function is to operate as a catalyst in a story about a man's initiation into psychosexual maturity.

In fact, a common quest pattern culminating in initiation in fairy tales involves a separation (a call to adventure, a threshold crossing into an otherworldly realm), an initiation (a ritual or test, resulting in a behavioral transformation), and the hero's return (a reincorporation into society) (Jones 2002, 15). N. J. Girardot describes the importance of this pairing of quest and initiation in greater detail in fairy tales whose plots unfold from an initial prologue and problem, to a separation, through a liminal period, and then culminate in a reincorporation and epilogue—likely a happily-ever-after resolution (1977, 282). "The Twelve Dancing Princesses" follows this format exactly: a cowboy becomes a self-directed young adolescent on a mission, eventually maturing into a married man who will be king.

Eyes Wide Shut, too, follows this structure as Bill is initiated into the reality of his marriage through a journey of self-awakening. His nighttime expedition into the sexual underside of New York City is a crucial liminal and transitory experience that involves chaotic "ordeals of a physical and psychological nature" suffered by the hero in isolation from the community or family (Girardot 1977, 282). These kinds of transitions are required when the hero lacks cultural knowledge and suffers from an abundance of innocence, naïveté, or ignorance about the world, or an extreme case of disavowal—a situation that reflects exactly Bill's eyes-wide-shut approach to life, love, and human nature.[17] Girardot describes this liminal phase as "a necessary prelude to any new creation or transition in life" (Ibid., 282). Progressing from taunts of homosexuality, to the threshold of adultery, to a ritualistic orgy complete with suggestions of human sacrifice, a traumatized Bill finally makes it back to the safety of the marital bed. It is only after he survives these ordeals and tests that he is ready to participate fully in rebuilding his relationship with Alice—rather than continuing to coast through it, alternately neglecting and misunderstanding his wife.

Accustomed to seeing the world and others through a dispassionate and detached clinical perspective, Bill now has his eyes opened wide to the power and danger of sexuality—his own desire, Alice's, and that of a cast of threatening strangers (men and women) lurking outside the safe harbor of his marriage. The initiation function is coupled with a cautionary warning about the dark dangers that exist in the unknown world beyond the boundaries of marriage/family/home. This same message is directed to curious girls and young women through "Little Red Riding Hood" and Bluebeard's wife because the two tales that feature them (or at least the best-known versions) also warn about the threats to personal safety that can result from venturing into unknown and forbidden territories, woods, or chambers.[18] In "The Twelve Dancing Princesses" and *Eyes Wide Shut*, warnings are issued to both men and women prohibiting the breaching of boundaries and breaking of social taboos that may threaten the functioning of both the individual and social bodies. By describing the plights of ineffective fathers with disobedient daughters running wild and dysfunctional families with neglected wives and philandering husbands, fairy tales

---

17 According to Beatriz E. Dujovne (2004), *disavowal* involves the failure to grasp fully the meaning of what is perceived; it is a psychological defense that deflects ideas that may endanger our views of the world and the self as we know them. Dujovne develops an analysis of Bill's extreme disavowal, denial, and neuroses that accounts for the crisis of masculinity in the film.

18 In the French text of "Little Red Riding Hood," published by Charles Perrault in 1697 (http://www.surlalunefairytales.com/authors/perrault.html), the appended moral makes the warning explicit but only alludes to sexuality: "Children, especially attractive, well bred young ladies, should never talk to strangers, for if they should do so, they may well provide dinner for a wolf. I say 'wolf,' but there are various kinds of wolves. There are also those who are charming, quiet, polite, unassuming, complacent, and sweet, who pursue young women at home and in the streets. And unfortunately, it is these gentle wolves who are the most dangerous ones of all" (http://www.pitt.edu/~dash/type0333.html; see also Warner 1990).

operate as cultural pedagogy, clearly demarcating cultural values, describing appropriate rewards and punishments, and defining heroism and what counts as happiness.

No Dream Is Ever Just a Dream: Cinematic Folklore as Cultural Analysis

The effectiveness of fairy tales and other forms of fantastic literature depends on the innovative manner in which we make the basic information of the tales relevant for the listeners and receivers of the tales. As our environment changes and evolves, so too do we change the media or modes of the tales to enable us to adapt to new conditions.

Jack Zipes, 2006b (152)

Kubrick's film is a modern, gothic, fairy tale film for adults that successfully incorporates the classic narrative structure of "The Twelve Dancing Princesses" and many of its motifs, reshaping them to tell a modernized, yet timeless, story. Though probably unintentionally and perhaps unconsciously, Kubrick's erotic thriller unfolds as "an age-old folk narrative decked out in the most up-to-the-minute guise" (Schechter 1988, 15). This film offers "a centuries-old story retold in terms that are consonant with the obsessions of our age,"—namely the preoccupied fascinations with sex, secrets, and power (Ibid., 23). Both "The Twelve Dancing Princesses" and *Eyes Wide Shut* are cautionary tales that develop the themes of the duplicity of women, masculinity in crisis, the irresistibility of pleasure infused with danger, and the difficulties of marital fidelity.

At the same time that Kubrick reveals the underside of domesticity and marriage among the elite, his film manages to reposition these social institutions as fixtures. In the film, as in the fairy tale, domesticity operates as cultural scaffolding, however flawed and dysfunctional for both genders. It provides support and a foothold in ever-changing times, and it is a control mechanism for the sexuality of both genders. It is then no surprise that both stories end with the image of marriage as panacea—although to be fair, *Eyes Wide Shut* does not present an unequivocally happy ending. This may at first appear to be a significant departure from fairy tale convention, but as Lutz Röhrich notes, it is an oversimplification to suggest that every fairy tale ends happily; instead, many stories have mildly unsettling and partial resolutions—with many questions left unanswered and loose strings dangling

(1991: 209). Certainly this describes the state of affairs between Bill and Alice as the lights come up.

10

Tim Burton and the Idea of Fairy Tales

Brian Ray

AMERICAN FILMMAKER TIM BURTON HAS, FOR NEARLY TWO DECADES, performed potent countermagic to Hollywood's syrupy adaptations of fairy tales and fables. While films like *Sleepy Hollow* (1999) and *Alice in Wonderland* (2010) illustrate the extent to which he has engaged the genre, Burton's links to towering figures like Washington Irving, Jacob and Wilhelm Grimm, Marie-Catherine D'Aulnoy, Walt Disney, and others run deeper than many realize. The visionary and "slightly twisted" (Tiffin 2008, 148)[1] auteur began using fairy tales quite early, when he was still slaving during the 1980s as an underappreciated cartoonist in the dungeons of Disney Studios. Since those days, his efforts have delivered evocative interpretations of works ranging from "Hansel and Gretel" (ATU 327B) to "Beauty and the Beast" (ATU 425C). The release of a new *Alice in Wonderland* further identifies Burton as more than an occasional visitor to the shores of fairy tales. And yet, despite this growing body of work, his films have gone largely unstudied.

Although few researchers have given his films much attention,[2] Burton's distinct style begs consideration of the way this artist has spurred "transformations in the institution" of the fairy tale (Zipes 2000, xxviii). *Edward Scissorhands* (1990), *Sleepy Hollow*, and *Corpse Bride* (2005), in particular, show the way Burton has worked to break what Jack Zipes calls "the

---

1   Jessica Tiffin is not the first to consider Burton's films disturbing (2008, 148). Her whirlwind tour of his engagement with fables, folktales, and fairy tales covers every groove of his oeuvre—albeit briefly—yet, as reflected in my essay, the list of secondary sources analyzing Burton is short.

2   An exception is Marina Warner, who mentions *Edward Scissorhands* as one of many variations of tale type 425C (1994, 314). A number of other articles and books refer to Burton's relationship to fairy tales and folktales but merely in passing.

Disney spell" (1994, 95). Through consideration of these films, I advocate for Burton's place among the many directors such as "Jim Henson, Tom Davenport, John Sayles, and others . . . [who have] sought to . . . bring about new perspectives on the fairy tale and society through cinematic experimentation" (Zipes 2000, xxxi). Though Burton is often left out of this critical conversation, his films have indeed done as much or more to challenge the status quo.

Many biographical pieces on Burton acknowledge his tedious apprenticeship as a young animator with Disney Studios—countless hours spent in futile efforts to draw cuddly animals for *The Fox and the Hound* (directed by Ted Berman, Richard Rich, and Art Stevens, 1981), in addition to aborted work for *The Black Cauldron* (directed by Ted Berman and Richard Rich, 1985). His enthusiasm and energy waned considerably due to this lack of creative freedom. While employed there, Burton has said, he tended to sleep between twelve and fourteen hours a day, a fair amount of his time on the job. To trick his employers, he often dozed upright with a pen in one hand (Salisbury 1995, 10). During this sluggish period, Burton produced some short films such as *Vincent* (1982), *Hansel and Gretel* (1982), and *Frankenweenie* (1984), which enjoyed mixed success. *Frankenweenie* was praised and slated to run in theatres alongside a rerelease of *Pinocchio* (directed by Hamilton Luske and Ben Sharpsteen, 1940). Yet when this live-action short, about a reanimated dog's corpse, received a PG rating (indicating that "some material may not be suitable for children" [Reasons for Movie Ratings 2000]), it was pulled and essentially shelved.

Fortunately, *Vincent* did gain Burton some exposure, winning the Critics' Prize at the Annecy International Animated Film Festival and going on to play at festivals throughout Europe and the United States. Yet Disney executives tried (and failed) to impose their ideologies here as well, pressing Burton to glue on a happy ending where the morbid child protagonist snaps out of his gloom when his father invites him to a baseball game. The executives disliked the original ending—Vincent faking his own death so his mother will leave him alone—because it violated the studio's general tendency to represent children as docile and innocent (Hanke 2000, 41). Disney, of course, has always promoted an idealized version of adolescence that Burton's aesthetic rejects. By 1984 Burton's work had attracted the attention of Paul Reubens, who was writing the script for *Pee-wee's Big Adventure* (1985). Their collaboration enabled the frustrated filmmaker a degree of expressive independence. His enormous success with *Batman*

(1989)—described as a "violent urban fairy tale" (Hinson 1989)—landed him in a strategic position to begin experimenting with concepts and characters as he had hoped to do at Disney. Indeed, Burton would never have enjoyed such license to, say, direct a major motion picture about a boy with scissors for hands without first becoming a household name.

Edward Scissorhands

Burton's first few films all draw on fairy tale motifs to a large extent and so qualify as what Jeana Jorgensen refers to as "fairy tale pastiches" (2007, 218). But *Edward Scissorhands* (1990) is Burton's first full-length motion picture explicitly to use a fairy tale type, although he did so on a smaller scale with *Hansel and Gretel* as well as a short live-action/animated version of *Aladdin and his Wonderful Lamp* (1986). Working with and against the "Beauty and the Beast" type, *Edward* sliced through theaters the same year Disney released its own *Beauty and the Beast* (directed by Gary Trousdale and Kirk Wise, 1991) and shortly following the cancellation of Ron Koslow's immensely popular CBS television series *Beauty and the Beast* (1987–90). In Burton's film, Burbank—a suburb of Los Angeles, California—symbolizes mainstream America during the 1950s and 1960s, oft remembered as "the Eisenhower-era world of mass conformity with its standardized houses and lockstep mentality," where all were "expected to do and believe and behave the same way" (Hanke 2000, 26). Burton's interpretation of the tale type may seem haphazard, but it possesses a surprising degree of complexity, upsetting many social conventions and gender preconceptions.

The first fairy tale versions of "Beauty and the Beast" developed from the oral tradition of salon games in seventeenth-century France. Folk versions had actually circulated for hundreds of years, but folklorists attribute the first literary telling to Madame D'Aulnoy, who worked the motif of an animal or monstrous bridegroom into several stories (Zipes 1994, 25). Her tales sought to critique the decadent practices of the French elite and prescribe in their place more admirable traits, such as sincerity and fidelity. The later versions written for children, such as a story by Madame Gabrielle de Villeneuve, published in 1740, and one by Madame Le Prince de Beaumont in 1756, were modeled on D'Aulnoy's archetypes. But these later authors added some important twists. Self-denial and repression, rather than sincerity and fidelity, became key elements, and the heroine placed social values and manners before her own wants. In fact, the story "has been especially instrumental in rationalizing male domination, gender polarity, and violation" since the 1800s (Ibid., 36).

Many revisions of the tale reverse some of these elements while also scrutinizing the Beast's patriarchal authority, not to mention Beauty's unquestioning subservience toward men in general. In some retellings, such as Guy Wetmore Carryl's poem "How Beauty Contrived to Get Square with the Beast" (1902, 65), the heroine even exacts revenge on her captors. In more contemporary times, several of Angela Carter's well-known stories in *The Bloody Chamber and Other Stories* (1979) also rework or reference the tale type. Carter's motivation for the retellings stems from a desire to "extract the latent content" of earlier versions and liberate them from Christian and bourgeois allegory (Haffenden 1985, 80).

Burton, however, has never made clear any feminist, psychoanalytic, or Marxist agendas. The inspiration for *Edward Scissorhands* "actually came from a drawing I did a long time ago. It was just an image that I liked. It came subconsciously and was linked to a character who wants to touch but can't" (quoted in Salisbury 1995, 87). The narrative framework proceeded from that concept; he did not necessarily begin with a desire to retell "Beauty and the Beast." Feminist elements in this film are due partly to Burton's recurring tendency toward feminine-styled heroes but, also, to screenwriter Caroline Thompson, who wrote the script for the film and later collaborated on *Corpse Bride*.[3]

Consequently, *Edward Scissorhands* departs from most retellings in the magnitude of its revision: a complete restructuring of the narrative, to begin with, and also a vast altering of character relationships. Two significant gender reversals are apparent even in the opening scenes. First, mother becomes father. Second, Beast becomes Beauty. In most versions of 425C, Beauty's father incurs the Beast's wrath by trespassing on his property. Burton's opening sequence follows this conventional setup except that the mother commits all of the acts the father previously did. Peg Boggs (Dianne Wiest) is the one who trespasses. She does not steal anything—contrary to most versions—but instead offers Edward (Johnny Depp) something (makeup). In this sense—working as a door-to-door seller from Avon—the mother also functions as merchant. Finally, she is not forced to stay in Edward's

---

3   Thompson could well serve as the subject of an article, but it is worth noting that she wrote the scripts for *The Addams Family* (directed by Barry Sonnenfeld, 1991) and *The Nightmare Before Christmas* (directed by Henry Selick, 1993). She also dated Burton's house musician, Danny Elfman (Page 2007, 80).

castle. Instead, she brings him home. Here begins the second gender reversal. In most versions, of course, the father brings his daughter to the Beast.
But Edward conversely winds up sleeping in Beauty's bed his first night in
the Boggses' house. Thus, this retelling quickly becomes a feminist critique
where Edward displaces his love interest, Kim Boggs (Winona Ryder), as the
"innocent persecuted heroine," a familiar archetype for female characters in
fairy tales and folktales.[4]

    If, in most versions, Beauty views her servitude to the Beast as an act
that simply trades one patriarchal figure—in this case, the inventor whom
Edward calls Father (Vincent Price)—for another, then Edward's move into
the Boggses' household trades a patriarchal figure for a matriarchal one. On
a broader level, Edward's physical journey from his gothic-style mansion
into the suburbs of Burbank also coincides with a psychological one toward
maturity and inner completion, goals usually reserved for Beauty.[5] Burton
establishes all of these complex plot and character shifts in the beginning
scenes, masking the structure so well that audiences may not realize for
some time the affinities between film and fairy tale.

    Although Edward behaves like an innocent persecuted heroine, he does
not exactly resemble one. His most monstrous attribute is his hands. They
provide powerful symbols for traditional themes in "Beauty and the Beast,"
in particular the idea of a young woman's ascension to adulthood. Because
gender operates largely as a social construction,[6] Edward's relationship to his
sexual self and his community has presumably suffered due to his long-term
isolation. Imagine a Beauty who not only must navigate an intricate web
of male desires but must also learn basic social skills in a dramatically short
time. Edward's sharp hands emphasize and complicate his incomplete initiation into the symbolic order, an important stage in psychosexual growth.[7]

---

4   Although Cristina Bacchilega (1993) does not include Beauty among her list of
      innocent persecuted heroines, this character does possess many of the traits she
      enumerates. Twentieth Century Fox executives favored Tom Cruise for the role of
      Edward. Tom Hanks and Michael Jackson were also possibilities (Page 2007, 80).

5   See also Ming-Hsun Lin's consideration in this volume of Harry Potter as Cinderella,
      another partial transgendering of a traditional figure.

6   In her chapter in this collection, Christy Williams references Judith Butler's notion of
      performative sexuality to discuss the construction of gender in her consideration of
      Cinderella. Also a persistent argument in my essay is that Burton's films do more than
      make empty appeals to feminism for ulterior purposes.

7   Jacques Lacan's mirror stage—and his general principle of movement among the
      realms of imaginary, symbolic, and real—chronicle the development of the human

Jacques Lacan's conception of the *Real*—that which resists immersion into the symbolic order—provides insight into Edward's problematic relationship to the conformist suburb of Burbank. Through Lacan's approach, we see that "Edward Scissorhands . . . epitomizes the postmodern subject" as one "condemned to pure gaze since he knows that touching the beloved will cause him or her unbearable pain" (Žižek 1991, 59–60).[8] And yet, like Beauty, Edward is subjected to others' inspection as well. He is made Other by his new family and their community. His journey to sexual adulthood deconstructs the moral that mainstream versions of "Beauty and the Beast" represent: the necessary subjection of women to patriarchy and fathers.

Traditionally, castration by the father enables a male's initiation into the symbolic order.[9] Edward missed castration since his creator died and left him stranded in adolescence. His phallic authority, moreover, is also undermined by the experiences that this authority prevents: touch, communication, and communion. From the struggle for acceptance to minute tasks like dressing, eating, or drinking, his phallic hands impede his desires. Yet at other times, they enable him to sculpt, groom pets, style hair, and unlock doors. They also serve as intentional and accidental weapons. Only in this way do they fulfill their function as phallus, and then only partially. Critics have even debated about whether Edward means to kill Kim's boyfriend, Jim (Anthony Michael Hall), at the end of the film (Page 2007, 89). The phallus inevitably becomes ambiguous; Edward appears androgynous, embodying aspects of both Beauty and Beast. He wears makeup at times to conceal his scars. His punkish hair—reminiscent of Lydia's hairdo in *Beetle Juice* (1988)—also blurs gender lines. Even more conspicuously, his voice sounds soft and feminine.

---

being, where he or she learns at six months of age to tie subjectivity to an image. The movement from the imaginary (preverbal) to the symbolic order occurs when the person learns no from the father, rather than yes from the mother. The phallus (not the imaginary one attributed to the mother) initiates humans at a young age to the symbolic realm, where language mediates between wants and that which can either grant or refuse them (Evans 1996, 83, 115–17, 159).

8   In Žižek's analysis of Lacan, this is the only reference he makes to Burton.

9   Lacan's theories do exclude the female from initiation into the symbolic order— somewhat problematically. Like Freud, he argued that the female's lack of a phallus leads to the desire for a child, which acts as a temporary substitute (Evans 1996, 118). Many scholars and philosophers have addressed this dilemma, but, in regard to a Lacanian reading of Burton, it becomes an opportunity. If Burton's films radically revise fairy tales like "Beauty and the Beast," then they also update Lacan by making the male almost completely androgynous.

Audiences can chronicle Edward's psychological development, his movement through the mirror stage of identity formation in particular. On his first day in the Boggses' house—while standing in Kim's bedroom, no less—he spends several seconds staring at his reflection and then reaches out to touch it. He remains docile and compliant throughout the first half of the film, largely because the multiple insults he receives simply do not register. Edward's first self-conscious, violent, and perhaps adult reaction occurs only after Kim's boyfriend, Jim, has taunted him: the first sign of male competition. He rampages through the house and winds up standing before the bathroom mirror, staring demonically into his own image as he shreds the wallpaper. In this scene, Edward acknowledges his reflection and, for the first time, equates his abnormal appearance with his identity. His angry expression also signals that he has identified his sexual desire for Kim, a realization that Burton represents as frightening. At this point, he momentarily enters the phallic realm where "cold silence itself starts to function as something infinitely more threatening than violent roars" (Žižek 1991, 58).

One historical figure, Kaspar Hauser, further illuminates Edward's roughshod road to maturity. An awkward young man, Hauser inexplicably appeared in Nuremburg Square in 1828 knowing little language aside from a few prayers and phrases and claimed he had grown up in a dark cave devoid of contact with the outside world. Hauser's existence threatens the symbolic order because it presents evidence of human beings existing outside or beyond the social. As Slavoj Žižek argues, "The Lacanian diagnosis of Kaspar can be succinctly put—he was the subject who had not been captured by his image in the mirror; in other words, *he was the subject without an ego.* . . . Hauser was thrown straight into the symbolic network, bypassing the imaginary (mis)recognition that enables one to experience oneself as a 'person'" (Ibid., 65–66). This story precisely describes Edward's condition. While Hauser never learned to identify his reflection, Edward does eventually accept his own image, a progression that symbolizes his attempt to gain acceptance in Burbank's rigid social structure.

Edward's innocence and docility—at odds with his appearance—become a vehicle for social commentary. Burton radically undermines the importance of manners and etiquette, a feature in many of the early literary versions of "Beauty and the Beast." Indeed, an attempt "to graft Edward back into family and community leads instead to the rupture of the community's own unarticulated sutures of desire" (Potter 1992, para. 5). In almost all early versions, the ugly bridegroom woos the heroine with displays of chivalry, manners, and general good breeding that hint at his social superiority.[10] The heroine, likewise, is a paragon of grace.

By contrast, Edward's profound naïveté and timidity persist in the face of enculturation. He does not conform, despite some genuine attempts. His interactions with others, in fact, often unmask the hypocrisy in the community and prompt audiences to interrogate Burbank's suburban social codes. During one of many dinner scenes, a neighbor uses etiquette as an excuse not to eat anything Edward serves because "he used his hands," blatantly neglecting her own manners. Meanwhile, Jim talks with his mouth full about how much he hates his father. Later, when Kim's father Bill (Alan Arkin) asks Edward what he would do if he found a large bag of money, Edward naïvely says he would "buy things for my loved ones." The entire family corrects him—except Kim, who voices a defense. "Isn't that a much nicer thing?" she asks. Even Edward's creator tries to school him in etiquette, reading to him from conduct books. "Should the man rise when he accepts his cup of tea?" the inventor blandly recites, only to leave the question unanswered when he gives up on the lesson, calling it "boring," in favor of poetry.

Most significantly, no external change occurs in the film. That Edward never obtains human hands violates the standard script and rejects the idea that a Beast needs to change. This lack of physical transformation encourages viewers to consider his internal alterations and find values in "Beauty and the Beast" that have largely given way to shallow aspirations toward wealth and conformity. This rejection of mainstream readings of the tale draws attention to Kim's internal development as well. Indeed, the transformation at the core of versions by D'Aulnoy "centers on the girl, not the beast'" (Bryant 1989, 448).[11] So much holds true, in part, for Kim Boggs. D'Aulnoy's versions of "Beauty and the Beast" hinge on emotional growth— namely the cultivation of sincerity, honesty, and trust. As in D'Aulnoy's tales, Kim's development surfaces in her ultimate decision to refute dominant social codes that threaten to destroy Edward. In the beginning, Kim

---

10   As Marina Warner points out, one exception occurs in Villeneuve's tale, where Beauty "finds [Beast] boring because he can utter only a few words and repeats them endlessly" (1994, 299).

11   Marina Warner, especially, finds a tendency in contemporary adaptations that resists the traditional transformation of Beast. "The Beast no longer needs to be disenchanted. Rather, Beauty has to learn to love the beast in him, in order to know the beast in herself" (1994, 312). In this context, *Edward Scissorhands* makes a brief appearance in Warner's work as a further example of a Beast who does not need to change.

Boggs differs little from one of a dozen stereotypical blond teenagers from TV sitcoms in the 1960s, '70s, and '80s. Burton prompts viewers, in fact, to identify her as a cheerleader brat—a stock character incapable of depth or change. Initially Kim acts spoiled, cynical, and selfish. She makes little effort to veil her dislike or fear of Edward. When they first meet, she bursts into obnoxious screams at the sight of him lying in her bed.

Kim never scolds her boyfriend, Jim, for making fun of Edward unless it somehow embarrasses her. She also causes Edward tremendous chagrin by failing to come forward when the Burbank police arrest him for breaking and entering, although she is the one who talked him into it. Her eventual guilt parallels the grief of the heroine in D'Aulnoy's "The Ram," where the beast bridegroom dies as a result of her prolonged absence (Zipes 1994, 27). Beauty in "The Ram" fails to keep her word, just as Kim fails to tell the truth. In that vein, the film also resists the popular fairy tale ending. Edward doesn't die or transform or marry but lives out the rest of his life hidden away inside his castle. While the community at large shares the blame, Kim's moral failure certainly contributes to the film's gray ending.

And yet Kim achieves a significant amount of positive agency, outsmarting the town into thinking Edward has died in order to protect him—therefore saving him, so to speak, and maintaining his role as innocent persecuted heroine. She is never rescued from her violent, controlling boyfriend but learns to save herself (albeit aided by Edward's accidental stabbing). In fact, the only other figure who needs saving is Kim's brother, Kevin (Robert Oliveri), whom Edward pushes from the path of Jim's van. Finally, Kim maintains narrative control of the film. The entire story unfolds within a framed narrative told to her granddaughter. So, in contrast to many adaptations of "Beauty and the Beast"—related from the perspective of a distant and often unidentified narrator—Kim can clearly articulate her own moral and psychological development. These numerous departures—from Edward's hybrid sexuality to Kim's elevated agency—show that *Edward Scissorhands* goes well beyond the "pop feminism" in many of its contemporaries (Craven 2002, 130). Beauty and Beast operate as roles that Edward and Kim both inhabit at various points, but they are not limited to them. The roles are blurred and traded—shared.

Sleepy Hollow

Burton's use of fairy tale ebbed after *Edward Scissorhands*. But though he moved away from the explicit use of tale types and motifs in subsequent films such as *Batman Returns* (1992), *Ed Wood* (1994), and *Mars Attacks!* (1996), the filmmaker returned to them with enthusiasm in the late 1990s, and he has largely remained there since. This trend has roots in *Sleepy Hollow*, his most free-associative retelling. With *Sleepy Hollow*, Burton began to take heat for his supposedly unfaithful incorporation of source material. But rather than attack his films for their disloyalty to urtexts, scholars might view them as prime examples of "new media texts" and search for latent value in their "schizophrenic instrumentalization of fairy tale matter" (Jorgensen 2007, 218).[12]

Burton's *Sleepy Hollow* straddles the border between dark parody and pastiche. The film provides adept commentary on authorship in fairy tales and folktales, one that requires some consideration of history. While Washington Irving's story remains the version most Americans know best, the early American writer drew on a number of sources. There is a surprising degree of cross-pollination among American, German, and Irish versions of the story of the headless horseman. In his collection *Irish Fairy and Folk Tales*, W. B. Yeats mentions a faerie known as the *dullahan*, a spirit that rides a headless horse or drives a stagecoach led by headless horses, brandishing a whip made from a human spine (2003, 118). Yeats only briefly describes this horseman, referring readers to the nineteenth-century Irish folklorist Thomas Crofton Croker, who devotes several stories to the *dullahan*. Croker's description anticipates Disney's fiery animation, a head which the horseman carries

> under [his] . . . right arm . . . and such a head no mortal ever saw before. It looked like a large cream cheese hung round with black puddings: no speck of colour enlivened the ashy paleness of the depressed features; the skin lay stretched over the unearthly surface almost like the parchment head of a drum. Two fiery eyes of prodigious circumference, with a strange and irregular motion, flashed like meteors . . .

---

12 In their essay in this volume, Cristina Bacchilega and John Rieder explore generic hybridization in several films that draw on aspects of fairy tales and folktales without incorporating specific plotlines. They study the rhetorical effects of genre hybridization, in particular, and make a case for Guillermo Del Toro's *Pan's Labyrinth* (2006) as one of the few films that genuinely deconstruct the dominant ideology of contemporary fairy tales.

and to complete all, a mouth reached from either extremity of two
ears, which peeped forth from under a profusion of matted locks of
lustreless blackness. (1825, 234–35)

In his notes to the story, Croker goes on to state that during "the early part
of the last century the headless horse was not unknown in England," taking
the motif back to the eighteenth century and perhaps earlier (Ibid., 240).

The Brothers Grimm translated Croker's *Fairy Legends and Traditions of
the South of Ireland* into German a year after its initial publication (Hennig
1946, 44). But even before reading Croker, the Grimms had collected a brief
account of a headless horseman that appears in *Deutsche Sagen,* originally
published in 1816 and later translated and edited by Donald Ward in 1981.
The Grimms' legend possesses little or no plotline, merely recounting an
incident where "a woman of Dresden" sees "a man without a head, dressed
in a long grey cloak and riding upon a grey horse" (Grimm 1981, 246).
The spirit eventually reveals himself as the ghost of a man named Hans
Jagenteufel, who is punished for his inhumane treatment of the poor. Ward
traces the appearance of headless ghosts in Euro-North American culture
all the way to Iceland, where during the Middle Ages, sightings of headless
living corpses were not uncommon (Ibid., 412).

But Irving undoubtedly plucked the ideas for his horseman from the
pages of an even earlier source than the Grimms: Johann Karl August
Musäus, author of a collection of German stories first published between
1782 and 1787. Irving traveled through Germany and Austria in 1822–23,
and his deep fascination with the land's folktales led him to Musäus, from
whom he borrowed heavily (Reichart 1957, 31). The horseman appears
briefly, but poignantly, in Musäus's fifth legend of Rübezahl, a German folk
spirit—first described as "a jet-black figure, of a size exceeding that of man,
crowned with a broad Spanish tippet; but what was the most suspicious cir-
cumstance in its whole appearance, was its being without a head" (Musäus
1791, 147). The strange figure turns out indeed to have a head but chooses
to carry it "under his arm, just as if it [were] a lap-dog" (Ibid., 150).

The terrified coach driver, conveying a countess through the moun-
tains haunted by Rübezahl, tries to greet the figure. But it "hurls" its head
at him, striking the driver "on the forehead" and causing him to fall "head-
long from the box over the fore-wheel." A lord by the name of Giantdale
(Rübezahl in disguise) saves the party from this specter, and once the "mask
and drapery were presently stripped away," an "ordinary fellow" appears

underneath—"just of the shape of an ordinary man" (Ibid., 153). The would-be robber, who attempts to steal the party's coach and horses, turns out to be a pauper by the name of Robin, who eventually appeals to the lord for amnesty. Thus, the horseman holds a relatively trivial place, functioning largely as a red herring.

In his retelling of Musäus, Irving abandoned many aspects of the original tale, although others such as "the fantastic adventure at midnight, the headless horseman who threw his detached head at Ichabod's skull, the unexpected denouement that implicates a disguised rival, and the hurled pumpkin" belong fundamentally to this German version (Reichart 1957, 31). Given the wide degree of variation among these tales, then, one can hardly fault Burton for any freewheeling improvisation.

Burton primarily discusses his familiarity with contemporary versions of the tale, giving a vague impression that he may never have read Irving's story that closely for inspiration. "I probably remember it more from the Disney cartoon actually," he has said (Kermode 2000, para. 4). "I talked to a lot of people who thought they knew the story" but retained—more than any literal memory—"the power of that image and the setting" (Ibid.). This eclecticism is typical for Burton, whose influences include movies adapted from Edgar Allan Poe, Mary Shelley, and Bram Stoker rather than the original literature. His brand of pastiche constitutes "a subjective interpretation of a half-informed memory," rather than a conscious revision (Hanke 2000, xvii). This form of influence characterizes in general Burton's style. While the 1920 film *The Cabinet of Dr. Caligari* (directed by Robert Wiene) influenced Burton's animated short *Vincent*, for example, he admits that he never saw the film beforehand—only posters and stills from magazines.

This cursory attention to sources leads some critics to see Burton as "sloppy, suggesting that he doesn't do his homework properly to reproduce slavishly the look of his film 'models'" (Ibid.). To counter such charges, Burton has spoken on one or two occasions about his influences, including fairy tales:

Because I never read, my fairy tales were probably those monster movies. To me they're fairly similar. I mean, fairy tales are extremely violent and extremely symbolic and disturbing, probably even more so than *Frankenstein* and stuff like that, which are kind of mythic and perceived as fairy tale like. But fairy tales, like the Grimms' fairy tales, are probably closer to movies like *The Brain That Wouldn't Die*, much rougher, harsher, full of bizarre symbolism. . . . I think I've

always liked the idea of fairy tales or folktales, because they're symbolic of something else. There's a foundation to them, but there's more
besides, they're open to interpretation. . . . So I think I didn't like fairy
tales specifically. I liked the *idea* of them more. (quoted in Salisbury
1995, 3)

The idea of the horseman—and but a few plot elements or character relationships—connects Musäus, the Brothers Grimm, Croker, Irving, Disney,
and Burton—who finally elevates the horseman from a legend that Von
Brunt (Casper Van Dien) exploits to a real supernatural killer: the Hessian
(Christopher Walken). Nonetheless, some of Burton's bold departures do
contribute a coherent agenda that underlies and facilitates his improvisa-
tional retelling.

Von Brunt's death serves as a vivid example of an ostensibly sloppy
break from source material that in fact constitutes a sophisticated act of
revision. Incorporating generic elements of mystery, suspense, and detective
stories, *Sleepy Hollow* makes the identity of the horseman a key question in
a way that Irving did not. Prior to the scene where Von Brunt dies, he is a
suspect—if not in Ichabod's mind, then at least for audiences who draw on
their prior knowledge of Irving's tale. The unexpected death severs audiences violently from such conjecture. Moreover, Von Brunt is the only victim of the horseman who does not lose his head. Rather, he is torn in half.
Not only is he removed as a suspect in a split second, but he is also clearly
not a prime target of the Hessian's killing spree and, therefore, not integral
to the plot. (The Hessian does not kill randomly and so tries to spare this
persistent hero.) In the end, Von Brunt plays a simplified role in Burton's
version of the tale that mirrors Musäus's use of the horseman: a red herring.

The fragmentation of themes and motifs in earlier versions (torn apart
like Von Brunt) also undergirds the relationships between characters, as well
as methods through which the story unfolds. Burton purposefully conflates
physical and psychological dislocation. The frequent decapitations and
other acts of violence provide more than a string of shocks: they coordinate
ideas and characters. The starkest example involves the symbiosis between
Ichabod and the Hessian. In Irving's version, no real character traits bind
them. The horseman is simply Von Brunt's alter ego. In Burton's adaptation,
however, they share a great deal that escapes an uncritical eye. To begin
with, they are both outsiders—the one a foreign mercenary, the other an
urbanite unaccustomed to rural life. The Hessian kills out of desire for his
head; he wishes to be a whole person. Ichabod tries to save lives through

criminal investigation to fulfill a similar hunger for unity. His journey to Sleepy Hollow awakens fragments of his past that he eventually pieces together. The Hessian's reunion with his skull corresponds to Ichabod's reconnection with his terrifying childhood, which he must confront to achieve emotional solidarity.

Burton's Ichabod has suffered intense psychological trauma as a child, watching his father brutally murder his mother in Puritan zeal. The figure of Ichabod's dead mother (Lisa Marie) may qualify as the film's single most gruesome image. Ichabod's history—like the Hessian's—unfolds through a series of violent and disjointed scenes that possess clear stylistic differences from the rest of the film. Cuts between shots in these flashbacks (Ichabod's as well as the Hessian's) are often sharp and jarring. Close-ups are quick and gruesome. These scenes are also devoid of dialogue. It follows, then, that the main conflict's resolution occurs when Ichabod, rather than escaping or defeating his adversary, delivers to him the desired skull without a second's hesitation. That he never even instructs the horseman to release Katrina Van Tassel (Christina Ricci) implies a kind of blind trust, or understanding, that a reconstituted body will end his killing spree.

Fragmentation also converges with ownership and authenticity. As with so many tales, Disney had by the mid-twentieth century all but copyrighted many classics and made them distinctly American, at least in the Euro-North American imagination. In the case of "The Legend of Sleepy Hollow," Disney had appropriated and commodified one of the few truly American tales. The effect is not unlike raiding a national treasure in the sense that Irving's intentions to comment on class and gender in the original story faded into the background of animation spectacle.[13] Speaking of this phenomenon, Burton says, "I think in America . . . there's not the wealth of stories, folktales and fairy tales, that there are in other countries. . . . [Irving's tale] was one of the only early American folktales and that's why I was drawn to it" (Kermode 2000, para. 4). A retelling of Irving's story

---

13 Stanley Orr identifies the original Ichabod Crane as "an emissary of metropolitan culture," noting the way Irving describes the schoolhouse as an "empire" or "realm" that brings civilization to the frontier (2003, 45). Disney's cartoon does not necessarily eliminate this aspect of Irving's story, but nonetheless the class tension between Ichabod and Von Brunt is buried in endless episodes of slapstick comedy. Additionally Orr argues that Burton and the screenplay's author, Andrew Kevin Walker, transformed the horseman from a paradoxical symbol of colonial harmony into a savage Other who reminds Sleepy Hollow of its "bloody colonial history" (Ibid., 47).

necessitates coming to terms, so to speak, with Disney's version, which is dominated by a chipper, sing-songy narrator and slapstick comedy.

Especially in relation to Disney's cartoon, Burton's *Sleepy Hollow* becomes a study in ownership and visual signature. Signs and signatures recur through Burton's film, which in fact opens with the image of a dis-embodied hand scrawling a signature across a will and sealing it with red wax. The hand belongs to Van Garrett senior (Robert Sella), whose murder sets the plot in motion, prompting the town leaders to scheme to obtain his property. Katrina Van Tassel, who ultimately inherits her father's estate, pro-tects Ichabod with pagan symbols (the evil eye) that denote control over a given space. In that sense, she signs his living quarters by chalking a symbol beneath his head, exercising ownership over it. Katrina tries the same evil-eye signature to protect her father (Michael Gambon), preventing the Hessian's entry into the town church, though the horseman manages to outsmart her. When Katrina's stepmother, Lady Van Tassel (Miranda Richardson), decapi-tates her servant, she fools Ichabod and the rest of Sleepy Hollow by slicing, or signing, the corpse's hand—to pass off the corpse as her own.

In all cases, Ichabod must learn to read these signs properly to solve the mystery, and his initial misreading of Katrina's symbols leads him to suspect her erroneously as the murderer. (A similar sign also drives Ichabod's pious father [Peter Guinness] to kill his mother.) While Ichabod initially inter-prets the evil eye as a threat, he chances to discover that the image provides "protection against evil spirits" by accidentally flipping to a passage in the spell book Katrina has given him as a gift. Furthermore, he uncovers the crux of the mystery in the public notary's office, a warehouse of signatures. The film closes on a now-familiar reference to writing—Lady Van Tassel's twitching hand as it protrudes from the Tree of Death.

Image, sign, and signature play a crucial role in one scene when the horseman (actually Von Brunt dressed as him) appears and emulates a famous scene from Disney's cartoon, complete with a frog that calls Ichabod's name before plopping into the water and a flaming jack-o'-lantern. This particular scene goes beyond mere homage. Typically, when Burton borrows images and concepts from other films, he does so with a degree of creative inter-pretation that can (as mentioned before) be mistaken for sloppiness. In few other places has the director gone into such detail to simulate a prior work. Here Burton seems to mock Disney's supposed ownership of the tale.

In some fairy tales, a magician may reverse or break a spell by read-ing it backward—a verbal mirror, so to speak. Through mirroring the cartoon, Burton breaks the Disney spell. Those who tried to erase Irving are now "forced to witness the grim spectacle of the Horseman's true menace" (Kevorkian 2003, 30).[14] Burton drives the message home when the horseman removes his costume, revealing Von Brunt. The entire scene is a hoax—an image—that hints that the cartoon is merely a joke and not authoritative in the least. Disney's mythologized version of Irving's tale is effectively demythologized. In the same way, the complete remodeling of the story reminds viewers and critics alike that no single urtext for these tales exists, and therefore one cannot dictate truly what distinguishes a faithful from an unfaithful retelling.

Corpse Bride

Burton's *Corpse Bride*, too, exemplifies a complex web of source material. A story by Howard Schwartz entitled "The Finger" is one of the most recent literary adaptations of tale type ATU 365, "The Dead Bridegroom Carries Off His Bride," and it in turn draws from a tale dating back to a much earlier story about the kabbalist Isaac Luria in a collection entitled *Shivhei ah-Ari (In Praise of the Ari).*[15] This original tale about Luria, first published in 1629, involves a young man who accidentally weds a demon rather than a corpse—and it concludes on a comparatively mundane note. Luria simply annuls the marriage and tells the demon to return to the underworld. The moral or meaning has to do with the rabbi's role as communal leader and his power over the spiritual and supernatural.

The tale also condemns acts of sacrilege. The Jewish story that *Corpse Bride* builds on incorporates the Venus-ring motif (accidental marriage to a statue), which provides a direct counterstatement to Chrys Ingraham's

---

14   Martin Kevorkian argues that the grinning jack-o'-lantern in the film's beginning "stands in for Irving's explanatory authority" (2003, 30), which heavily suggests that the horseman does not exist. He notes the conspicuous absence of the term "legend" in Burton's title. Disney's film, likewise, heavily implies that Von Brunt is the horseman's alter ego.

15   Many sources on the Web and in print, ranging from a major Tim Burton fan site (the Tim Burton Collective) to the *Village Voice* (Atkinson 2005), have misattributed the source of Burton's film to a vague nineteenth-century retelling of the original version. Jewish folktale expert Howard Schwartz assured me in an e-mail on May 12, 2008, that his short story, "The Finger," in his collection entitled *Lilith's Cave,* is the first adaptation of the Venus-ring motif to make the bride a corpse, rather than a demon. He did so "to make it more of a tale of terror." Furthermore, Schwartz's story is the only version that Burton and Warner Bros. officially acknowledge as inspiration.

notion of "the wedding-industrial complex" that Disney—among many
other entities—perpetuates through films and merchandising (2008,
87–89).[16] If contemporary versions of popular tales trivialize marriage as an
institution, as many scholars have noted, then Burton's adaptation of this
old story both critiques and affirms marriage. His portrayal of the corpse
bride offers a corrective on somewhat misogynistic elements of older stories
about accidental matches.

In *Reimagining the Bible: Storytelling of the Rabbis,* Howard Schwartz
discusses the demon bride motif at length, citing several versions, including
"The Queen of Sheeba," where a demoness seduces a shopkeeper, and "The
Demon in the Tree," where a young man slips a ring on a demon's finger,
mistaking it for a friend with whom he is playing hide-and-seek (1998). The
demon in the latter narrative haunts the man for the rest of his life, killing
successive wives until the third wife arranges a compromise to share their
husband. These versions, according to Schwartz, became popular in the sixteenth century (Ibid., 68). The tale structure seems to have circulated in and
out of popularity for the following two centuries.

The Jewish theme of the demon or corpse bride borrows from an even
older story that circulated through Europe during the medieval period,
involving the marriage of a man to a statue of Venus. In all variations of the
Venus-ring tale, a priest manages to save this irresponsible or naïve young
man from his dim fate. The story provides some excellent commentary on
the hybridization of pagan and Christian cultures during the eleventh and
twelfth centuries, and it is also an interesting counter-tale to type 425—
"The Search for the Lost Husband." In the various versions of 425C especially, readers may note irony in the fact that a woman earns rewards for
loyalty and devotion to an ugly husband, whereas a man who commits sacrilege and winds up accidentally betrothed to a statue, demon, or corpse only
needs to consult his local rabbi or priest to restore harmony. The original
tales—outside of "The Demon in the Tree"—deliver little consequence or
punishment to the husband.

Venus herself has embodied numerous and often competing themes
over the past thousand years. In the earliest known version of the narrative
by William of Malmesbury, circa 1125, a member of the Roman nobility
places his wedding ring on a statue of Venus while playing an athletic game.

---

16   For an extended discussion of the way the dominant trends in the fairy tale film
     industry reinforce gender norms through their representation of marriage and wedding
     ceremonies, see Linda Pershing and Lisa Gablehouse's essay in this volume.

The statue seizes the ring and will not let it go, and later that night the god-dess appears in bed with him and his wife. To regain his ring and save his marriage, the nobleman must consult a priest named Palumbus, who knows how to perform black magic. Subsequent versions, like one appearing in the mid-twelfth-century epic German poem *Kaiserchronik* (Ziolkowski 1977, 29), further demonize Venus by making her a seductress, rather than a nui-sance. She cons the young man—Astrolabius in this version—out of his ring. He then suffers spiritually and emotionally—hypnotized by the devil-like spirit—until a priest can work countermagic to save his soul.

The Venus-ring tale was "one of the most popular legends of late medi-eval and early Renaissance Europe" (Ibid., 31). The story subsequently faded in and out of popularity with a revival in the 1800s, when Venus signified the dark forces of nature that threaten rationality and order—notions that evolved during the Enlightenment. By the end of the nineteenth century, Venus "embodies the power of primitive passion in contrast to the sterility of civilization . . . either positively or negatively depending on the standpoint of the writer" (Ibid., 75). For authors like Henry James, "the statue repre-sents a dangerous intrusion into the order of nineteenth-century society, a threat to order and civilization" (Ibid.). Essentially the motif has undergone a series of mutations to promote the values of the hour, like many tales.

Burton's version re-eroticizes the Venus figure but also humanizes her. His film portrays her as innocently sexual, sensitive, and expressive. Despite her decay, Emily appears markedly more erotic than Victor's fiancée. Victoria Everglot wears her hair in a bun, for example, while Emily's hair streams behind her when she dances—something Victoria never does. She makes jokes, for example, when she stands at an overlook in the underworld. "Isn't the view beautiful?" she asks. "It takes my breath away. Well, it would if I had any." Emily plays the piano. Victoria plays no instrument, by contrast, and she makes no jokes or puns outside of chuckling at Lord Barkis when he discovers her family's secret poverty. Her mother has forbidden her to express herself beyond cordialities. "Mother won't let me near the piano," Victoria says on the day of her wedding rehearsal. "Music is improper for a young lady. 'Too passionate,' she says.'" Finally, Victoria's face, lips, and eyebrows move much less than Victor's or Emily's when they act or speak. Her arms remain somewhat motionless as well.

Female agency becomes a subtle theme as the Venus figure is human-ized and plays off of audience expectations. Like Edward, Emily assumes the role of the Real, resisting symbolism and classification. What is she, a villain or an innocent persecuted heroine? In some ways, she fits the "castrating bitch" archetype that Laura Sells sees as the quintessential villain of many Disney films (1995, 181). Although Emily's demeanor is benevolent, she holds Victor in wedlock against his will, and her temper flares when he tries to escape to Victoria. As the film progresses, audiences recognize elements of the innocent persecuted heroine when they hear a disturbing song that recounts her death at the hands of a vagabond trickster. Here the film coyly implies that the answer to Victoria's problems lie—through "the wedding-industrial complex"—in marriage (Ingraham 2008, 87–89). If only some-one else would marry the poor corpse bride, then all of the film's external conflicts would fade away, permitting Victor's freedom.[17] Audiences may indeed expect Victor to go search for a more suitable suitor than himself, perhaps Rhett Butler's corpse.

Such is not the case, fortunately. Only after the demise of her killer, Barkis Bittern, and a Hamlet-like acceptance of mortality and fate, can Emily achieve final peace, the best ending she can hope for. In a way similar to the moral of *Pan's Labyrinth*, it is a hard lesson for child and adult view-ers alike: death cannot be reversed by dislodging a chunk of poison apple or waking someone with a kiss. Death is a permanent transformation and also a phase in a cycle, a message driven home by Victoria's sudden and surpris-ing dissolution into butterflies.

In a final and important twist to earlier stories that use the Venus-ring motif, Emily leaves the living couple of her own accord—neither exorcised by a religious authority figure, compromised with, nor placated. As *Corpse Bride* illustrates, Burton's heroines indeed possess a lioness's share of agency. They tell their own stories and resolve their own problems. They do not rely exclusively on men or authority figures. And their independence—con-trasted with the timidity of their male companions—appears a good deal more genuine than that of many other contemporary heroines.

Burton also breaks with tradition by pushing the tale's male protago-nist through a stage of emotional development. Even Schwartz's tale largely relieves its main character, Reuven, of consequences. He simply crawls to the elder rabbis, who, after some deliberation, declare the marriage "null

---

17   Cristina Bacchilega points out the patriarchal constraints, as well as the social construction of gender, within the subgenre of innocent persecuted heroine stories that push women through narratives toward fulfillment of a hero's desire, not their own (1993, 5). *Corpse Bride* questions such constructions of gender, as this essay argues.

and void" (1998, 52). Afterward Reuven appears largely unchanged despite his encounter. By contrast, significant transformations occur in Victor that are similar to those experienced by Beauty in tale type 425C. Internally he overcomes his fear of commitment and the social anxieties that have previously marred his vows.[18] Most importantly, he also accepts the corpse bride midway through the film, agreeing to kill himself so his marriage to Emily will become permanent. Victor's ultimate commitment to "drink the wine of ages" parallels the transformation that D'Aulnoy privileges in her versions of "Beauty and the Beast": trust and honesty. In this way, the film subverts the moral in most tales using the Venus-ring motif—all problems supernatural and spiritual can be solved by visiting one's local priest or rabbi.

Accordingly, another difference between film and folklore lies in the clergy's portrayal. In demon-bride and Venus-ring tales alike, the priest can manipulate the supernatural world and command the spirits. The early tales promoted confidence and faith in religious authority. *Corpse Bride* saps this power from its only clergy member, Pastor Galswells, whom Victoria consults after discovering Victor's "unholy" marriage. "You are the only one in the village who knows of what awaits beyond the grave," she implores. "Can the living marry the dead? There must be some way to undo what's been done." She begs Galswells for help like all protagonists of previous versions. But not only does he lack the power to resolve the problem; he exacerbates it by returning Victoria to her grouchy parents. "She's speaking in tongues," he exclaims, "of unholy alliances. Her mind has come undone, I fear." In this scene, Burton undermines expectations perhaps more consciously than ever before. Additionally Galswells fails to keep a mass of the dead from entering his church to attend Emily and Victor's wedding. "Be gone, ye demons from Hell. Back to the void from whence you came," he proclaims, brandishing his staff. "You shall not enter here." The only response comes in the form of a joke: "Keep it down," says one of the skeletons. "We're in a church." Meanwhile the crowd moves calmly past.

Burton may remain more deeply influenced by the idea of fairy tales than the tales themselves, but he has nonetheless contributed to a growing body of work that rejects many of the diminishing effects of the sanitized

---

18 According to Theodore Ziolkowski (1977), Western tales using the Venus-ring motif were often a metaphor for cold feet or anxiety regarding sexual performance on the wedding night. In Burton's version, especially, we can see Victor's fear of disappointing Victoria as a husband. While the film makes no overt references to sexuality, adult viewers should not find this a huge deductive leap.

fairy tale. His 2010 interpretation of *Alice in Wonderland*—surprisingly produced and distributed in collaboration with Disney—will likely not be the last time he draws on tales and fables for ideas. The sudden cooperation of Burton and Disney, furthermore, implies a new direction for the longtime perpetuators of safe, predictable stories. It appears that Burton's dungeon days are behind him, and he has finally secured the creative authority to lead Disney onto new paths—if ever so tenuously.

List of Tale Types and Literary Stories

Aarne-Thompson-Uther Tale Types

"The Animal as Bridegroom," ATU 425A

"The Beautiful and the Ugly Twinsisters," ATU 711

"Babes in the Woods," ATU 327A

"Beauty and the Beast," ATU 425C

"Bluebeard," ATU 312

"The Boy Steals the Ogre's Treasure," ATU 328

"The Brothers and the Ogre," ATU 327B

"Cinderella"/"Peau d'âne" ("Donkeyskin")/"Catskin"/"All-Kinds-of-Fur,"
    ATU 510, 510A, and 510B

"The Clever Farmgirl," ATU 875

"The Dead Bridegroom Carries Off His Bride," ATU 365

"East of the Sun and West of the Moon," ATU 425A

"Faithful Johannes," ATU 516

"The Frog King"/"Iron Heinrich," ATU 440

"The Gingerbread Man"/"Runaway Pancake," ATU 2025

"Hansel and Gretel," ATU 327A

"Hop o' My Thumb," ATU 327B

"The Juniper Tree," ATU 720

"Kate Crackernuts," ATU 306/711

"The Little Red Ox," ATU 511A

"Little Red Riding Hood"/"Little Red Cap"/"The Story of Grandmother,"
    ATU 333

"The Magic Flight," ATU 313

"Molly Whuppie," ATU 327B

"Muncimeg," ATU 327B/328/711

"Peg Bearskin," ATU 306/327B/328/711

"Puss in Boots," ATU 545B

"Rapunzel," ATU 310

"Rescue by the Sister," ATU 311

"The Search for the Lost Husband," ATU 425

"Six Swans"/"Little Brother and Little Sister," ATU 450

"Sleeping Beauty," ATU 410

"Snow White," ATU 709

"Tatterhood," ATU 711

"The Three Little Pigs"/"Blowing the House In," ATU 124

"The Twelve Dancing Princesses"/"The Danced-Out Shoes"/"The Secret Ball"/"The Shoes That Were Danced to Pieces"/"The Worn-Out Dancing Shoes," ATU 306

Literary Tales

Andersen, Hans Christian. "The Little Mermaid" (1836); "The Ugly Duckling" (1844); "The Red Shoes" (1845).

Barrie, J. M. *Peter Pan* (1904).

Baum, L. Frank. *The Wonderful Wizard of Oz* (1900).

Carroll, Lewis. *Alice's Adventures in Wonderland* (1865).

Collodi, Carlo. *Pinocchio: The Adventures of a Puppet* (1882).

Gaiman, Neil. *MirrorMask* (2005).

Goldman, William. *The Princess Bride* (1973).

Irving, Washington. "The Legend of Sleepy Hollow" (1819).

Rowling, J. K. *Harry Potter and the Philosopher's Stone* (1997); *Harry Potter and the Chamber of Secrets* (1998); *Harry Potter and the Prisoner of Azkaban* (1999); *Harry Potter and the Goblet of Fire* (2000); *Harry Potter and the Order of the Phoenix* (2003); *Harry Potter and the Half-Blood Prince* (2005); *Harry Potter and the Deathly Hallows* (2007).

Schwartz, Howard. "The Finger" (1998).

Steig, William. *Shrek!* (1990).

Bibliography

Aarne, Antti, and Stith Thompson. 1961. *The Types of the Folktale: A Classification and Bibliography.* 2d rev. ed. Helsinki: Academia Scientarum Fennica.

———. 1999. From *The Types of the Folktale: A Classification and Bibliography.* In *The Classic Fairy Tales,* ed. Maria Tatar, 373–78.

Abrahams, Roger D. 1980. *Between the Living and the Dead.* Folklore Fellows Communications 225. Helsinki: Suomalainen Tiedakatemia.

Acevedo-Munoz, Ernesto R. 2002. Don't Look Now: Kubrick, Schnitzler, and "The Unbearable Agony of Desire." *Literature Interpretation Theory* 13, no. 2: 117–37.

Adler, Shawn. 2007. 'Enchanted' Disney Spoofs: Past Princesses, Familiar Restaurants, Cleaning Cockroaches: Susan Sarandon, James Marsden, Amy Adams Pick Their Favorite Hidden References. MTV News, November 13. Available online at http://www.vh1.com/movies/news/articles/1574092/20071112/story.jhtml?rsspartner=rssMozilla

Alderson, Brian. 1993. The Spoken and the Read: German Popular Stories and English Popular Diction. In *The Reception of the Grimms' Fairy Tales: Responses, Reactions, Revisions,* ed. Donald Haase, 59–77.

Alison, Jane. 2003. Stanley Kubrick's *Eyes Wide Shut:* A Masque in Disguise. *Post Script* 23, no. 1: 3–13.

Andersen, Hans Christian. 1846. "The Little Mermaid." In *Danish Fairy Legends and Tales,* trans. Caroline Peachey, 44–82. London: William Pickering.

Andrew, James Dudley. 1984. *Concepts in Film Theory.* Oxford: Oxford University Press.

Andrews, David. 2006. Sex Is Dangerous, So Satisfy Your Wife. *Cinema Journal* 45, no. 3: 59–89.

Anime and Popular Culture: An Interview with Bill Ellis. 2007. *Theofantastique,* September 24. Available online at http://theofantastique.blogspot.com/2007/09/anime-and-popular-culture-interview.html

Arendt, Hannah. 2006. *Eichmann in Jerusalem: A Report on the Banality of Evil.* New York: Penguin Group, Inc.

Armitt, Lucie. 1997. The Fragile Frames of The Bloody Chamber. In *The Infernal Desires of Angela Carter,* ed. Joseph Bristow and Trev Lynn Broughton, 88–99.

Árnason, Jón. 1993. Bakkadraugurinn. In *Íslenzkar Þjóðsögur og Ævintýri,* eds. Árni Böðvarsson and Bjarni Vilhjálmsson, Vol. 1: 274-76. 6 vols. Reykjavík: Þjóðsaga..

Arroyo, Jose. 2006. Girl Interrupted. *Sight & Sound,* December. Available online at http://www.bfi.org.uk/sightandsound/feature/49337

Artz, L. 2004. The Righteousness of Self-Centred Royals: The World According to Disney Animation. *Critical Arts* 18, no. 1: 116–46.

Ashe, Marie. 1997. "Bad Mothers" and Welfare Reform in Massachusetts: The Case of Claribel Ventura. In *Feminism, Media & the Law,* ed. Martha A. Fineman and Martha T. McCluskey, 203–16. New York: Oxford University Press.

Ashliman, D. L. 2002. Maria, the Wicked Stepmother, and the Seven Robbers. Available online at http://www.pitt.edu/~dash/type0709.html#maria

———. Folklinks: Folk and Fairy Tale Sites. Available online at http://pitt.edu/~dash/ashliman.
    html
Atkinson, Michael. 2005. Death Becomes Her. Review of *Corpse Bride* by Tim
    Burton. *Village Voice*, September 6. Available online at http://www.villagevoice.
    com/2005-09-06/film/death-becomes-her/
———, ed. 2003b. *The Emperor's Old Groove: Decolonizing Disney's Magic Kingdom*. New
    York: Peter Lang.
Auerbach, Nina, and U. C. Knoepflmacher, eds. 1992. *Forbidden Journeys: Fairy Tales and
    Fantasies by Victorian Women Writers*. Chicago: University of Chicago Press.
Axelrod, Mark. 2003. Beauties and Their Beasts and Other Motherless Tales from the
    Wonderful World of Walt Disney. In *The Emperor's Old Groove: Decolonizing Disney's
    Magic Kingdom*, ed. Brenda Ayres, 29–38.
Ayres, Brenda. 2003a. The Wonderful World of Disney. In *The Emperor's Old Groove:
    Decolonizing Disney's Magic Kingdom*, ed. Brenda Ayres, 15–25.
Bacchilega, Cristina. 1993. An Introduction to the "Innocent Persecuted Heroine" Fairy
    Tale. *Western Folklore* 52, no. 1: 1–12.
———. 1997. *Postmodern Fairy Tales: Gender and Narrative Strategies*. Philadelphia:
    University of Pennsylvania Press.
———. 2008. Extrapolating from Nalo Hopkinson's *Skin Folk*: Reflections on
    Transformation and Recent English-Language Fairy Tale Fiction by Women. In
    Contemporary Fiction and the Fairy Tale, ed. Stephen Benson, 178–203.
Baldassarre, Angela. 1993. Myth and magic pervade Icelandic tale. *Eye* (Feb 11).
Barr, Marleen S. 2000. Biology Is Not Destiny; Biology Is Fantasy: *Cinderella*, or the
    Dream Disney's "Impossible"/Possible Race Relations Dream. In *Fantasy Girls:
    Gender in the New Universe of Science Fiction and Fantasy Television*, ed. Elyce Rae
    Helford, 187–99. Lanham, MD: Rowman & Littlefield.
Barzilai, Shuli. 1990. Reading "Snow White": The Mother's Story. *Signs: Journal of Women
    in Culture and Society* 15, no. 3: 515–34.
Basile, Giambattista. 1932. "The Young Slave." In *The Pentamerone of Giambattista Basile*,
    ed. N. M. Penzer, 192–96. New York: Dutton and Company.
Bauman, Zygmunt. 2007. *Liquid Life*. Cambridge: Polity Press.
Bean, Kellie. 2003. Stripping Beauty: Disney's "Feminist Seduction." In *The Emperor's Old
    Groove: Decolonizing Disney's Magic Kingdom*, ed. Brenda Ayres, 53–64.
Beauvoir, Simone de. 1953. *The Second Sex*. Trans. H. M. Parshley. New York: Knopf.
Bell, Elizabeth, Lynda Haas, and Laura Sells, eds. 1995. *From Mouse to Mermaid: The
    Politics of Film, Gender, and Culture*. Bloomington: Indiana University Press.
Ben-Amos, Dan. 1971. Toward a Definition of Folklore in Context. *Journal of American
    Folklore* 84, no. 331: 3–15.
Bendix, Regina. 1993. Seashell Bra and Happy End: Disney's Transformation of "The Little
    Mermaid." *Fabula* 34, nos. 3/4: 280–90.
Benson, Stephen, ed. 2008. *Contemporary Fiction and the Fairy Tale*. Detroit: Wayne State
    University Press.
Berland, David I. 1982. Disney and Freud: Walt Meets the Id. *Journal of Popular Culture*
    15, no. 1: 93–104.
Berry, Sarah. 1999. Genre. In *Companion to Film Theory*, ed. Toby Miller and Robert Stam,
    25–43. London: Blackwell.
Bettelheim, Bruno. 1976. *The Uses of Enchantment: The Meaning and Importance of Fairy
    Tales*. New York: Knopf.

Beyard-Tyler, Karen C., and Howard J. Sullivan. 1980. Adolescent Reading Preferences for Type of Theme and Sex of Character. *Reading Research Quarterly* 16, no. 1: 104–20.

Blackford, Holly. 2007. PC Pinocchios: Parents, Children, and the Metamorphosis Tradition in Science Fiction. In *Folklore/Cinema: Popular Film as Vernacular Culture,* ed. Sharon R. Sherman and Mikel J. Koven, 74–92. Logan: Utah State University Press.

Blake, Richard. A. 1999. For Better or Worse? Review of *Eyes Wide Shut. America* 181, no. 5: 22.

Bottigheimer, Ruth B. 1986. Silenced Women in the Grimms' Tales: The "Fit" between Fairy Tales and Society in Their Historical Context. In *Fairy Tales and Society: Illusion, Allusion and Paradigm,* ed. Ruth B. Bottigheimer, 113–31. Philadelphia: University of Pennsylvania Press.

———. 1987. *Grimms' Bad Girls & Bold Boys: The Moral and Social Vision of the Tales.* New Haven, CT: Yale University Press.

———. 2004. Fertility Control and the Birth of the Modern European Fairy Tale Heroine. In *Fairy Tales and Feminism: New Approaches,* ed. Donald Haase, 37–51.

Bould, Mark. 2002. The Dreadful Credibility of Absurd Things. *Historical Materialism* 10, no. 4: 51–88.

Bourdieu, Pierre. 1985. The Market of Symbolic Goods. *Poetics* 14: 13–44.

Bowles, Scott. 2007. *Enchanted* Casts Spell Over Thanksgiving Box Office. *USA Today,* November 25. Available online at http://www.usatoday.com/life/movies/news/2007-11-25-box-office_N.html

Bristow, Joseph, and Trev Lynn Broughton, eds. 1997. *The Infernal Desires of Angela Carter.* New York: Addison Wesley Longman.

Brown, Sarah. 2004. Deceased Wife's Sister Act. *The Literary Encyclopedia.* Available online at http://www.litencyc.com/php/stopics.php?rec=true&UID=1430

Bryant, Sylvia. 1989. Re-constructing Oedipus through "Beauty and the Beast." *Criticism* 31, no. 4 (fall): 439–53.

Brydon, Anne. 2005. Icelanders. In *Encyclopedia of the World's Minorities,* ed. Carl Skutsch, 2: 581–83. New York: Routledge.

Bryman, Alan. 2004. *The Disneyization of Society.* London: Sage Publications.

Bullen, Elizabeth. 2009. Inside Story: Product Placement and Adolescent Consumer Identity in Young Adult Fiction. *Media, Culture and Society* 31, no. 3: 497–508.

Burr, Ty. 1999. The shoe fits. *Entertainment Weekly,* March 5, issue 475: 68-70.

Busty Bot for Lonely Hearts. 2008. *The Age.* Available online at http://www.theage.com.au/news/technology/busty-bot-for-lonely-hearts/2008/06/18/1213468466750.html

Butler, Judith. [1990] 1999. *Gender Trouble: Feminism and the Subversion of Identity.* Repr. New York: Routledge. Text citations are to the 1999 edition.

Byatt, A. S. 2004. Introduction to *The Annotated Brothers Grimm,* ed. Maria Tatar, xvii–xxvi.

Campbell, Joseph. 1968. *The Hero with a Thousand Faces.* Princeton, NJ: Princeton University Press.

Card, Orson Scott. 1990. *How to Write Science Fiction and Fantasy.* Cincinnati: Writer's Digest.

Carryl, Guy Wetmore, and Albert Levering. 1902. *Grimm Tales Made Gay.* New York: Houghton Mifflin.

Carter, Angela. 1979. *The Bloody Chamber and Other Stories.* London: Vintage.

———, ed. 1990. *The Virago Book of Fairy Tales.* London: Virago.

———. 1991. *Sleeping Beauty and Other Favourite Fairy Tales.* Boston: Otter Books.

Cheadle, Dave. 2007. *Victorian Fairies and the Enchanting Little People of a Romantic Age.* Nashville: Premium Press America.

Chodorow, Nancy. 1976. Oedipal Asymmetries and Heterosexual Knots. *Social Problems* 23, no. 4: 454–68.

Clover, Carol. 1992. *Men, Women, and Chain Saws: Gender in the Modern Horror Film.* Princeton, NJ: Princeton University Press.

———. 1996. Her Body, Himself: Gender in the Slasher Film. In *The Dread of Difference: Gender and the Horror Film,* ed. B. K. Grant, 66-180. Austin: University of Texas Press.

Code, Lorraine, ed. 2000. *Encyclopedia of Feminist Theories.* New York: Routledge.

Collodi, Carlo. [1883] 1973. *Pinocchio.* Trans. M. Murray. London: Aldine Press.

Comyns, Barbara. 1985. *The Juniper Tree.* New York: St. Martin's Press.

Crane, Thomas Frederick. 1885. *Italian Popular Tales.* New York: Houghton Mifflin.

Craven, Allison. 2002. Beauty and the Belles: Discourses of Feminism and Femininity in Disneyland. *European Journal of Women's Studies* 9, no. 2: 123–42.

Creed, Barbara. 1993. *The Monstrous-Feminine: Film, Feminism, Psychoanalysis.* London: Routledge.

Croker, Thomas Crofton. 1825. *Fairy Legends and Traditions of the South of Ireland.* London: J. Murray.

Day, Aidan. 1998. *Angela Carter: The Rational Glass.* Manchester, UK: Manchester University Press.

Decter, Midge. 1999. The Kubrick Mystique. *Commentary* 108, no. 2: 52–55.

Dégh, Linda. 1991. What Did the Grimm Brothers Give to and Take from the Folk? In *The Brothers Grimm and Folktale,* ed. James M. McGlathery, 66–90. Urbana: University of Illinois Press.

———. 1994. *American Folklore and the Mass Media.* Bloomington: Indiana University Press.

De Lauretis, Teresa. 1987. *Technologies of Gender: Essays on Theory, Film, and Fiction.* Bloomington: Indiana University Press.

Delicka, Magdalena. 1997. American Magical Realism: Crossing the Borders in Literatures of the Margins. *Journal of American Studies of Turkey* no. 6,. Available online at http://www.bilkent.edu.tr/~jast/Number6/Delicka.html

Denby, David. 2000. The Last Waltz. *The New Yorker* 75, no. 20: 84–86.

Deszcz, Justyna. 2002. Beyond the Disney Spell, or Escape into Pantoland. *Folklore* 113, no. 1: 83–91.

Disney Movies Versus Fairy Tales. n.d. SurLaLune Fairy Tale Discussion Board. Available online at http://www.surlalunefairytales.com/boardarchives/2004/jul2004/disney-movies1.html

Disney princess. 2008. Disney Shopping. Available online at http://disneyshopping.go.com/webapp/wcs/stores/servlet/CategoryDisplay?catalogId=10002&storeId=10051&categoryId=13925&langId=-1&N=0&Ntk=p_categoryID&Ntt=13925&Nu=p_productID

Doane, Mary Ann. 1991. *Femmes Fatales: Feminism, Film Theory, Psychoanalysis.* New York: Routledge.

———. 2000. Film and the Masquerade: Theorizing the Female Spectator. In *Feminism and Film,* ed. E. Ann Kaplan, 418–36. New York: Oxford University Press.

Dogar, Rana. 1997. Here Comes the Billion Dollar Bride. *Working Woman* 22, no. 5 (May): 32–35, 69–70.

Doja, Albert. 2006. The Predicament of Heroic Anthropology. *Anthropology Today* 22, no. 3: 18–22.

Do Rozario, Rebecca-Anne C. 2004. The Princess and the Magic Kingdom: Beyond Nostalgia, the Function of the Disney Princess. *Women's Studies in Communication* 27, no. 1: 34–59.

Doughty, Terri. 2004. Locating Harry Potter in the "Boys' Book" Market. In *The Ivory Tower and Harry Potter: Perspectives on a Literary Phenomenon,* ed. Lana A. Whited, 243–57. Columbia: University of Missouri Press.

Douglas, Susan J. 1994. *Where the Girls Are: Growing Up Female with the Mass Media.* New York: Times Books (Random House).

Dresang, Eliza T. 2004. Hermione Granger and the Heritage of Gender. In *The Ivory Tower and Harry Potter: Perspectives on a Literary Phenomenon,* 211–42.

Dujovne, Beatriz E. 2004. Disavowal and the Culture of Deadening: Revisiting Stanley Kubrick's *Eyes Wide Shut. Psychoanalytic Psychology* 21, no. 4: 633–37.

Duncker, Patricia. 1984. Reimagining the Fairy Tales: Angela Carter's Bloody Chambers. *Literature and History* 10, no. 1: 3-14.

———. 1992. *Sisters and Strangers: An Introduction to Contemporary Feminist Fiction.* Oxford: Blackwell.

Dundes, Alan. 1965. *The Study of Folklore.* Englewood Cliffs, NJ: Prentice-Hall.

———. 1989. Interpreting "Little Red Riding Hood" Psychoanalytically. In *Little Red Riding Hood: A Casebook,* ed. Alan Dundes, 192–238. Madison: University of Wisconsin Press.

Ebert, Roger. 2005. Review of *MirrorMask. Chicago Sun-Times,* September 30.

Edwards, Lee R. 1979. The Labors of Psyche: Toward a Theory of Female Heroism. *Critical Inquiry* 6, no. 1: 33–49.

Ellis, John M. 1983. *One Fairy Story Too Many: The Brothers Grimm and Their Tales.* Chicago: University of Chicago Press.

Eliot, Marc. 1993. *Walt Disney: Hollywood's Dark Prince.* New York: Carol Publishing Group.

Enchanted. 2008. Disney Shopping. Available online at http://disneyshopping.go.com/webapp/wcs/stores/servlet/CategoryDisplay?catalogId=10002&storeId=10051&categoryId=42001&langId=-1&N=0&Ntk=p_categoryID&Ntt=42001&Nu=p_productID

Enchanted. 2007. El Capitan Theatre, November 2007–January 2008. Available online at http://disney.go.com/DisneyPictures/el%5Fcapitan

Enchanted Box Office Earnings. 2007. Box Office Mojo. Available online at http://www.boxofficemojo.com/movies/?id=enchanted.html

Enchanted's Princess Giselle Debuts at Disney-MGM Studios. 2007. Walt Disney World News, December 27. Available online at http://www.wdwnews.com/ViewImage.aspx?ImageID=108400

Enchanted. 2007. Reviews. Rotten Tomatoes. Available online at http://www.rottentomatoes.com/m/enchanted/reviews_mycritics.php

Enchanted. 2007. Reviews at Metacritic. Available online at http://www.metacritic.com/film/titles/enchanted?q=*Enchanted* - critics

Eng, David L. 2000. Melancholia in the Late Twentieth Century. *Signs: Journal of Women in Culture and Society* 25, no. 4: 1275–81.

Evans, Dylan. 1996. An Introductory Dictionary of Lacanian Psychoanalysis. New York: Routledge.

Falassi, Alessandro. 1980. *Folklore by the Fireside: Text and Context in the Tuscan Veglia.* Austin: University of Texas Press.

Faludi, Susan. 1991. *Backlash: The Undeclared War against American Women.* New York: Crown Publishers.

Faris, Wendy. 1995. Scheherazade's Children: Magical Realism and Postmodern Fiction. In *Magical Realism: Theory, History, Community,* eds. Lois P. Zamora and Wendy B. Faris, 163–90. Durham, NC: Duke University Press.

Faye, Dennis. 2009. In the Garden of Good and Evil. Writers Guild of America West. Available online at http://www.wga.org/content/default.aspx?id=3076

Felski, Rita. 2003. *Literature after Feminism.* Chicago: University of Chicago Press.

Film Ratings. Motion Picture Association of America. Available online at http://www.mpaa.org/FilmRatings.asp

Fjellman, Stephen M. 1992. *Vinyl Leaves: Walt Disney World and America.* Boulder, CO: Westview Press.

Flowers, Stephen. 1989. *The Galdrabók: An Icelandic Grimoire.* York Beach, MN: Samuel Weiser.

Freeman, Elizabeth. 2002. *The Wedding Complex: Forms of Belonging in Modern American Culture.* Durham, NC: Duke University Press.

Freud, Sigmund. 1960. *Jokes and Their Relation to the Unconscious.* Trans. and ed. by James Strachey. New York: W. W. Norton.

Frow, John. 2005. *Genre.* New York: Routledge.

Gaiman, Neil. 2005. *MirrorMask.* Illustrated by Dave McKean. New York: HarperCollins.

Gallardo-C., Ximena, and C. Jason Smith. 2003. "Cinderfella": J. K. Rowling's Wily Web of Gender. In *Reading Harry Potter: Critical Essays,* ed. Giselle Liza Anatol, 191–205. London: Praeger.

Gardner, Martin. 1960. *The Annotated Alice.* New York: Clarkson N. Potter.

Genette, Gérard. 1997. *Palimpsests: Literature in the Second Degree.* Trans. Channa Newman and Claude Doubinsky. Lincoln: University of Nebraska Press.

Gilbert, Sandra M., and Susan Gubar. 1979. The Queen's Looking Glass: Female Creativity, Male Images of Women, and the Metaphor of Literary Paternity. In *The Madwoman in the Attic: The Woman Writer and the Nineteenth-Century Literary Imagination,* 3–44. New Haven, CT: Yale University Press.

Girardot, N. J. 1977. Initiation and Meaning in the Tale of "Snow White and the Seven Dwarfs." *Journal of American Folklore* 90, no. 357: 274–300.

Giroux, Henry A. 1997. Are Disney Movies Good for Your Kids? In *Kinderculture: The Corporate Construction of Childhood,* eds. Shirley R. Steinberg and Joe L. Kincheloe, 53–68. Boulder, CO: Westview Press.

———. 1999. *The Mouse That Roared: Disney and the End of Innocence.* New York: Rowman & Littlefield.

———. 2009. Disney, Casino Capitalism and the Exploitation of Young Boys: Beyond the Politics of Innocence. *Truthout,* April 15. Available online at http://www.truthout.org/041509J

Glass, Philip. n.d. Compositions: *The Juniper Tree.* Available online at http://www.philip-glass.com/html/compositions/the-juniper-tree.html

Gonzenbach, Laura. 1870. Maria, die böse Stiefmutter und die sieben Räuber. In *Sicilianische Märchen: Aus dem Volksmund gesammelt,* vol 1, ed. Otto Hartwig, 4–7. Leipzig: Verlag von Wilhelm Engelmann.

Greenhill, Pauline. 2008. Fitcher's [Queer] Bird: A Fairytale Heroine and Her Avatars. *Marvels & Tales* 22, no. 1: 143–67.

Greenhill, Pauline, and Emilie Anderson-Grégoire with Anita Best. Forthcoming. Queering Gender: Transformations in "Peg Bearskin" and Related Tales. In *Transgressive Tales: Queer Sexualities, Grimm Sex, and Transgender,* eds. Kay Turner and Pauline Greenhill, Detroit: Wayne State University Press.

Greenhill, Pauline, and Steven Kohm. 2009. Little Red Riding Hood and the Pedophile in Film: *Freeway, Hard Candy* and *The Woodsman. Jeunesse: Young People, Texts, Cultures* 1, no. 2: 35-65.

Grimm, Jacob and Wilhelm. [1812] 1890. *Childhood and Household Tales.* Trans. Andrew Lang. Available online at http://www.surlalunefairytales.com

———. 1981. *The German Legends of the Brothers Grimm.* Trans. Donald Ward. Philadelphia: Institute for the Study of Human Issues.

———. 1992. Cinderella. In *The Complete Fairy Tales of the Brothers Grimm,* trans. and ed. Jack Zipes, 86–92. New York: Bantam.

———. 2004. *The Annotated Brothers Grimm.* Trans. and ed. Maria Tatar. New York: W. W. Norton.

Grover, Ron. 1991. *The Disney Touch: How a Daring Management Team Revived an Entertainment Empire.* Homewood, IL: Business One Irwin.

Gruner, Elisabeth Rose. 2003. Saving "Cinderella": History and Story in *Ashpet* and *Ever After. Children's Literature* 31: 142–54.

Guenther, Irene. 1995. "Magic Realism, New Objectivity, and the Arts during the Weimer Republic." In *Magical Realism: Theory, History, Community,* eds. Lois P. Zamora and Wendy B. Faris, 33–73.

Gunnarsson, Gísli. 1983. *Monopoly Trade and Economic Stagnation: Studies in the Foreign Trade of Iceland 1602–1787.* Lund: Ekonomiske Historiska Foreningen.

Haas, Lynda. 1995. "Eight-Six the Mother": Murder, Matricide, and Good Mothers. In *From Mouse to Mermaid: The Politics of Film, Gender, and Culture,* eds. Elizabeth Bell, Lynda Haas, and Laura Sells, 193–211. Bloomington: Indiana University Press.

Haase, Donald. 1993a. Yours, Mine, or Ours? Perrault, the Brothers Grimm, and the Ownership of Fairy Tales. In *Once upon a Folktale: Capturing the Folktale Process with Children,* ed. Gloria T. Blatt, 63–79. New York: Teachers College Press.

———. 1993b. Response and Responsibility in Reading Grimms' Fairy Tales. In *The Reception of the Grimms' Fairy Tales: Responses, Reactions, Revisions,* ed. Donald Haase, 230-49. Detroit: Wayne State University Press.

———, ed. 2004a. *Fairy Tales and Feminism: New Approaches.* Detroit: Wayne State University Press.

———. 2004b. Feminist Fairy Tale Scholarship. In *Fairy Tales and Feminism: New Approaches,* 1–36.

———. 2006. Hypertextual Gutenberg: The Textual and Hypertextual Life of Folktales and Fairy Tales in English-Language Popular Print Editions. *Fabula* 47, no. 3/4: 222–30.

Haffenden, John. 1985. *Novelists in Interview.* New York: Routledge.

Halberstam, Judith. 1998. *Female Masculinity.* Durham, NC: Duke University Press.

Hallmundsson, May, and Hallberg Hallmundsson. 1987. *Icelandic Folk and Fairy Tales.* Reykjavík: Iceland Review Library.

Hanhardt, John G. 1990. Video Art: Expanded Forms. *Leonardo* 23, no. 4: 437–39.

Hanke, Ken. 2000. *Tim Burton: An Unauthorized Biography of the Filmmaker.* Los Angeles: Renaissance Books.

Haring, Lee. 2008. Hybridity, Hybridization. In *The Greenwood Encyclopedia of Folktales and Fairy Tales,* ed. Donald Haase, vol. 2, 463–67. Westport, CT: Greenwood.

Harries, Elizabeth Wanning. 2001. *Twice Upon a Time: Women Writers and the History of the Fairy Tale.* Princeton, NJ: Princeton University Press.

Heilman, Elizabeth E. 2003. "Blue Wizards and Pink Witches": Representations of Gender Identity and Power. In *Harry Potter's World: Multidisciplinary Critical Perspectives,* ed. Elizabeth E. Heilman, 221–39. New York: Routledge Falmer.

Heiner, Heidi Anne. SurLaLune Fairy Tales Web site. Available online at http://www.surlalunefairytales.com

Helmetag, Charles. 2003. Dream Odysseys: Schnitzler's *Traumnovelle* and Kubrick's *Eyes Wide Shut. Literature/Film Quarterly* 31, no. 4: 276–86.

Henke, Jill Birnie, Diane Zimmerman Umble, and Nancy J. Smith. 1996. Construction of the Female Self: Feminist Readings of the Disney Heroine. *Women's Studies in Communication* 19, no. 2: 229–49.

Hennig, John. 1946. The Brothers Grimm and T. C. Croker. *Modern Language Review* 41, no. 1: 44–54.

Hensher, Philip. 1999. Masque of the Dead Flesh. *Times Literary Supplement,* September 17, 20.

Hines, Susan, and Brenda Ayres. 2003. Introduction: (He)gemony Cricket! Why in the World Are We Still Watching Disney? In *The Emperor's Old Groove: Decolonizing Disney's Magic Kingdom,* 1–12.

Hinson, Hal. 1989. Review of *Batman* by Tim Burton. *Washington Post,* June 23. Available online at http://www.washingtonpost.com/wpsrv/style/longterm/movies/videos/batmanpg13hinson_a07fb8.html

Hoerrner, Keisha L. 1996. Gender Roles in Disney Films: Analyzing Behaviors from Snow White to Simba. *Women's Studies in Communication* 19, no. 2: 213–28.

Holbek, Bengt. 1998. *Interpretation of Fairy Tales: Danish Folklore in a European Perspective.* Helsinki: Academia Scientiarum Fennica.

Holden, Stephen. 1998. No Helpless, Wimpy Waif Filling This Glass Slipper. *New York Times,* July 31, arts section.

hooks, bell. 1992. *Black Looks: Race and Representation.* Cambridge, MA: South End Press.

———. 2000. *Feminism Is for Everybody: Passionate Politics.* Cambridge, MA: South End Press.

Hreinsson, Viðar, Robert Cook, Terry Gunnell, Keneva Kunz, and Bernard Scudder, eds. 1997. *The Complete Sagas of Icelanders.* 5 vols. Reykjavík: Leifur Eiríksson Publishing Ltd.

Hubner, Laura. 2007. *Pan's Labyrinth:* Fear and the Fairy Tale. Paper presented at the Fear, Horror and Terror at the Interface first global conference, September 10–12, Mansfield College, Oxford, UK.

Hurley, Dorothy. 2005. Seeing White: Children of Color and the Disney Fairy Tale Princess. *Journal of Negro Education* 74, no. 3: 221–32.

Hutcheon, Linda. 2000. *A Theory of Parody: The Teachings of Twentieth-Century Art Forms.* Urbana: University of Illinois Press. (Orig. pub. 1985.)

———. 2006. *A Theory of Adaptation.* New York: Routledge.

Ingraham, Chrys. 2008. *White Weddings: Romancing Heterosexuality in Popular Culture.* 2d ed. New York: Routledge.

Irigaray, Luce. 1985. *This Sex Which Is Not One.* Trans. Catherine Porter. New York: Cornell University Press.

Jackson, Rosemary. 1981. *Fantasy: The Literature of Subversion.* New York: Methuen.

Jacobs, Alexandra. 2001. Love, Honor, Obey and . . . oh. *New York Observer,* February 12. Available online at http://www.observer.com/node/38356

Jacobs, Joseph. 1967a. Kate Crackernuts. In *English Fairy Tales,* collected by Joseph Jacobs, 198–202. New York: Dover.

———. 1967b. Molly Whuppie. In *English Fairy Tales,* collected by Joseph Jacobs, 125–30. New York: Dover.

———. 1975. Catskin. In *English Fairy Tales,* collected by Joseph Jacobs, 268–71. London: The Bodley Head.

Jones, Steven Swann. 1993. The Innocent Persecuted Heroine Genre: An Analysis of Its Structure and Themes. *Western Folklore* 52, no. 1: 13–41.

———. 2002. *The Fairy Tale: The Magic Mirror of the Imagination.* London: Routledge.

Joralemon, Donald. 2000. The Ethics of the Organ Market. In *Biotechnology and Culture: Bodies, Anxiety, Ethics,* ed. Paul Brodwin, 224–40. Bloomington: Indiana University Press.

Jorgensen, Jeana. 2007. A Wave of the Magic Wand: Fairy Godmothers in Contemporary American Media. *Marvels & Tales* 21, no. 2: 216–27.

The Juniper Tree. 1990. The Internet Movie Database. Available online at http://imdb.com/title/tt0138545/

Kam, Nadine. 2007. Pouf! Costume Magic: The Wardrobe in Disney's New Film Pulls off the Cartoon-to-Real World Theme. *Star Bulletin,* November 15. Available online at http://starbulletin.com/2007/11/15/features/story01.html

Kaplan, E. Ann. 1997. The Politics of Surrogacy Narratives. In *Feminism, Media & the Law,* ed. Martha A. Fineman and Martha T. McCluskey, 193–202.

———. 2000. The Case of the Missing Mother. In *Feminism & Film,* ed. E. Ann Kaplan, 466–78. New York: Oxford University Press.

Karpin, Isabel. 1997. Pop Justice: TV, Motherhood, and the Law. In *Feminism, Media & the Law,* 120–36.

Karras, Irene. 2002. The Third Wave's Final Girl: Buffy the Vampire Slayer. *Thirdspace,* vol 1, 2. Available online at www.thirdspace.ca/articles/karras.html

Keene, Nietzchka. n.d. Fulbright Application.

———. 1990. *The Juniper Tree.* Undated script. Collection, Wisconsin Center for Film and Theater Research.

———. 2002. Interview. *The Juniper Tree* DVD. Rhino Home Video.

Kelts, Roland. 2006. *Japanamerica: How Japanese Pop Culture Has Invaded the U.S.* New York: Palgrave MacMillan.

Kenway, Jane, and Elizabeth Bullen. 2001. *Consuming Children: Education, Entertainment, Advertising.* Buckingham: Open University Press.

Kermode, Mark. 2000. Interview with Tim Burton. *The Guardian,* January 6. Available online at http://www.guardian.co.uk/film/2000/jan/06/guardianinterviewsatbfisouthbank3

Kevorkian, Martin. 2003. "You Must Never Move the Body!" Burying Irving's Text in *Sleepy Hollow. Literature/Film Quarterly* 31, no. 1: 27–32.

Kracauer, Siegfried. 1997. *Theory of Film: The Redemption of Physical Reality.* Princeton, NJ: Princeton University Press.

Kristeva, Julia. 1980. *Desire in Language.* Trans. Leon S. Roudiez. New York: Columbia University Press.

———. 1982. *Powers of Horror.* New York: Columbia University Press.

———. 1989. *Black Sun: Depression and Melancholia.* Trans. Leon S. Roudiez. New York: Columbia University Press.

Krum, Sharon. 2006. Beware! Queen Kong Is Coming. *The Guardian,* February 24. Available online at http://www.guardian.co.uk/world/2006/feb/24/gender.oscars2006

Labrie, Vivian. 1997. Help! Me, S/he, and the Boss. In *Undisciplined Women: Tradition and Culture in Canada,* eds. Pauline Greenhill and Diane Tye, 151–66. Montreal: McGill-Queen's University Press.

Lang, Andrew, ed. [1890] 1966. Twelve Dancing Princesses. *The Red Fairy Book.* New York: Dover. Available online at http://www.surlalunefairytales.com/twelvedancing/stories/lang.html

Langer, Beryl. 2002. Enchantment: Children and Consumer Capitalism. *Thesis Eleven* 69, no. 1: 67–81.

Langlois, Janet. 1985. Belle Gunness, the Lady Bluebeard: Narrative Use of a Deviant Woman. In *Women's Folklore, Women's Culture,* eds. Rosan A. Jordan and Susan J. Kal ik, 109–24. Philadelphia: University of Pennsylvania Press.

———. 1993. Mothers' Double Talk. In *Feminist Messages: Coding in Women's Folk Culture,* ed. Joan Newlon Radner, 80–97. Urbana: University of Illinois Press.

Lapine, James. 1988. Writer/Director. *Performing Arts Journal* 11, no. 1: 54–55.

Lappas, Catherine. 1996. Seeing Is Believing, but Touching Is the Truth: Female Spectatorship and Sexuality in *The Company of Wolves. Women's Studies* 25, no. 2: 115–35.

Lau, Kimberly J. 2008. Erotic Infidelities: Angela Carter's Wolf Trilogy. *Marvels & Tales* 22, no. 1: 77–94.

Laub, Dori. 1992. Bearing Witness or the Vicissitudes of Listening. In *Testimony: Crises of Witnessing in Literature, Psychoanalysis and History,* eds. Shoshana Felman and Dori Laub, 57–74. New York: Routledge.

Lee, Hermione. 1994. A Room of One's Own or a Bloody Chamber?: Angela Carter and Political Correctness. In *Flesh and the Mirror: Essays on the Art of Angela Carter,* ed. Lorna Sage, 308–20. London: Virago.

Lieberman, Marcia R. 1972 "Some Day My Prince Will Come": Female Acculturation through the Fairy Tale. *College English* 34, no. 3: 383–95.

Liedl, Nathaniel. 2004. Comm Arts Dealt Tragedy. *Badger Herald (University of Wisconsin-Madison),* October 26. Available online at http://badgerherald.com/news/2004/10/26/comm_arts_dealt_trag.php

List of Disney References in *Enchanted.* Wikipedia. Available online at http://en.wikipedia.org/wiki/List_of_Disney_references_in_*Enchanted*

Loren, Scott. 2004. What Are the Implications of the Virtual for the Human? An Analytical Ethics of Identity in Pop Culture Narratives. *European Journal of American Culture* 23, no. 3: 173–85.

Loudermilk, Kim. 2004. *Fictional Feminism: How American Bestsellers Affect the Movement for Women's Equality.* New York: Routledge.

Lundell, Torborg. 1986. Gender-Related Biases in the Type and Motif Indexes of Aarne and Thompson. In *Fairy Tales and Society: Illusion, Allusion and Paradigm,* ed. Ruth B. Bottigheimer, 149–63.

Lurie, Alison. 1970. Fairy Tale Liberation. *New York Review of Books* 15 no. 11, December 17: 42–44.

———. 1971. Witches and Fairies: Fitzgerald to Updike. *New York Review of Books* 17 no. 9, December 2, 6–11.

Macleod, Dianne Sachko. 2003. The Politics of Vision: Disney, Aladdin, and the Gulf War. In *The Emperor's Old Grove: Decolonizing Disney's Magic Kingdom,* ed. Brenda Ayres, 179–92.

Maio, Kathi. 1998. Disney's Dolls. *The New Internationalist* 308, December: 12–14. Available online at http://www.newint.org/issue308/dolls.html

Maitland, Sara. 1987. *A Book of Spells*. London: Joseph.

Makinen, Merja. 2008. Theorizing Fairy Tale Fiction: Reading Jeanette Winterson. In *Contemporary Fiction and the Fairy Tale,* ed. Stephen Benson, 144–77.

Mankin, Nan. 1988. Contemporary Performance: The Emergence of the Fairy Tale. *Performing Arts Journal* 11, no. 1: 48–53.

Manovich, Lev. 1999. What Is Digital Cinema? In *The Digital Dialectic: New Essays on New Media,* ed. Peter Lunenfeld, 172–92. Cambridge, MA: MIT Press.

Marr, Marisa. 2007. Disney Reaches to the Crib to Extend Princess Magic. *Wall Street Journal,* November 19. Available online at http://online.wsj.com/public/article/SB119543097711697381.html

Martin, Ann. 2006. *Red Riding Hood and the Wolf in Bed: Modernism's Fairy Tales.* Toronto: University of Toronto Press.

Martin, Sara. 2001. Little Red Riding Hood Meets the Werewolf: Genre and Gender Tensions in Neil Jordan's *The Company of Wolves. Journal of the Fantastic in the Arts* 12, no. 1: 18–33.

Mathews, Richard. 1997. *Fantasy: The Literature of Imagination.* New York: Twayne Publishers.

Matrix, Sidney Eve. 2006. "I-Do" Feminism Courtesy of *Martha Stewart Weddings* and HBCs Vow to Wow Club: Inventing Modern Matrimonial Tradition with Glue Sticks and Cuisinart. *Ethnologies* 28, no. 2: 53–80.

Mattessich, Stefan. 2000. Grotesque Caricature: Stanley Kubrick's *Eyes Wide Shut* as the Allegory of Its Own Reception. *Postmodern Culture* 10, no. 2. Available online at http://muse.jhu.edu/journals/pmc/v010/10.2.r_mattessich.html

Mazierska, Ewa. 2000. Between the Sacred and the Profane, the Sublime and the Trivial: The Magic Realism of Jan Jakub Kolski. *Scope,* January. Available online at http://www.scope.nottingham.ac.uk/article.php?issue=jan2000&id=281&section=article

McCallum, Robyn, and John Stephens. n.d. Film and Fairy Tales. Available online at http://www.answers.com/topic/film-and-fairy tales

McCarthy, Todd. 1991. Review of *The Juniper Tree. Variety* 342, February 18: 70.

McCormick, Moira. 1999. Fox's 'Ever After' Push Takes Multiple Paths to Reach Female Buyers. *Billboard,* March 20.

McDougall, Joyce. 2004. Freud and Female Sexualities. In *Dialogues on Sexuality, Gender, and Psychoanalysis,* ed. Iréne Matthis, 23–40. London: Karmac Books.

McGowan, Todd, and Sheila Kunkle, eds. 2004. *Lacan and Contemporary Film.* New York: Other Press.

McMahan, Alison. 2005. *The Films of Tim Burton: Animating Live Action in Contemporary Hollywood.* New York: Continuum.

Memorial Resolution of the Faculty of the University of Wisconsin-Madison on the Death of Professor Nietzchka Keene. 2005. February 7. Available online at http://www.secfac.wisc.edu/senate/2005/0207/1825(mem_res).pdf

Meph, Johannes. 1997. Stresses and Strains: New Music from Leipzig, Berlin, Vienna, Munich & Wittener. *The Musical Times* 138, no. 1852: 42–44.

Metz, Christian. 2004. From *The Imaginary Signifier.* In *Film Theory and Criticism,* eds. Leo Braudy and Marshall Cohen, 820–36. 6th ed. New York: Oxford University Press.

Morrissey, Thomas. 2004. Growing Nowhere: *Pinocchio* Subverted in Spielberg's *A.I: Artificial Intelligence. Extrapolation* 16, no: 3: 249–62.

Mosley, Leonard. 1990. *Disney's World.* Lanham, MD: Scarborough House.

Mulvey, Laura. 1975. Visual Pleasure and Narrative Cinema. *Screen* 16, no. 3 (autumn): 6–18.

Murray, Rebecca. n.d. Amy Adams Transforms into a Princess for *Enchanted*. About Movies. Available online at http://movies.about.com/od/enchanted/a/enchanted111507.html

Musäus, Johann Karl. 1791. *Popular Tales of the Germans*. Trans. William Beckford. London: J. Murray.

Nagy, Joseph Falaky. 1979. Rites of Passage in "The Juniper Tree." *Southern Folklore Quarterly* 43, no. 1/2: 253–65.

———. 1984. Vengeful Music in Traditional Narrative. *Folklore* 95, no. 2: 182–90.

Napier, Susan J. 2005. *Anime from Akira to Howl's Moving Castle: Experiencing Contemporary Japanese Animation*. New York: Palgrave Macmillan.

Narváez, Peter, ed. 1991. *The Good People: New Fairylore Essays*. New York: Garland.

Narváez, Peter, and Martin Laba, eds. 1986. *Media Sense: The Folklore-Popular Culture Continuum*. Bowling Green, OH: Bowling Green State University Popular Press.

Nashawaty, Chris. 2008. Knight Fever. *Entertainment Weekly*, August 1, issue 1008: 20.

Nikolajeva, Maria. 1998. Exit Children's Literature? *Lion and the Unicorn* 22, no. 2: 221–36

———. 2003. Fairy Tale and Fantasy: From Archaic to Postmodern. *Marvels & Tales* 17, no. 1: 138–56.

O'Brien, Pamela Colby. 1996. The Happiest Films on Earth: A Textual and Contextual Analysis of Walt Disney's *Cinderella* and *The Little Mermaid*. *Women's Studies in Communication* 19, no. 2: 155–83.

Opie, Iona, and Peter Opie. 1992. *The Classic Fairy Tales*. Oxford: Oxford University Press.

Orme, Jennifer. 2008 Disobedient Desire: Narrative vs. Sexual Desire in *Pan's Labyrinth*. Paper presented at the Popular Culture Association/American Culture Association conference, March 19–22, San Francisco.

———. Forthcoming. Happily Ever After...According to Our Tastes: Jeanette Winterson's Twelve Dancing Princesses and Queer Possibility. In *Transgressive Tales: Queer Sexualities, Grimm Sex, and Transgender*, eds. Kay Turner and Pauline Greenhill, Detroit: Wayne State University Press.

Orr, Stanley. 2003. "A Dark Episode of Bonanza": Genre, Adaptation, and Historiography in *Sleepy Hollow*. *Literature/Film Quarterly* 31, no. 1: 44–49.

Ostry, Elaine. 2004. Is He Still Human? Are You? Young Adult Science Fiction in the Posthuman Age. *The Lion and the Unicorn* 28, no. 2: 222–46.

Otnes, Cele C., and Elizabeth Hafkin Pleck. 2003. *Cinderella Dreams: The Allure of the Lavish Wedding*. Berkeley: University of California Press.

Overstreet, Jeffrey. 2007. Fear Not *The Compass*. *Christianity Today*, November 30. Available online at http://www.christianitytoday.com/movies/commentaries/fearnot-thecompass.html

Page, Edwin. 2007. *Gothic Fantasy: The Films of Tim Burton*. London: Marion Boyars.

Pan's Labyrinth Official Podcast. 2006. Episode One, December 12. Available online at http://www.panslabyrinth.com/podcast.html

Perrault, Charles. 1961. *Complete Fairy Tales*. Trans. A. E. Johnson. New York: Dodd, Mead.

———. 2001. "Cinderella"; or, "The Little Glass Slipper." In *The Great Fairy Tale Tradition: From Straparola and Basile to the Brothers Grimm*, trans. and ed. Jack Zipes, 449–54.

Petrie, Duncan, ed. 1993. *Cinema and the Realms of Enchantment: Lectures, Seminars and Essays by Marina Warner and Others.* London: British Film Institute.

Pinterics, Natasha. 2001. Riding the Feminist Waves: In with the Third? *Canadian Woman Studies* 20/21, no. 4/1: 15–21.

Pocock, Judy. 2000. Collaborative Dreaming: Schnitzler's *Traumnovelle,* Kubrick's *Eyes Wide Shut,* and the "Paradox of the Ordinary." *Arachne: An Interdisciplinary Journal of Language and Literature* 7, no. 1/2: 76–93.

Potter, Russell. 1992. Edward Schizohands: The Postmodern Gothic Body. *Postmodern Culture* 2, no. 3: . Available online at http://pmc.iath.virginia.edu/text-only/issue.592/potter.592

Powdermaker, Hortense. 1950. Celluloid Civilization. *Saturday Review of Literature,* October 14, 9–10, 43–45.

Preston, Cathy Lynn. 2004. Disrupting the Boundaries of Genre and Gender: Postmodernism and the Fairy Tale. In *Fairy Tales and Feminism: New Approaches,* ed. Donald Haase, 197–212. Detroit: Wayne State University Press.

Propp, Vladímir. 1968. *Morphology of the Folktale.* Trans. Laurence Scott. Austin: University of Texas Press.

Rabkin, Eric S. 1976. *The Fantastic in Literature.* Princeton, NJ: Princeton University Press.

Rasmussen, Randy. 2001. *Stanley Kubrick: Seven Films Analyzed.* New York: McFarland & Co.

Reasons for Movie Ratings. 2000. Available online at http://www.filmratings.com/

Reichart, Walter A. 1957. *Washington Irving and Germany.* Ann Arbor: University of Michigan Press.

Reider, Noriko T. 2005. *Spirited Away:* Film of the Fantastic and Evolving Japanese Folk Symbols. *Film Criticism* 29, no. 3, 4–27.

Rieti, Barbara. 1991. *Strange Terrain: The Fairy World in Newfoundland.* St. John's, NL: Institute of Social and Economic Research.

Riviere, Joan. 1929. Womanliness as a Masquerade. *International Journal of Psychoanalysis* 10: 36–44.

Roberts, Sheila. 2006. Guillermo del Toro Interview, *Pan's Labyrinth.* Movies Online. Available online at http://www.moviesonline.ca/movienews_10799.html

Robertson, Gail. 1998. Snow Whitey: Stereotyping in the Magical Kingdom. *Canadian Dimension* 32, no. 5: 42–44.

Röhrich, Lutz. 1986. Introduction to *Fairy Tales and Society: Illusion, Allusion and Paradigm,* ed. Ruth B. Bottigheimer, 1–9.

———. 1991. *Folktales and Reality.* Bloomington: Indiana University Press.

Rose, Jacqueline. 1988. Paranoia and the Film System. In *Feminism and Film Theory,* ed. Constance Penley, 141–58. New York: Routledge.

Rowe, Karen E. 1986. "Feminism and Fairy Tales." In *Don't Bet on the Prince: Contemporary Feminist Fairy Tales in North America and England,* ed. Jack Zipes, 209–26.

Rowling, J. K. 1997. *Harry Potter and the Philosopher's Stone.* London: Bloomsbury.

———. 1998. *Harry Potter and the Chamber of Secrets.* London: Bloomsbury.

———. 1999. *Harry Potter and the Prizoner of Azkaban.* London: Bloomsbury.

———. 2000. *Harry Potter and the Goblet of Fire.* London: Bloomsbury.

———. 2003. *Harry Potter and the Order of the Phoenix.* London: Bloomsbury.

———. 2005. *Harry Potter and the Half-Blood Prince.* London: Bloomsbury.

———. 2007. *Harry Potter and the Deathly Hallows.* London: Bloomsbury.

Rozen, Leah and Tom Gliatto. 1998. Picks & Pans: Screen. *People* 50, no. 4, August 9, 31-5.

Rubin, Gayle. 1975. The Traffic in Women: Notes on the "Political Economy" of Sex. In
    Toward an Anthropology of Women, ed. Rayna Reiter, 157-210. New York: Monthly
    Review Press.
Russ, Joanna. 1973. Speculations: The Subjunctivity of Science Fiction. *Extrapolation* 15,
    no. 1: 51–59.
Ryan, Tim. 2007. Critical Consensus: *Enchanted* bewitches, *Hitman* misses, *No Country* is
    certified fresh. *Rotten Tomatoes,* November 20. Available online at http://www.rotten-
    tomatoes.com/m/mist/news/1690522/
Sæmundsson, Matthías Víðar. 1992. *Galdrar á Íslandi: íslensk galdrabók.* Reykjavík:
    Almenna bókafélagið.
The Sagas of Icelanders: A Selection. 2000. Preface by Jane Smiley; introduction by Robert
    Kellogg. London: Penguin Books.
Salisbury, Mark. 1995. *Burton on Burton.* London: Faber and Faber.
Sanders, Julie. 2006. *Adaptation and Appropriation.* Abingdon, UK: Routledge.
Saur, Pamela S. 2001. *Eyes Wide Shut* and its Literary Forebear: Tom Cruise Got Off Easy.
    Lamar Journal of the Humanities 26, no. 2: 53–61.
Schafer, Elizabeth D. 2000. Potter as Legend. In *Exploring Harry Potter*, 148–49. Osprey,
    FL: Beacham.
Schechter, Harold. 1988. *The Bosom Serpent: Folklore and Popular Art.* Iowa City:
    University of Iowa Press.
Schickel, Richard. 1968. *The Disney Version: The Life, Times, Art, and Commerce of Walt
    Disney.* New York: Simon and Schuster.
Schoefer, Christine. 2000. Harry Potter's Girl Trouble. *Salon,* January 13. Available online
    at http://dir.salon.com/story/books/feature/2000/01/13/potter/
Schwartz, Howard. 1988. *Lilith's Cave.* New York: Oxford University Press.
———. 1998. *Reimagining the Bible: Storytelling of the Rabbis.* New York: Oxford
    University Press.
Schwarzbaum, Lisa. 1998. Legend of the Ball. *Entertainment Weekly,* August 7, issue 444:
    52.
Sedgwick, Eve Kosofsky. 1987. *Between Men.* New York: Columbia University Press.
Sells, Laura. 1995. "Where Do the Mermaids Stand?": Voice and Body in *The Little
    Mermaid.* In *From Mouse to Mermaid: The Politics of Film, Gender, and Culture,* ed.
    Elizabeth Bell, Lynda Haas, and Laura Sells, 175–92.
Segal, Lore, and Maurice Sendak, comp. 1973. *The Juniper Tree and Other Tales from
    Grimm.* 2 vols. New York: Farrar, Straus and Giroux.
Seymour, Gene. 2007. Review of *Enchanted. Newsday,* November 21. Available online at
    http://www.newsday.com/entertainment/movies/ny-kdtues5468767nov21,0,992492.
    story
Simpson, Jacqueline. 1972. *Icelandic Folktales and Legends.* Berkeley: University of
    California Press.
Smelik, Anneke. 1998. *And the Mirror Cracked: Feminist Cinema and Film Theory.* New
    York: St. Martin's Press.
Smith, Kevin Paul. 2007. *The Postmodern Fairytale: Folkloric Intertexts in Contemporary
    Fiction.* New York: Palgrave MacMillan.
Smith, Paul Julian. 2007. *Pan's Labyrinth (El laberinto del fauno). Film Quarterly* 60, no. 4:
    4–9.
Smoodin, Eric, ed. 1994. *Disney Discourse: Producing the Magic Kingdom.* New York:
    Routledge.

Snyder, Midori. 2002. The Monkey Girl. In *Mirror, Mirror on the Wall: Women Writers Explore Their Favorite Fairy Tales,* ed. Kate Bernheimer, 325–33. 2d ed. New York: Anchor Books.

Stam, Robert. 2004. *Literature and Film: A Guide to the Theory and Practice of Film Adaptation.* London: Blackwell.

Stephens, John. 1992. *Language and Ideology in Children's Fiction.* Essex, UK: Longman.

Stephens, John, and Robyn McCallum. 2002. Utopia, Dystopia, and Cultural Controversy in *Ever After* and *The Grimm Brothers' Snow White. Marvels & Tales* 16, no. 2: 201–13.

Stone, Kay. 1985. The Misuses of Enchantment: Controversies on the Significance of Fairy Tales. In *Women's Folklore, Women's Culture,* eds. Rosan A. Jordan and Susan J. Kalçik, 125–45. Philadelphia: University of Pennsylvania Press.

———. 1998. *Burning Brightly: New Light on Old Tales Told Today.* Peterborough: Broadview Press.

———. 2004. Fire and Water: A Journey into the Heart of a Story. In *Fairy Tales and Feminism: New Approaches,* ed. Donald Haase, 113–28. Detroit: Wayne State University Press.

———, with Marvyne Jenoff and Susan Gordon. 1997. Difficult Women in Folktales: Two Women, Two Stories. In *Undisciplined Women: Tradition and Culture in Canada,* eds. Pauline Greenhill and Diane Tye, 250–65.

Strauss, Gary. 2004. Princesses Rule the Hearts of Little Girls. *USA Today,* March 2. Available online at http://www.usatoday.com/life/lifestyle/2004-03-02-princess_x.html

Suvin, Darko. 2003. Theses on Dystopia 2001. In *Dark Horizons: Science Fiction and the Dystopian Imagination,* ed. Raffaella Baccolini and Tom Moylan, 187–203. New York: Routledge.

Tatar, Maria. 1985. From Nags to Witches: Stepmothers in the Grimms' Fairy Tales. In *Opening Texts: Psychoanalysis and the Culture of the Child,* eds. Joseph H. Smith and William Kerrigan, 28–41. Baltimore: Johns Hopkins University Press.

———. 1987. *The Hard Facts of the Grimms Fairy Tales.* Princeton, NJ: Princeton University Press. Revised and expanded, 2003.

———. 1992. *Off with Their Heads: Fairy Tales and the Culture of Childhood.* Princeton, NJ: Princeton University Press.

———, ed. 1999. *The Classic Fairy Tales: Texts, Criticism.* New York: W. W. Norton.

———. 2003. *The Hard Facts of the Grimms Fairy Tales.* Exp. 2nd ed. Princeton, NJ: Princeton University Press.

———, ed. and trans. 2004. *The Annotated Brothers Grimm.* New York: W. W. Norton.

Taylor, Bruce. n.d. Mr. Magical Realism: The Magic Realist Writers International Network. Available online at http://www.pantarbe.com/mrmagicrealism/mrfilms.html

Tiffin, Jessica. 2008. Tim Burton. In *The Greenwood Encyclopedia of Folktales and Fairy Tales,* ed. Donald Haase, 1:148–49.

Todorov, Tzvetan. 1973. *The Fantastic: A Structural Approach to a Literary Genre.* Cleveland: Press of Case Western Reserve University.

Tosenberger, Catherine. 2008a. Homosexuality at the Online Hogwarts: Harry Potter Slash Fanfiction. *Children's Literature* 36: 185–207.

———. 2008b. "Oh My God, the Fanfiction!": Dumbledore's Outing and the Online Harry Potter Fandom. *Children's Literature Association Quarterly* 33, no. 22: 200–206.

Toumani, Meline. 2007. Blog entry in response to Barbara Ehrenreich's essay, Bonfire of the Disney Princesses. *The Nation,* December 17. Available online at http://www. thenation.com/doc/20071224/ehrenreich

Traversi, Derek Antona. 1976. *T. S. Eliot: The Longer Poems.* London: Bodley Head.

Trifonova, Temenuga. 2006. The Fantastic Redemption of Reality. *Quarterly Review of Film and Video* 23, no. 1: 55–78.

Tuana, Nancy. 1993. *The Less Noble Sex: Scientific, Religious, and Philosophical Conceptions of Woman's Nature.* Bloomington: Indiana University Press.

Turan, Kenneth. 1998. Cinderella as the Original Spice Girl. *Los Angeles Times,* July 31, guide section.

Uther, Hans-Jörg. 2004. *The Types of International Folktales: A Classification and Bibliography.* 3 vols. Helsinki: Academia Scientiarum Fennica.

Valenti, Jessica. 2007. *Full Frontal Feminism: A Young Woman's Guide to Why Feminism Matters.* Emeryville, CA: Seal Press.

Verdier, Yvonne. 1980. Le Petit chaperon rouge dans la tradition orale. *Le Debat* 3, juillet-août: 31–56.

von Franz, Marie-Louise. 1972. *The Feminine in Fairytales.* Dallas, TX: Spring Publications.

———. 2002. *Animus and Anima in Fairy Tales.* Toronto: Inner City Books.

Waldby, Catherine, and Robert Mitchell. 2006. *Tissue Economies: Blood, Organs and Cell Lines in Late Capitalism.* Durham, NC: Duke University Press.

Ward, Donald. 1991. New Misconceptions about Old Folktales: The Brothers Grimm. In *The Brothers Grimm and Folktale,* ed. James M. McGlathery, 91–100. Urbana: University of Illinois Press.

Warner, Marina. 1990. Goose Tales: Female Fiction, Female Fact? *Folklore* 101, no. 1: 3–25.

———. 1993. *Cinema and the Realms of Enchantment: Lectures, Seminars and Essays.* Ed. Duncan Petrie. London: British Film Institute.

———. 1994. *From the Beast to the Blonde: On Fairy Tales and Their Tellers.* London: Vintage.

———. 1998. *No Go the Bogeyman: Scaring, Lulling, and Making Mock.* New York: Farrar, Straus and Giroux.

———. 2004. *Signs & Wonders: Essays on Literature and Culture.* London: Virago.

Washington, Julie E. 2007. Fairy Tale to Real Woman Plot Challenged *Enchanted's* Costume Designer Mona May. *The Plain Dealer,* November 23. Available online at http://www.cleveland.com/entertainment/plaindealer/index.ssf?/base/entertainment-0/1195810501231580.xml&coll=2

Wasko, Janet. 2001. *Understanding Disney: The Manufacture of Fantasy.* Cambridge: Polity Press.

Waters, Fiona. 2002. *Wizard Tales.* London: Pavilion Children's Books.

Watts, Steven. 1995. Walt Disney: Art and Politics in the American Century. *Journal of American History* 82, no. 1: 84–110.

———. 1997. *The Magic Kingdom: Walt Disney and the American Way of Life.* Columbia: University of Missouri Press.

Wells, Jennifer. 2008. Battlelines Harden on the Gender Front. *Globe and Mail,* March 8, A22.

Welsh, James M., and Peter Lev, eds. 2007. *The Literature/Film Reader: Issues of Adaptation.* Toronto: Scarecrow Press.

Whelehan, Imelda. 2005. *The Feminist Bestseller.* New York: Palgrave MacMillan.

Whitinger, Raleigh, and Susan Ingram. 2003. Schnitzler, Kubrick, and "Fidelio." *Mosaic* 36, no. 3: 55–72.

Williams, Linda. 2000. Something Else Besides a Mother: *Stella Dallas* and the Maternal Melodrama. In *Feminism & Film,* ed. E. Ann Kaplan, 479–504.

———. 2005. *The Erotic Thriller in Contemporary Cinema.* Bloomington: Indiana University Press.

Wilmington, Michael. 1998. "Ever After" Takes Fairy Tale to New Age. *Chicago Tribune,* July 31, entertainment section.

Wilson, Rawdon. 1995. "The Metamorphoses of Fictional Space: Magical Realism." In *Magical Realism: Theory, History, Community,* ed. Lois P. Zamora and Wendy B. Faris, 209–233.

Windling, Terri. 2001. On Tolkien and Fairy Stories. In *Journal of Mythic Arts,* Endicott Studio. Available online at http://www.endicott-studio.com/rdrm/fortolkn.html

Wise, Christopher. 2003. Notes from the Aladdin Industry: Or, Middle Eastern Folklore in the Era of Multi-national Capitalism. In *The Emperor's Old Groove: Decolonizing Disney's Magic Kingdom,* ed. Brenda Ayres, 105–14.

Wisker, Gina. 1997. Revenge of the Living Doll: Angela Carter's Horror Writing. In *The Infernal Desires of Angela Carter,* eds. Joseph Bristow and Trev Lynn Broughton, 116–31.

Wolf, Naomi. [1995] 1999. Brideland. In *Women: Images and Realities, a Multicultural Anthology,* eds. Amy Kesselman, Lily D. McNair, and Nancy Schniedewind, 58–60. Repr. Mountain View, CA: Mayfield.

Wood, Buddy. 2008. Interview with Kevin Lima: *Enchanted.* Urban Cine File, May 29. Available online at http://www.urbancinefile.com.au/home/view. asp?a=14351&s=Interviews

Yeats, W. B., and Paul Muldoon. 2003. *Irish Fairy and Folk Tales.* New York: Modern Library.

Zamora, Lois P., and Wendy B. Faris. 1995. Introduction to *Magical Realism: Theory, History Community,* 1–11.

Ziolkowski, Theodore. 1977. *Disenchanted Images: A Literary Iconology.* Princeton, NJ: Princeton University Press.

Zipes, Jack. 1979. *Breaking the Magic Spell: Radical Theories of Folk and Fairy Tales.* London: Heinemann.

———. 1983. *The Trials and Tribulations of Little Red Riding Hood: Versions of the Tale in Sociocultural Context.* South Hadley, MA: Bergin & Garvey.

———. 1986. *Don't Bet on the Prince: Contemporary Feminist Fairy Tales in North America and England.* New York: Methuen.

———. 1994. *Fairy Tale as Myth, Myth as Fairy Tale.* Lexington: University of Kentucky Press.

———. 1995. Breaking the Disney Spell. In *From Mouse to Mermaid: The Politics of Film, Gender, and Culture,* ed. Elizabeth Bell, Lynda Hass, and Laura Sells, 21–42.

———. 1996. Towards a Theory of the Fairy Tale Film: The Case of Pinocchio. *The Lion and the Unicorn* 20, no. 1: 1–24.

———. 1997. *Happily Ever After: Fairy Tales, Children, and the Culture Industry.* New York: Routledge.

———. 2000. *The Oxford Companion to Fairy Tales: The Western Fairy Tale Tradition from Medieval to Modern.* New York: Oxford University Press.

————. 2001. Cross-Cultural Connections and the Contamination of the Classical Fairy Tale. In *The Great Fairy Tale Tradition: From Straparola and Basile to the Brothers Grimm*, trans. and ed. by Jack Zipes, 845–69. New York: W. W. Norton.

————, ed. and trans. 2002a. *The Complete Fairy Tales of the Brothers Grimm*. 3rd ed. New York: Bantam Books.

————. 2002b. *Sticks and Stones: The Troublesome Success of Children's Literature from Slovenly Peter to Harry Potter*. London: Routledge.

————. 2006a. *Fairy Tales and the Art of Subversion: The Classical Genre for Children and the Process of Civilization*. 2d ed. New York: Routledge.

————. 2006b. *Why Fairy Tales Stick: The Evolution and Relevance of a Genre*. New York: Routledge.

————. 2007. *When Dreams Come True: Classical Fairy Tales and Their Tradition*. 2d ed. New York: Routledge.

————. 2008. Review of *Pan's Labyrinth*. *Journal of American Folklore* 121, no. 480: 236–40.

————. 2009. *Relentless Progress: The Reconfiguration of Children's Literature, Fairy Tales, and Storytelling*. New York: Routledge.

————. 2010. *The Enchanted Screen: A History of Fairy Tales on Film*. New York: Routledge.

Žižek, Slavoj. 1991. Grimaces of the Real, or When the Phallus Appears. *October* 58, Autumn: 44–68.

Zucker, Carole. 2000. Sweetest Tongue Has Sharpest Tooth: The Dangers of Dreaming in Neil Jordan's *The Company of Wolves*. *Literature/Film Quarterly* 28, no. 1: 66–71.

Filmography

Across the Universe. 2007. Directed by Julie Taymor. U.S.A.: Revolution Studios.
The Addams Family. 1991. Directed by Barry Sonnenfeld. U.S.A: Orion Pictures
    Corporation.
AI: Artificial Intelligence. 2001. Directed by Steven Spielberg. U.S.A.: Warner Bros.
    Pictures.
Aladdin. 1992. Directed by Ron Clements and John Musker. U.S.A.: Walt Disney Pictures.
Aladdin and His Wonderful Lamp. TV movie, 1986. Directed by Tim Burton. U.S.A.:
    Gaylord Productions.
Alice in Wonderland. 2010. Directed by Tim Burton. U.S.A.: Walt Disney Pictures.
Aliens. 1986. Directed by James Cameron. U.S.A.: Twentieth Century Fox.
Baba Yaga. 1973. Directed by Corrado Farina. Italy/France: Luglio Cinematografica/
    Allouche.
Barbe-bleue (Bluebeard). 1901. Directed by Georges Méliès. France: Star Film.
Barefoot to Jerusalem. 2008. Directed by Nietzchka Keene. U.S.A.: Keene Productions.
Basic Instinct. 1992. Directed by Paul Verhoeven. U.S.A.: Canal+.
Batman. 1989. Directed by Tim Burton. U.S.A.: Warner Bros. Pictures.
Batman Returns. 1992. Directed by Tim Burton. U.S.A.: Warner Bros. Pictures.
Beauty and the Beast. TV series, 1987–90. Created by Ron Koslow. CBS.
Beauty and the Beast. 1991. Directed by Gary Trousdale and Kirk Wise. U.S.A.: Walt
Disney Pictures.
Beetle Juice. 1988. Directed by Tim Burton. U.S.A.: Geffen Pictures.
La Belle et la bête. 1946. Directed by Jean Cocteau. France: DisCina.
The Black Cauldron. 1985. Directed by Ted Berman and Richard Rich. U.S.A.: Walt
    Disney Pictures.
Bluebeard. 1972. Directed by Edward Dmytryk and Luciano Sacripanti. France/Italy/West
    Germany: Gloria Film.
Buffy the Vampire Slayer. TV series, 1997–2003. Created by Joss Whedon. U.S.A.:
    Twentieth Century Fox.
The Cabinet of Dr. Caligari. 1920. Directed by Robert Wiene. Germany: Decla-Bioscop
    AG.
Cinderella. 1922. Directed by Walt Disney. U.S.A.: Laugh-O-Gram Films.
Cinderella. 1950. Directed by Clyde Geronimi, Wilfred Jackson, and Hamilton Luske.
    U.S.A.: Walt Disney Pictures.
A Cinderella Story. 2004. Directed by Mark Rosman. USA: Warner Bros. Pictures.
Cinderella Up-to-Date. 1909. Directed by Georges Méliès. U.S.A.: Georges Méliès.
Cinderfella. 1960. Directed by Frank Tashlin. U.S.A.: Jerry Lewis Productions.
Cendrillon. 1899. Directed by Georges Méliès. France: Star Film.
Cendrillon ou La Pantoufle merveilleuse. 1912. Directed by Georges Méliès. France: Star
    Film.
The Chronicles of Narnia: The Lion, the Witch, and the Wardrobe. 2005. Directed by Andrew
    Adamson. U.S.A./U.K.: Walt Disney Pictures.

The Chronicles of Narnia: Prince Caspian. 2008. Directed by Andrew Adamson. U.S.A./ U.K.: Walt Disney Pictures.

The Company of Wolves. 1984. Directed by Neil Jordan; cowriter Angela Carter. U.K.: Incorporated Television Company.

Corpse Bride. 2005. Directed by Tim Burton; cowriters Caroline Thompson and Pamela Pettler. U.K./U.S.A.: Warner Bros. Pictures.

Dirty Dancing. 1987. Directed by Emile Ardolino. U.S.A.: Great American Films Limited Partnership.

Edward Scissorhands. 1990. Directed by Tim Burton; cowriter Caroline Thompson. U.S.A.: Twentieth Century Fox.

Ed Wood. 1994. Directed by Tim Burton. U.S.A.: Touchtone Pictures.

Enchanted. 2007. Directed by Kevin Lima. U.S.A.: Walt Disney Pictures.

Eréndira. 1983. Directed by Ruy Guerra. France/Mexico/West Germany: Atlas Saskia Film.

Ever After. 1998. Directed by Andy Tennant. U.S.A.: Twentieth Century Fox.

Eyes Wide Shut. 1999. Directed by Stanley Kubrick. U.K./U.S.A.: Hobby Films.

Faerie Tale Theatre. TV series, 1982–87. Directors various, including Roger Vadim, Nicholas Meyer, Tim Burton, and Francis Ford Coppola. U.S.A.: Gaylord Productions.

Fantasia. 1940. Directors James Algar, Samuel Armstrong. Ford Beebe, Norman Ferguson, Jim Handley, T. Hee, Wilfred Jackson, Hamilton Luske, Bill Roberts, Paul Satterfield, and Ben Sharpsteen. U.S.A.: Walt Disney Pictures.

Fatal Attraction. 1987. Directed by Adrian Lyne. U.S.A.: Paramount Pictures.

Field of Dreams. 1989. Directed by Phil Alden Robinson. U.S.A.: Gordon Company.

The Fox and the Hound. 1981. Directed by Ted Berman, Richard Rich and Art Stevens. U.S.A.: Walt Disney Pictures.

Frankenweenie. 1984. Directed by Tim Burton. U.S.A.: Walt Disney Pictures.

Freeway. 1996. Directed by Matthew Bright. U.S.A.: Kushner/Locke Company.

The Gingerdead Man. 2005. Directed by Charles Band. U.S.A.: Shoot Production Company.

Ginger Snaps. 2000. Directed by John Fawcett. Canada/USA: Copper Heart Entertainment.

The Golden Compass. 2007. Directed by Chris Weitz. U.S.A./U.K.: New Line Cinema.

Hable con ella (Talk to Her). 2002. Directed by Pedro Almodóvar. Spain: El Deseo S.A.

Hansel and Gretel. 1982. Directed by Tim Burton. U.S.A.: Walt Disney Pictures.

Hansel & Gretel. 2002. Directed by Gary Tunnicliffe. U.S.A.: Broomstick Entertainment.

Hard Candy. 2005. Directed by David Slade. U.S.A.: Vulcan Productions.

Harry Potter and the Sorcerer's Stone/Harry Potter and the Philosopher's Stone. 2001. Directed by Chris Columbus; cowriter J. K. Rowling. U.K.: 1492 Pictures.

Harry Potter and the Chamber of Secrets. 2002. Directed by Chris Columbus; cowriter J. K. Rowling. U.S.A./U.K./Germany: 1492 Pictures.

Harry Potter and the Prisoner of Azkaban. 2004. Directed by Alfonso Cuarón; cowriter J. K. Rowling. U.K./U.S.A.: Warner Bros. Pictures.

Harry Potter and the Goblet of Fire. 2005. Directed by Mike Newell; cowriter J. K. Rowling. U.K./U.S.A.: Warner Bros. Pictures.

Harry Potter and the Order of the Phoenix. 2007. Directed by David Yates; cowriter J. K. Rowling. U.K./U.S.A.: Warner Bros. Pictures.

Harry Potter and the Half-Blood Prince. 2009. Directed by David Yates; cowriter J. K. Rowling. U.K./U.S.A.: Warner Bros. Pictures.

Heroine of Hell. TV movie, 1996. Directed by Nietzchka Keene. U.S.A.: Independent Television Service (ITVS).

Into the Woods. TV movie, 1991. Directed by James Lapine. U.S.A.: Brandman Productions.

The Juniper Tree. 1990. Directed and written by Nietzchka Keene. U.S.A.: Keene Productions.

King Kong. 1933. Directed by Merian C. Cooper and Ernest B. Schoedsack. U.S.A.: RKO Radio Pictures.

Kung Fu Panda. 2008. Directed by Mark Osborne and John Stevenson. U.S.A.: Dreamworks.

Kvitebjørn Kong Valemon (The Polar Bear King). 1991. Directed by Ola Solum. Norway/Sweden/Germany: Svensk Filmindustri.

Labyrinth. 1986. Directed by Jim Henson. U.S.A.: Sony Pictures.

Lady in the Water. 2006. Directed by M. Night Shyamalan. U.S.A.: Warner Bros. Pictures.

The Legend of Sleepy Hollow. 1949. Directed by Clyde Geronimi and Jack Kinney. U.S.A.: Walt Disney Pictures.

Like Water for Chocolate (Como agua para chocolate). 1992. Directed by Alfonso Arau. Mexico: Arau Films Internacional.

The Lion King. 1994. Directed by Roger Allers and Rob Minkoff. U.S.A.: Walt Disney Pictures.

The Little Mermaid. 1989. Directed by Ron Clements and John Musker. U.S.A.: Silver Screen Partners.

Little Red Riding Hood. 1922. Directed by Walt Disney. U.S.A.: Laugh-O-Gram Films.

Little Red Riding Hood. 1997. Directed by David Kaplan. U.S.A.: Caruso/Mendelsohn Productions.

The Lord of the Rings: The Fellowship of the Ring. 2001. Directed by Peter Jackson. New Zealand/U.S.A.: New Line Cinema.

The Lord of the Rings: The Two Towers. 2002. Directed by Peter Jackson. U.S.A./New Zealand/Germany: New Line Cinema.

The Lord of the Rings: The Return of the King. 2003. Directed by Peter Jackson. U.S.A./New Zealand/Germany: New Line Cinema.

Maid in Manhattan. 2002. Directed by Wayne Wang. U.S.A.: Revolution Studios.

Mars Attacks!. 1996. Directed by Tim Burton. U.S.A.: Warner Bros. Pictures.

The Matrix. 1999. Directed by Andy Wachowski and Larry Wachowski. U.S.A.: Groucho II Film Partnership.

MirrorMask, 2005. Directed by Dave McKean. U.K./U.S.A.: Jim Henson Productions.

The Muppet Show. TV series, 1976–81. Directed by Peter Harris and Philip Casson. U.S.A./U.K.: Associated Television (ATV).

The NeverEnding Story (Die unendliche Geschichte). 1984. Directed by Wolfgang Petersen. West Germany/U.S.A.: Neue Constantin Film.

The Nightmare Before Christmas. 1993. Directed by Henry Selick. U.S.A: Skellington Productions.

964 Pinocchio. 1991. Directed by Shozin Fukui. Japan: n.p.

Notorious. 1946. Directed by Alfred Hitchcock. U.S.A.: Vanguard Films.

101 Dalmatians. 1996. Directed by Stephen Herek. U.S.A.: Walt Disney Pictures.

Pan's Labyrinth. 2006. Directed by Guillermo del Toro. Mexico/Japan/U.S.A.: Tequila Gang.

Peau d'âne (Donkeyskin). 1970. Directed by Jacques Demy. France: Marianne Productions.

Pee-wee's Big Adventure. 1985. Directed by Tim Burton. U.S.A: Warner Brothers.

Peter Pan. 1953. Directed by Clyde Geronimi, Wilfred Jackson, and Hamilton Luske. U.S.A.: Walt Disney Pictures.

Le Petit chaperon rouge (Little Red Riding Hood). 1901. Directed by Georges Méliès. France: Star Film.

The Piano. 1993. Directed and written by Jane Campion. Australia/New Zealand/France: Australian Film Commission.

Le Piège d'Issoudun. 2003. Directed by Micheline Lanctôt. Canada: Radio-Canada.

Pinocchio. 1940. Directed by Hamilton Luske and Ben Sharpsteen. U.S.A.: Walt Disney Pictures.

Pretty Woman. 1990. Directed by Garry Marshall. U.S.A.: Silver Screen Partners.

The Princess and the Frog. 2009. Directed by Ron Clements and John Musker. U.S.A.: Walt Disney Pictures.

The Princess Bride. 1987. Directed by Rob Reiner. USA: Act III Communications.

Puss in Boots. 1922. Directed by Walt Disney. U.S.A.: Laugh-O-Gram Films.

The Red Shoes. 1948. Directed by Michael Powell. U.K.: The Archers.

The Red Shoes (Bunhongsin). 2005. Directed by Yong-gyun Kim. South Korea: Tartan Video.

Robots. 2005. Directed by Chris Wedge and Carlos Saldanha. U.S.A.: Twentieth Century Fox Animation.

Secret Beyond the Door. 1948. Directed by Fritz Lang. U.S.A.: Diana Productions.

The Secret of My Succe$s. 1987. Directed by Herbert Ross. U.S.A.: Rastar Pictures Production.

Sex and the City. 2008. Directed by Michael Patrick King. U.S.A.: New Line Cinema.

Shark Tale. 2004. Directed by Bibo Bergeron, Vicky Jenson, and Rob Letterman. U.S.A.: Dreamworks.

She's All That. 1999. Directed by Robert Iscove. U.S.A: All That Productions.

Shrek. 2001. Directed by Andrew Adamson and Vicky Jenson. U.S.A.: Dreamworks Animation.

Shrek 2. 2004. Directed by Andrew Adamson, Kelly Asbury and Conrad Vernon. U.S.A.: Dreamworks SKG.

Shrek the Third. 2007. Directed by Chris Miller and Raman Hui. U.S.A.: Dreamworks Animation.

Sleeping Beauty. 1959. Directed by Clyde Geronimi. U.S.A.: Walt Disney Pictures.

Sleepy Hollow. 1999. Directed by Tim Burton. U.S.A./Germany: Paramount Pictures.

Snow White and the Seven Dwarfs. 1937. Directed by David Hand. U.S.A.: Walt Disney Pictures.

Snow White: A Tale of Terror. 1997. Directed by Michael Cohn. U.S.A.: Polygram Filmed Entertainment.

Snow White: The Fairest of Them All. TV movie, 2001. Directed by Caroline Thompson; writers Caroline Thompson and Julie Hickson. Canada/U.S.A./Germany: Babelsberg International Film Produktion.

The Sound of Music. 1965. Directed by Robert Wise. U.S.A.: Twentieth Century Fox.

Spirited Away. 2002. (English version of *Sen to Chihiro no kanikakushi,* directed by Hayao Miyazaki. Studio Ghibli, 2001.) Directed by Hayao Miyazaki and Kirk Wise. U.S.A.: Walt Disney Pictures.

Splash. 1984. Directed by Ron Howard. U.S.A.: Touchstone Pictures.

Star Wars. 1977. Directed by George Lucas. U.S.A.: Lucasfilm.

The Stepford Wives. 1975. Directed by Bryan Forbes. U.S.A.: Fadsin Cinema.

The Storyteller. TV movie, 1988. Directed by Steve Barron and Jim Henson. U.K.: Henson Associates.

Sydney White. 2007. Directed by Joe Nussbaum. U.S.A.: Morgan Creek.

10 Things I Hate About You. 1999. Directed by Gil Junger. USA: Touchstone Pictures.

The 10th Kingdom. TV movie, 2000. Directed by David Carson and Herbert Wise. U.K./Germany/U.S.A.: Babelsberg Film und Fernesehen.

The Texas Chain Saw Massacre. 1974. Directed by Tobe Hooper. U.S.A.: Vortex.

The Thief of Bagdad. 1924. Directed by Raoul Walsh. U.S.A.: Douglas Fairbanks Pictures.

Trois places pour le 26. 1988. Directed by Jacques Demy. France: Renn Productions.

Vanilla Sky. 2001. Directed by Cameron Crowe. U.S.A: Paramount Pictures.

Vincent. 1982. Directed by Tim Burton. U.S.A.: Walt Disney Pictures.

Who Framed Roger Rabbit? 1988. Directed by Robert Zemeckis. U.S.A.: Walt Disney Pictures.

The Wizard of Oz. 1939. Directed by Victor Fleming. U.S.A.: Metro-Goldwyn-Mayer.

The Woodsman. 2004. Directed by Nicole Kassell. U.S.A.: Dash Films.

Working Girl. 1988. Directed by Mike Nichols. U.S.A.: Twentieth Century Fox.

Contributors

CRISTINA BACCHILEGA is professor of English at the University of Hawai'i at Mānoa, where she teaches folklore and literature, fairy tales and their adaptations, and cultural studies. Her most recent book is *Legendary Hawai'i and the Politics of Place: Tradition, Translation, and Tourism*. With historian Noelani Arista and translator Sahoa Fukushima, she studied nineteenth-century translations of *The Arabian Nights* into Hawaiian. She is review editor of *Marvels & Tales: Journal of Fairy Tale Studies*, and her current book project focuses on the poetics and politics of twenty-first-century fairy tale adaptations.

ANNE BRYDON is associate professor and chair of anthropology at Wilfrid Laurier University, Waterloo, Canada. Her work focuses on the anthropology of modernist imaginaries with specific attention to representation, visual studies, ethnographic writing, and the aesthetics of knowing. Her ongoing research concerns nationalism and the cultural politics of environmentalism in Iceland as well as the study of visual arts and material culture. Currently she is investigating how contemporary visual artists working in Iceland are re-imagining changing social relations between nature, science, and technology.

LISA GABLEHOUSE is a former elementary school teacher and children's book author. Her areas of expertise in the classroom include reading and language arts, creating engaging work centers, and English as a second language and dual-language instruction from prekindergarten through the third grade.

PAULINE GREENHILL is professor of women's and gender studies at the University of Winnipeg, Manitoba, Canada. She was co-editor with Liz Locke and Theresa Vaughan of *Encyclopedia of Women's Folklore and Folklife*. Her most recent book is *Make the Night Hideous: Four English-Canadian Charivaris, 1881-1940*. Her work has appeared in *Signs*, *Marvels & Tales*, *Resources for Feminist Research*, *Journal of American Folklore*, *Canadian Journal of Women and the Law*, and *parallax*, among others.

MING-HSUN LIN obtained her first M.A. in theatre studies from the University of Manchester and her second M.A in comparative literature from University College London. Currently she is a Ph.D. student at the University of Manchester studying gender, fairy tales, fantastic and children's literature, and film, with reference to Harry Potter.

SIDNEY EVE MATRIX is Queen's National Scholar and assistant professor of film and media at Queen's University in Kingston. She teaches mass communications and popular film. Her research involves digital technology cultural and consumer trends.

LINDA PERSHING is a women's studies professor at California State University San Marcos. Author of *The Ribbon around the Pentagon: Peace by Piecemakers, Sew to Speak: The Fabric Art of Mary Milne*, and co-editor of *Feminist Theory and the Study of Folklore*, her areas of expertise include feminist folklore studies, the gendered dimensions of war and peace, and the politics of culture.

BRIAN RAY is currently completing his PhD at University of North Carolina at Greensboro, where he teaches composition and literature. He earned his MFA from the University of South Carolina in 2007. His prize-winning first novel, *Through the Pale Door*, was published by the Hub City Writers Project in 2009.

JOHN RIEDER is professor of English at the University of Hawai'i, Mānoa, where he teaches critical theory and cultural studies. He is the author of *Colonialism and the Emergence of Science Fiction* and *Wordsworth's Counterrevolutionary Turn*. Recent essays appear in *Red Planets: Marxism and Science Fiction* and *The Routledge Companion to Science Fiction*; forthcoming are essays on genre theory, on Jules Verne and Stanley Kubrick, and on science fiction and the Western.

NAARAH SAWERS is a post-doctoral scholar at Deakin University, Australia. Her research explores the intersections between narrative and bioethics, particularly in relation to texts for children and young people. She has published in a variety of journals, including *Papers: Explorations into Children's Literature, Children's Literature in Education, Children's Literature Association Quarterly*, and *Continuum: Journal of Media and Cultural Studies*.

KIM SNOWDEN is an instructor in the women's and gender studies program at the University of British Columbia where she teaches courses on feminist literature, fairy tales, and popular culture. She is the co-founder and, until January 2009, was chief co-editor of *thirdspace: a journal of feminist theory and culture*. Her current research looks at contemporary vampire films and literature with a focus on the representation of women's bodies as monstrous, vampire reproduction and birth, and the sexual transmission of affect.

TRACIE LUKASIEWICZ is a graduate of the University of Miami's film studies master's program. Her work primarily focuses on femininity and masculinity in the cinema, especially with regard to action films. Most recently, she presented her study of sound and music in the film *There Will Be Blood* at the Literature on Screen conference in Amsterdam. She is currently conducting research that contributes to the scholarly conversation regarding feminism and film in a society of post-identities.

CHRISTY WILLIAMS is an instructor of English at Hawai'i Pacific University and a doctoral student at the University of Hawai'i. She specializes in fairy tale studies, focusing on the gender and narrative interventions made by contemporary and postmodern fairy tales. Her work on fairy tale retellings can be found in the journals *The Comparatist* and *Marvels & Tales* and the collection *Beyond Adaptation: Essays on Radical Transformations of Original Works*, which she co-edited with Phyllis Frus.

JACK ZIPES is professor emeritus of German and comparative literature at the University of Minnesota. His more recent publications include *Sticks and Stones: The Troublesome Success of Children's Literature from Slovenly Peter to Harry Potter, Fairy Tales and the Art of Subversion, Why Fairy Tales Stick: The Evolution and Relevance of a Genre*, and *Relentless Progress: The Reconfiguration of Children's Literature, Fairy Tales, and Storytelling*. He has also translated a collection of Kurt Schwitters' fairy tales, *Lucky Hans and Other Merz Fairy Tales*.

Index

Titles of folktales are in quotation marks, titles of books and films in italics. Where original titles of non-English-language films appear in square brackets after the English title they are ignored for filing purposes. Titles beginning with numbers are filed as pronounced.

the Beast (Trousdale & Wise); *Cinderella* (Geronimi, Jackson, & Luske); *The Chronicles of Narnia: The Lion, the Witch, and the Wardrobe* (Adamson); *The Chronicles of Narnia: Prince Caspian* (Adamson); *Enchanted* (Lima); *Fantasia* (Algar et al.); *The Fox and the Hound* (Berman, Rich, & Stevens); *Frankenweenie* (Burton); *Hansel and Gretel* (Burton); *The Legend of Sleepy Hollow* (Geronimi & Kinney); *The Lion King* (Allers & Minkoff); *101 Dalmatians* (Herek); *Peter Pan* (Geronimi, Jackson, & Luske); *Pinocchio* (Luske & Sharpsteen); *Sleeping Beauty* (Geronimi); *Snow White and the Seven Dwarfs* (Hand); *Spirited Away* (Miyazaki & Wise); *Vincent* (Burton); *Who Framed Roger Rabbit?* (Zemeckis)
Disney films, xi, 6–7, 10, 12, 15, 17, 20, 21, 24, 27, 33, 49, 82–83, 137–56 *passim*, 161–64, 216; antifeminism in, 164; homophobia in, 145; princess characters, 137–56 *passim*; racism in, 146; xenophobia in, 145
Disney, Walt, ix–x, xi, 1 n. 1, 5, 6, 83, 145, 155, 198; *Little Red Riding Hood*, 5; *Puss in Boots*, 5; *Cinderella* (1922), 5; *The Legend of Sleepy Hollow*, 207–13 *passim. See also* under titles of later films produced by the Disney Corporation, as above
disobedience, 34, 71, 178, 182, 185, 189, 195
dispatchers, 80
Dmytryk, Edward. See *Bluebeard* (Dmytryk & Sacripanti)
Do Rozario, Rebecca-Anne C., 149
Doane, Mary Ann, 105, 188-189
Dogar, Rana, 141 n. 8
Doja, Albert, 122
dolls, 37–38, 81, 167, 172
"Donkeyskin," 11, 84 n. 10, 183, 187 n. 9
Donkeyskin (Peau d'âne) (Demy), 11, 168
donors, 80
double vision, 66. *See also* second sight
dragons, 13, 28–29, 39, 65
dramatis personae, 80, 81, 86
draugars, 119 n. 4
dream sequences, x, 14
Dream Story [Traumnovelle] (Schnitzler), 179
DreamWorks. See *Kung Fu Panda*; *Shark Tale*; *Shrek* series
Dresang, Eliza T., 79
Dreyer, Carl, 121
Dujovne, Beatriz E., 195 n. 17
Dulac, Edmund, 5

dullahans, 207
Duncker, Patricia, 84, 158 n. 2, 169
Dundes, Alan, 182 n. 5
duplicity, 178, 187, 196
duty, 33. *See also* obedience; disobedience
Duvall, Shelley, *Faerie Tale Theatre*, xii, 7–8
dwarfs, 13, 82, 85 n. 12. *See also* "Snow White"
dystopias, 7, 37, 43, 46, 48, 49, 52, 58. *See also* utopias
"East of the Sun and West of the Moon," 184
Ebert, Roger, 36
Ed Wood (Burton), 207
Edward Scissorhands (Burton), 4 n. 5, 12, 20, 198, 200–06
Eisner, Michael, 140, 149
elves, 125
Enchanted (Lima), 4 n. 5, 9, 10, 19, 27, 28–32, 38, 83 n. 7, 137–56
Eréndira (Guerra), 64
erotic thrillers, 8, 12, 15, 181 n. 4, 183, 185 esp. n. 8, 190–96 *passim*
eroticism, 34
escapes, 48
Ever After: A Cinderella Story (Tennant), 21, 23–24, 26, 30, 37, 60, 99–115, 160
evil, 9, 10, 14, 36, 49, 60, 70 n. 7, 73 n. 11, 75, 88 n. 14, 133, 138, 146, 162, 212; banality of, 75; punishment of, 61, 74, 129, 192. *See also* devils; female evil; good against evil; villains
expectation (and anticipation), x, xii–xiii, 15–16, 60, 121, 161
experimentation, xii
Eyes Wide Shut (Kubrick), 4 n. 5, 9, 12, 17, 20, 173 n. 20, 178–97
Faerie Tale Theatre (Duvall), xii, 7–8
fairies, 13, 44, 49, 70 n. 7, 163; depicted like insects, 69–70
fairy godmothers, 60, 70, 94–95, 102, 112–13, 114, 154 n. 27
fairy tale fragments. See fairy tales, hybridization
fairy tale pastiche, 25–26, 200
fairy tale web, 25
fairy tale world, distinguished from world of magical realism, 67 esp. n. 5
fairy tales, editorial activity, effect of, 2–3; hybridization, 19, 25–26, 40; hybridization with other genres, 24 n. 1; influence on film in general, x; interconnections between, 25; internationality of, 1; Märchenstil [fairy tale

Lau, Kimberly J., 165 n. 12
Lee, Hermione, 169; "The Legend of Sleepy
    Hollow" (Irving), 207–13. See also *Sleepy
    Hollow*
The Legend of Sleepy Hollow (Geronimi &
    Kinney), 207–13 *passim*
legends, distinguished from folktales, 23–24,
    104
leprechauns, 70 n. 7
Letterman, Rob. See *Shark Tale*
Lewis, C. S., 21. See also *The Chronicles of
    Narnia*
Lieberman, Marcia R., 83, 100
Like Water for Chocolate [*Como agua para
    chocolate*] (Arau), 65
Lima, Kevin. See *Enchanted*
The Lion King (Allers & Minkoff), 43, 162
    n. 10
"The Little Mermaid" (Andersen), 1 n.1,
    12, 191; as source for *Harry Potter and the
    Goblet of Fire*, 96; as source for *Lady in the
    Water* (Shyamalan), 14
The Little Mermaid (Clements & Musker), 1
    n. 1, 139, 141, 149, 151
"Little Red Cap," 185
"The Little Red Ox," 93
"Little Red Riding Hood," 5, 13, 14, 17, 26,
    82; Grimm brothers' version, 161; Perrault
    version, 161, 167, 168, 170, 176, 195 n. 18
Little Red Riding Hood (Disney), 5
Little Red Riding Hood (Kaplan), 18 n. 14
Little Red Riding Hood [*Le Petit chaperon
    rouge*] (Méliès), xi, 5
locales. See carnivals; forests; labyrinths
The Lord of the Rings trilogy (Jackson), 10;
    *The Lord of the Rings: The Fellowship of the
    Ring* (Jackson), 10; *The Lord of the Rings:
    The Return of the King* (Jackson), 10; *The
    Lord of the Rings: The Two Towers* (Jackson),
    10
The Lord of the Rings (Tolkien), 67
Loudermilk, Kim, 160
love. See romantic love
Lucas, George, *Star Wars*, 10, 14
Lundell, Torborg, 94
Luria, Isaac, 213
Lurie, Alison, 20, 84, 100, 101
Luske, Hamilton. See *Cinderella* (Geronimi
    et al.); *Fantasia*; *Peter Pan* (Geronimi et al.);
    Pinocchio (Luske & Sharpsteen)
Lyne, Adrian, *Fatal Attraction*, 193
Madonna/whore dichotomy, 192

magic, 23, 30, 61 n. 3, 122, 125–26, 135–36.
    See also commodification of magic
"The Magic Flight," 18
magical realism, 63–65, 67; distinguished
    from fairy tale world, 67 esp. n. 5. See also
    neomagical realism
Maitland, Sara, 84
Maid in Manhattan (Wang), 12, 60
male parturition, 129, 130 n. 17
manga, 38
Mankin, Nan, 118
Manovich, Lev, 10 n. 9
manufactured humans. See humans, artificial
Märchenstil [fairy tale style], 118 n. 3
"Maria, the Wicked Stepmother, and the
    Seven Robbers," 81
Marquez, Gabriel Garcia, 67
marriage, 20, 138, 162, 164, 167, 180–96
    passim. See also weddings
Mars Attacks! (Burton), 207
Marshall, Garry, *Pretty Woman*, 12, 60
Martin, Ann, 163, 166
Martin, Sara, 168, 174, 177 n. 25
marvelous, 64, 66, 117–18; distinguished
    from the fantastic and the uncanny, 63
Marxist criticism, 30
masculine helpers. See helpers
masks (and masquerade), 36–38, 105–08,
    115, 187–89, 208
matricide, 6, 135, 183
Matrix, Sidney Eve, 142 n. 9
The Matrix (Wachowski & Wachowski), 14
maturity (and maturation), 33, 38, 133, 134,
    171–72, 176, 203. See also youth
mazes, contrasted with labyrinths, 61
McCallum, Robyn, 24 n. 1, 100–04 *passim*,
    138 n. 2
McKean, Dave. See *MirrorMask*
melancholia, 19, 120, 125, 134–36
Méliès, George, ix–xi, 5, 10; *The Adventures of
    Baron Munchausen*, x; *The Arabian Nights*, x;
    Bluebeard (*Barbe-bleue*) (1901), 5; *Cinderella*
    [*Cendrillon ou La Pantoufle merveilleuse*]
    (1912), 5; *Cinderella* [*Cendrillon*] (1899), 5;
    Cinderella Up-to-Date (1909), 5; *Little Red
    Riding Hood* [*Le Petit chaperon rouge*], xi, 5;
    "Snow White" adaptation, xi
melodramas, 11
Merlin, 93 n. 15
mermaids (and mermen), Harry Potter as, 96.
    See also "The Little Mermaid"
metacommentary, 143